ROCKY MOUNTAIN MAMMALS

ROCKY MOUNTAIN MAMMALS

A Handbook of Mammals of Rocky Mountain National Park and Vicinity

Revised Edition

by David M. Armstrong
Natural Science Program and University Museum
University of Colorado, Boulder

with drawings by Bill Border

COLORADO ASSOCIATED UNIVERSITY PRESS
in cooperation with
ROCKY MOUNTAIN NATURE ASSOCIATION

TO THE JESSUPS OF SYLVAN DALE RANCH
Dear friends, like the gentle hills, last forever

CONTENTS

LIST OF TABLES

CHECKLIST OF MAMMALS OF ROCKY MOUNTAIN NATIONAL PARK AND VICINITY

*Extirpated within historic time; **introduced in Colorado.

Southern Rocky Mountains. *Cartography by Kenneth Erickson*

I. INTRODUCTION

THIS IS A handbook of mammals of Rocky Mountain National Park and adjacent areas. It was written with a single overriding consideration: to allow visitors to increase their understanding of the mammals of the area—their diversity, their habits, and their complex relationships with the natural environment.

I think that the more we know about any aspect of our surroundings, the more we can enjoy it. The more we enjoy any resource, the more tenacious we are in protecting it for our own continuing enjoyment and that of generations to come. I hope that this handbook will not only serve visitors, but will also serve our native fauna and its precarious habitat.

Organization.—The bulk of this handbook is composed of accounts of species. Some 66 species of mammals occur in Rocky Mountain National Park and Arapahoe National Recreation Area (or are strongly suspected to occur there, or have occurred there within historic times). Accounts of species treat distribution and habitat, appearance and field recognition, and natural history. Selected references are noted at the end of each account. These citations will lead interested readers to useful reviews or technical monographs. In keeping with an orientation toward a lay audience, citations to the technical literature generally are omitted from accounts of species.

Although our interest is focused specifically on mammals of Rocky Mountain National Park and immediately adjacent areas, this handbook has a far wider application. It applies without exception to mountainous parts of north-central Colorado and adjacent Wyoming. Elsewhere in the Southern Rockies a similar fauna is present, although there is a gradual attenuation of the ranges of some species southward. In mountainous areas to the north and west (in the Middle Rocky Mountains of Wyoming and Utah), our coverage becomes progressively less complete. The reader interested in mammals of Colorado as a whole should consult Lechleitner (1969) or Armstrong (1972). Mammals of the Great Plains to the east were treated by Jones et al. (1983, 1985), and Armstrong (1982) described mammals of the Colorado Plateau to the west.

Wherever possible, data in accounts of species are from local studies. Measurements are of Coloradan animals and are given in metric units. (Conversion scales between metric and "English" units are found on page 224.)

A rather extensive, general introduction precedes the accounts of species. The section entitled, "What is a Mammal?" describes mammals in general and attempts to put our local fauna in perspective in time with respect to other vertebrate animals. "Mammalian Distribution" establishes our fauna in its spatial context. Comments on ecological distribution are intended to aid the reader in selecting those areas of Rocky Mountain National Park that are best suited to the development of certain mammalian communities. "How to Observe Mammals" offers a few hints for the prospective mammal-watcher to help the visitor enjoy our unique and fascinating faunal resources.

Explanation of Terminology. – This is a popular handbook. By "popular" I do not imply that it is a "best-seller," but that it was written for people, lay people, not for professional naturalists or others with extensive formal training in biology. Nonetheless, some scientific vocabulary has been used, and scientific names are included for each species. Why?

First of all, it has *not* been used to impress – and certainly not to discourage – the interested amateur. As paleontologist H. E. Wood once wrote: "The justification for the technical terminology of any specialty is not to serve as a hog latin by which initiates may mystify and exclude hoi polloi. . . ." Rather, technical vocabulary allows precise statements where the simpler or more familiar words of everyday language might be misleading. Technical terms are defined in a glossary at the end of this handbook.

What about scientific names? Here again, precision is the overriding criterion. A scientific name generally permits unequivocal reference to a particular species. Vernacular ("common") names often do not. Consider as an example the vernacular name "gopher." To the biologist, the word "gopher" connotes a pocket gopher, any member of the Family Geomyidae. "Gopher" in this sense is not a very restrictive term — there are some 40 species of pocket gophers. However, lay persons often use the term "gopher" to designate any burrowing rodent. The "Golden Gopher" of Minnesota is not a geomyid but the 13-lined ground squirrel. That same species is called "gopher" (or "picket-pin") in northeastern Colorado. In northwestern Colorado, however, the 13-lined ground squirrel is called "corn weasel"; there "picket-pin" designates the Wyoming ground squirrel, a widely different kind of ground squirrel. In Florida, "gopher" does not refer to a mammal at all, but designates a kind of tortoise. That leaves the local pocket gopher without a common name, so Floridians call them "salamanders"!

Use of scientific names prevents the confusion inherent in a loose system of common names. Scientific names are formulated and proposed under stringent international rules to which the systematic biologists of the world all subscribe voluntarily. Each species of animal or plant has a unique name. The complete name of a species consists of two words. The first word (capitalized) designates the genus to which a species belongs. Often several species comprise a genus and the generic name in common indicates close evolutionary affinity of one species with another. The second word (not capitalized) is unique and refers to a single species. Because they are in a foreign language, scientific names are conventionally printed in italic type.

What is an animal species? To the lay person (and probably to most zoologists), species are groups of individuals that look alike. In most — but by no means all — cases this definition is quite adequate. However, some species look very much alike, especially externally (the Colorado and Uinta chipmunks are examples in Rocky Mountain National Park). On the other hand, individuals within a species may look very different from one another. Siblings from the same litter may differ widely in color or pattern. For example, Abert's squirrels may be black, brown, or gray; "red" foxes may be reddish or "silver" (actually a frosty black);

and "black" bears may be brown. In addition, species vary geographically; in the eastern United States, our "red" squirrels (also called chickarees or pine squirrels) are indeed reddish in color, but here they are not red at all, but a sort of bluish brown. Clearly, a criterion for species more meaningful than mere appearance is needed. Modern zoologists consider species to be groups of actually or potentially reproducing individuals, reproductively isolated from other such groups. Species are thus defined by reproductive continuity, not merely by appearance.

This book is about species of mammals (with brief comments on the families and orders in which the species are classified). Recognized scientific names are used to allow a fixed point of reference for those who might wish to pursue their interest in a species into the technical literature. For those who are interested, the derivations of scientific names (where known to me) are included in Appendix III. Vernacular names usually follow Jones et al. (1982). Where appropriate, some alternative common names are included to make conversation with local naturalists possible. Species are treated in conventional phylogenetic sequence from orders through genera. Species within genera are arranged alphabetically. Descriptions of continental ranges generally follow Hall (1981) and those of ranges in Colorado are based on Armstrong (1972).

Measurements. – Measurements of mammals are given in metric units. (Some incidental measurements are in the so-called "English" system.) This arrangement should not prove confusing, and it may be instructive. The metric system is the world scientific standard and, except in the United States, has become the official commercial standard as well. Philosophically, the metric system is far more satisfying than our traditional system of measurement. The meter is based (roughly) on the circumference of Earth rather than on the length of some forgotten monarch's arm. Also, once one gets used to "thinking metric," it is a much easier system to use than the English system, because everything is based on multiples of ten: 10 millimeters to the centimeter, 100 centimeters to the meter, 1000 meters to the kilometer, 1000 grams to the kilogram, 1000 kilograms to the metric ton. Conversion factors and a table of English-metric equivalents appear in the back of this book.

Acknowledgments. – Numerous readers made comments or corrections on the first edition of this book that have been incorporated into this revision. In particular I thank for their comments several dozen students in "Ecological Mammalogy" at Rocky Mountain Biological Laboratory, Gothic, Colorado, and several hundred students in mammalogy at the University of Colorado, Boulder. Peer review of the manuscript of the first edition (Armstrong, 1975) was provided by David R. Stevens, Dwight L. Hamilton, John R. Douglass, and David B. Butts of Rocky Mountain National Park, and the late Douglas L. Gilbert of Colorado State University. The present edition was further improved by additional criticism from Dave Stevens, Park Biologist at Rocky Mountain National Park, but I continue to claim all errors as my own. I extend special thanks to Laura Armstrong, who typed portions of this revised edition, and to John Armstrong, who participated in numerous field trips to various parts of the Park that improved this edition. For this and other matters I thank Susan for her patience.

Mule Deer doe with twin fawns.

II. WHAT IS A MAMMAL?

Historical. – Mammals are vertebrate animals with hair. The mammals arose from a primitive group of reptiles (the therapsids) in the Triassic period, some 200 million years ago. The earliest mammals mostly were small animals and they probably were of relatively little importance in the ecosystems of their day. In the Triassic period, the ruling reptiles, or "dinosaurs," were coming to dominate the land and shallow seas, a position they were to occupy for over 100 million years. During the Age of Reptiles, mammals remained obscure and relatively unimportant, all the while perfecting the adaptations that are the hallmarks of the mammalian grade of organization. Toward the end of the Cretaceous period (70 million years ago), for reasons that arouse considerable debate, the vast majority of dinosaurs became extinct. Today they are survived only by the crocodiles and their kin (and an early and specialized side branch, the birds). Mammals seized upon the demise of ruling reptiles and diversified rapidly, rising quickly to a dominant position on the land and assuming an important role in freshwater and marine communities as well. Because of this dominance, the Cenozoic era, the past 70 million years, is aptly termed the "Age of Mammals."

Anatomical. – To define mammals as "vertebrate animals with hair" is an obvious understatement. Mammals certainly are far more than reptiles glorified with hair, but hair was a most important evolutionary "invention." In the first place, hair is an insulator. With a hairy coat separating the body from the environment, maintenance of a high and relatively constant body temperature is possible. Endothermy, or warm-bloodedness—as such temperature maintenance usually is called—allows an animal to remain active despite the ambient temperature. The cold-blooded (ectothermic) reptiles, on the other hand, can be active only when environmental temperatures rise well above freezing. Today reptiles are diverse only in tropical and subtropical areas of Earth. Mammals, on the other hand, have successfully occupied the cold environments of high latitudes and high elevations, areas completely beyond the tolerance of most reptiles. (For example, at most 11 species of reptiles and amphibians occur in Rocky Mountain National Park, less than 20% of the mammalian fauna.)

Coupled with the insulation provided by hair, mammals have evolved a highly efficient circulatory system. As in birds, the heart consists of four chambers. There are completely separate routes for blood to the body and blood to the lungs. Blood arriving at the tissues is rich in oxygen, allowing high rates of metabolism and a high level of activity.

The name "mammal" is derived from the Latin word *mamma*, "teat," and alludes to another hallmark of the class. Female mammals produce milk to nourish their young. Milk is secreted by specialized glands thought to represent highly modified sweat glands. Since sweat glands are peculiar to mammals and are associated with hair, the elaboration of mammary glands re-emphasizes the importance of hair in the evolution of mammals.

Milk is the food of young mammals immediately after birth. Milk varies in composition from species to species, but generally contains fats, sugar, and protein. On this rich diet—balanced to the needs of each particular species—young mammals grow until they are able to obtain their own food. But suckling allows more than a simple head-start. It permits a period of contact between the mother and her offspring. The nursing period allows the parent to train the young. By complex means such as imitative play, the young receive information learned through experience by the parental generation. In animals that show no parental care, communication between generations can only be by way of the genes, the biological inheritance. In mammals (and to a much lesser extent in birds) training can take place.

The possibility for training during a period of maternal dependence has made it advantageous for mammals to increase the size and complexity of learning centers in the brain, generally at the expense of lower centers concerned with innate (in-born or instinctive) behavioral patterns. Mammals as a class have a behavioral plasticity unmatched by other animal groups.

Another advance of mammals over their reptilian forebears is the presence of specialized teeth. Mammalian teeth are set in sockets (a condition termed "thecodont"). This provides mechanical strength for tearing, gnawing, or grinding. From front to back within the toothrow, the teeth are specialized for various functions ("heterodont"). One kind of tooth design is better for gnawing or nipping, another superior for grinding or crushing. Specialization of individual teeth within the toothrow allows far greater efficiency in collecting food and preparing it for digestion than does a dentition in which all teeth are the same ("homodont"). Four sorts of teeth are recognizable in most mammals—incisors, canines, premolars, and molars. Teeth of mammals are described numerically in terms of a "dental formula," which describes the upper and lower dentition in one side of the jaw. Thus, the dental formula of ancestral mammals was: incisors, 3/3; canines, 1/1; premolars, 4/4; molars, 3/3; total teeth, 44. Dental formulas of mammals of Rocky Mountain National Park are shown in Table 1.

Mammalian teeth differ greatly with feeding habits. The cheekteeth of some voles grow throughout life, an adaptation to an abrasive diet of grasses. The teeth of squirrels are suited to crushing and grinding seeds. Rodents have no canine teeth, because the food of most species is plants. Mammals that feed on other animals (most members of the Order Carnivora, for example) have well-developed canine teeth to grasp and hold the prey. The cats (and to a lesser extent, other carnivores as well) have a highly efficient shearing mechanism between upper and lower cheekteeth. The evolution from a common ancestor of species adapted to perform specialized ecological roles is termed "adaptive radiation." The diversity of mammalian dental patterns is a classic example of this phenomenon.

Adaptive radiation also has occurred in means of locomotion. Primitive mammals have five toes on each foot, both fore and aft. In modern mammals the number of toes may be reduced to one on each foot (and in some of the marine mammals, toes are lost completely). The primitive stance probably was plantigrade (as in humans and bears), with

Table 1. Dental formulas of mammals of Rocky Mountain National Park and vicinity (I = incisors, C = canines, P = premolars, M = molars).

I 3/3, C 1/1, P 4/4, M 2/3 = 42	*Ursus,* * *Canis, Vulpes, Urocyon*
I 3/3, C 1/1, P 4/4, M 2/2 = 40	*Procyon, Bassariscus*
I 2/3, C 1/1, P 3/3, M 3/3 = 38	*Myotis*
I 3/3, C 1/1, P 4/4, M 1/2 = 38	*Martes, Gulo*
I 2/3, C 1/1, P 2/3, M 3/3 = 36	*Lasionycteris, Plecotus*
I 3/3, C 1/1, P 4/3, M 1/2 = 36	*Lutra*
I 3/3, C 1/1, P 3/3, M 1/2 = 34	*Mustela, Mephitis, Taxidea, Spilogale*
I 0/3, C 1/1, P 3/3, M 3/3 = 34	*Cervus*
I 2/2, C 1/1, P 2/2, M 3/3 = 32	*Homo*
I 2/3, C 1/1, P 1/2, M 3/3 = 32	*Eptesicus*
I 3/1, C 1/1, P 3/1, M 3/3 = 32	*Sorex*
I 1/3, C 1/1, P 2/2, M 3/3 = 32	*Lasiurus*
I 0/3, C 0/1, P 3/3, M 3/3 = 32	*Odocoileus, Alces, Bison, Antilocapra, Ovis, Oreamnos*
I 3/3, C 1/1, P 2–3/2, M 1/1 = 28 or 30	*Felis*
I 2/1, C 0/0, P 3/2, M 3/3 = 28	*Lepus, Sylvilagus*
I 2/1, C 0/0, P 2/2, M 3/3 = 26	*Ochotona*
I 1/1, C 0/0, P 2/1, M 3/3 = 22	*Marmota, Spermophilus, Tamias, Tamiasciurus, Cynomys, Sciurus* *
I 1/1, C 0/0, P 1/1, M 3/3 = 20	*Castor, Erethizon, Thomomys*
I 1/1, C 0/0, P 1/0, M 3/3 = 18	*Zapus*
I 1/1, C 0/0, P 0/0, M 3/3 = 16	*Neotoma, Phenacomys, Clethrionomys, Microtus, Peromyscus, Lemmiscus, Ondatra*

*May have one upper premolar missing.

the toes, foot bones, and parts of the ankle and wrist in contact with the ground. The stance of modern mammals may be digitigrade (only the digits on the ground, as in dogs) or unguligrade (only the tips of the toes—protected by an ungule or hoof—on the ground), as in horses and cattle.

Diversity has evolved not only in stance, but in the mode of progression, or gait. Primitive mammals probably were ambulatory (walkers). In open habitats, swift cursorial (running) locomotion is at a premium among larger animals, and smaller species in such situations often are saltatorial (jumping). Natatorial (swimming) mammals represent a number of groups; the whales are so modified to marine life that they are completely helpless ashore. Invading the trees, some mammalian groups became scansorial (climbers). Some scansorial groups (for example, the flying squirrels) have adapted for efficient glissant (gliding) locomotion, but only one order, the bats, is volant (that is, capable of true, powered flight). The diversity of locomotor adaptations points out how plastic the basic mammalian body plan has been. Mammals compete successfully not only with other terrestrial groups, but with birds and fishes as well.

Reproductive. – Reptiles advanced over their amphibian ancestors and successfully invaded the land by evolving the shelled egg. The land egg has a number of membranes. Just within the shell is the chorion, which protects the developing embryo from desiccation. Two membranous bags attach to the belly of the embryonic reptile. The yolk sac contains stored food and the allantois serves to collect wastes from the embryo. Closely surrounding the embryo is another membrane, the fluid-filled amnionic sac. The amnionic fluid provides the developing reptile with protection from temperature change, chemical insult, and mechanical shock. In short, the land egg provides the embryonic reptile with its own "private pond."

Mammals took the basic structure of the reptilian egg and went a few steps farther. Among living mammals, only the monotremes (the duck-billed platypus of Australia and the spiny anteaters of Australia and New Guinea) lay shelled eggs. In all other mammals the shelless eggs are retained within the reproductive tract of the mother. The membranes of the reptilian egg remain, however. The amnionic sac and its fluid protect the developing mammals, and parts of the allantois and yolk sac form the umbilical cord. The chorion – the outer membrane of the cleidoic egg – comes into contact with the wall of the uterus. The chorion and the adjacent allantois are well supplied with blood vessels and through these vessels essential nutrients and oxygen pass from the blood of the mother to that of the embryo. Waste gases and fluids pass back in the opposite direction. The complex of embryonic and maternal membranes that permits this two-way exchange of materials is called the placenta. A placenta is characteristic of the largest group of mammals, the Eutheria; the marsupials (Metatheria – pouched mammals, such as the opossum) lack a true placenta. In many mammalian groups the placenta is passed with the newborn young at birth, and is termed the "afterbirth."

In most mammals, reproduction occurs during only a part of the year, the so-called "breeding season." In females, hormones secreted by the ovaries and the pituitary gland regulate the reproductive cycle. Interplay of these hormones produces a sequence of events known as the estrous cycle. Estrus (commonly called "heat") often coincides with ovulation, the release of eggs from the ovaries. During estrus, the female is receptive to the male. An interval termed proestrus precedes the period of heat. During proestrus, follicles on the ovaries are stimulated by pituitary hormones to produce egg cells (ova). The ovarian follicle produces a hormone (estrogen) that stimulates the growth of the lining of the uterus. After the ovum is shed from the follicle, the ruptured follicle forms a structure known as a corpus luteum ("yellow body"), which secretes the hormone progesterone. Progesterone causes the uterus to become quiescent, ready for the implantation of the embryos, should fertilization occur. If fertilization does take place, the embryos develop within the uterus for a variable length of time, the gestation period. During gestation, progesterone is secreted by the placenta to help maintain the quiescence of the uterus.

The length of the gestation period varies from a few days in some small rodents to nearly two years in the African elephant. In a number of mammals, embryonic development does not begin immediately after fertilization. Rather, the fertilized egg (zygote) undergoes a few cell divisions and then development is suspended, frequently for a number of months. Later the early embryo is implanted in the uterine wall and development continues. This phenomenon is known as delayed implantation.

Mammals which breed but once a year are termed "monoestrous"; those which breed more than once a year are described as "polyestrous." In many polyestrous mammals the estrous cycle ceases temporarily during gestation and lactation (nursing). However, some rodents exhibit a "post-partum estrus" and mate immediately after giving birth (parturition). Females of species with post-partum estrus can be lactating and gestating at the same time.

Generally the sexual activity of males also is seasonal. Sperm are produced only during the time of the year when females are reproductively active. Active testes are situated in a sack, the scrotum, outside the body cavity. Here the cooler temperatures necessary for sperm production can be maintained. When active spermatogenesis (sperm-production) is not taking place, the testes of many species return to lie within the abdominal cavity.

The timing of reproduction depends on specific annual rhythms. The annual cycle may be endogenous (that is, it may be specifically encoded in the genetic program of the animal). Endogenous rhythms continue in the laboratory in the absence of external environmental stimuli. Other rhythms are exogenous. Exogenous rhythms depend upon environmental cues, such as day length (photoperiod) and environmental temperature. Annual rhythms control not only the reproductive cycle, but such periodic phenomena as hibernation and migration as well.

Selected General References. – Anderson and Jones (1984); Eisenberg (1981); Vaughan (1986); Nowak and Paradiso (1983).

III. MAMMALIAN DISTRIBUTION

The Ecological Context. – Mammals are not distributed at random over the Earth. On a broad scale, long-term evolutionary sequences and geologic accidents determine which species occur where. More locally, the most important factor in mammalian distribution is the character of the vegetation. Vegetation provides mammals with cover and food (either directly or indirectly). The best predictor of the presence or absence of a species in a particular locality is the character of the local plant community. Thus, description of mammalian habitats in Rocky Mountain National Park (as indicated in Table 2) is important. Within the local species population, distribution of mammals is non-random also. The area covered by an individual in its daily round of activity is called the "home range." The home range varies in size from a fraction of a hectare for small mammals, such as shrews and some rodents, to many square kilometers for some large carnivores, such as grizzly bears.

A part of the home range may be defended against other members of the species. The defended area is termed a "territory." Two basic kinds of territories are commonly observed: the breeding territory and the foraging territory. Territoriality results in dispersion of individuals over

Table 2. Ecological distribution of mammals in Rocky Mountain National Park and vicinity.

	Ponderosa Pine Woodland	Subalpine Forest	Meadows	Aspen Woodland	Streambank/ Shoreline	Alpine Meadow/ Fellfield	Mountain Brush	Sagebrush
Masked Shrew	X	X	X	X	X	X		
Pygmy Shrew		X			X	X		
Merriam's Shrew								X
Montane Shrew	X	X	X	X	X			
Dwarf Shrew	X	X	X	X		X	X	X
Water Shrew					X	X		
Long-eared Myotis	X							
Little Brown Bat	X		X	X	X		X	
Small-footed Myotis							X	
Fringed Myotis	X							
Long-legged Myotis	X			X	X		X	
Silver-haired Bat	X	X		X				
Big Brown Bat	X			X			X	
Hoary Bat	X	X		X	X			
Townsend's Big-eared Bat	X						X	
Pika						X		
Nuttall's Cottontail	X	X	X	X	X		X	X
Snowshoe Hare		X		X	X			
White-tailed Jackrabbit	X	X	X	X		X	X	X
Least Chipmunk	X	X	X	X		X		X
Colorado Chipmunk	X						X	
Uinta Chipmunk		X	X					
Yellow-bellied Marmot	X	X	X	X		X		X
Wyoming Ground Squirrel	X		X					X
Golden-mantled Ground Squirrel	X	X	X	X		X	X	X
Rock Squirrel	X						X	
Abert's Squirrel	X							
Chickaree	X	X						
Northern Pocket Gopher	X	X	X	X		X	X	X
Beaver		X	X	X	X			
Rock Mouse	X						X	
Deer Mouse	X	X	X	X		X	X	X
Bushy-tailed Woodrat	X	X				X	X	

Mexican Woodrat	X						X	
Southern Red-backed Vole		X						
Heather Vole		X						
Long-tailed Vole	X	X	X	X	X	X		X
Montane Vole	X	X	X	X	X	X		X
Sagebrush Vole								X
Muskrat					X	X		
Western Jumping Mouse		X	X	X	X	X		
Porcupine	X	X					X	X
Coyote	X	X	X	X	X	X	X	X
Red Fox			X	X	X			
Gray Fox	X						X	
Raccoon					X	X		
Ringtail	X						X	
Black Bear	X	X		X	X		X	
Marten		X				X		
Ermine		X	X	X	X	X		
Long-tailed Weasel	X	X	X	X	X	X	X	X
Black-footed Ferret		X						X
Mink						X		
Wolverine		X						
Badger	X		X			X	X	X
Western Spotted Skunk							X	
Striped Skunk	X	X	X	X	X	X	X	X
River Otter						X		
Mountain Lion	X						X	
Lynx		X						
Bobcat	X	X				X	X	X
Wapiti	X	X	X	X	X	X		X
Mule Deer	X	X	X	X	X	X	X	X
White-tailed Deer					X			
Moose					X			
Pronghorn								X
Bighorn Sheep	X		X			X	X	

available habitat. As a result the resources of the ecosystem are not overtaxed by an over-concentrated population. In Rocky Mountain National Park, where some populations may have access to artificially great resources (garbage dumps, campgrounds, picnic areas, and scenic viewpoints, for example), unnatural concentrations of animals may congregate. Under such circumstances normal territorial behavior may break down.

The kind of biotic community in which a mammal lives is termed its "habitat." Because the habitat requirements of any particular species tend to be rather narrow, the experienced observer can simply look at a natural community and predict with considerable accuracy the kinds of animals that might occur. Major criteria involved in the description of habitats are vegetation, cover, soil, and moisture relationships. A complete description of a habitat would involve all characteristics of an animal's physical and biotic surroundings. Two or more species may share the same basic habitat. For example, both porcupines and Abert's squirrels occupy trees of the ponderosa pine woodland.

The functional role of an animal in a community is termed its "ecological niche." The terms habitat and niche sometimes are used interchangeably, but that is unfortunate. The niche is a complex and distinctive concept. Eminent ecologist E. P. Odum contrasted habitat and niche nicely: habitat is a species' "address"; niche is a species' "occupation." Description of habitat may be relatively simple; description of a niche is notoriously complex. The role of any species is sufficiently complicated that it probably is fair to say that for no species has the niche been described thoroughly.

A given ecological niche is occupied by a single species. Where two or more species have the same or closely similar demands on the environment (broad niche overlap), one species will eventually displace the other, a phenomenon known as competitive exclusion. The result may be the extinction of one species, its restriction to areas from which the competing species is absent, or changes in behavioral patterns that allow co-existence without direct competition. In this manner, the resources of an ecosystem are partitioned among the species that occupy the system.

Altitudinal Distribution.—The person who travels from the eastern plains (at Loveland, Longmont, or Boulder, for example) to the top of Trail Ridge Road will have passed in a space of tens of kilometers (and about 2000 meters of elevation) through a remarkably wide range of ecological conditions. To encompass a comparable range of conditions traveling northward with no change in elevation, one would need to go nearly 3200 kilometers (2000 miles), from Colorado to the Canadian Arctic. Approaching the Park from the west the effects of elevation are less apparent (because elevational change is less abrupt), but the effects are there, nonetheless.

A striking effect of increasing elevation (or increasing latitude) is the zonation of biotic communities. Approaching the Park from the east, for example, one passes from plains grassland through a narrow shrub zone, upward through various kinds of forest, to the alpine zone. Why are biotic communities zoned? For a start, recall that each species has a genetic program. That program specifies a range of tolerance for the species, a range of conditions (within the broader range of environmental conditions) within which it can exist. Each species-specific range of tolerance is characterized by a minimum, a maximum, and (in most cases) an optimum—a point on the scale where conditions are best for survival and reproduction. The environment provides a range of resources and conditions. For virtually any environmental factor that one might wish to investigate—temperature, rainfall, growing season, sunlight, available minerals, and so on) a range of conditions could be discovered. Species array themselves along resource gradients by occupying those areas that are most favorable.

In the complex web of competitive interactions that typifies natural communities there is a tendency for species to be restricted to a relatively narrow set of conditions ranging around the optimum. At the extremes of its range of tolerance, a given species may be less competitive than another species with a different genetic optimum.

In mountainous areas, many environmental factors vary with elevation. Doubtless the most obvious of these is temperature, but the amount of sunlight, actual and effective precipitation, composition of the atmosphere, texture of the soil, and other factors also change with elevation. Even relatively obscure factors, such as the mineral content of soils, may vary with elevation, for water is the great natural transport medium in ecological systems, and water flows downhill, changing concentrations of materials as it goes.

Physical factors of the environment are zoned with elevation. Organisms respond to the gradient of physical factors by occupying areas where they are most competitive, where conditions range closely about the optima for their needs. Where physical factors occur as altitudinal belts or bands so—as a direct consequence—do biotic communities.

Early workers in Colorado (and elsewhere in western North America) described elevational zonation in terms of formal "life zones." Recently, more informal systems of zones have been developed which are applicable to our area. The lowest of the vegetational zones is the *montane* woodland or forest, a relatively open community dominated by ponderosa pine or Douglas-fir, depending on local site qualities. The mon-

Ponderosa pine woodland; Mt. Meeker and Longs Peak in the distance. *National Park Service*

tane zone occurs at elevations from about 6000 to 9000 feet (roughly 2000 to 3000 meters). Between 9000 feet and about 11,500 feet (300–3700 meters) is a zone of *subalpine* forest, dominated by Engelmann spruce and subalpine fir. The upper limit of the subalpine is treeline. Above treeline is the *alpine* zone. For detailed description of the plants of these zones, the interested reader should consult Ruth Ashton Nelson's *Plants of Rocky Mountain National Park*, William A. Weber's *Rocky Mountain Flora*, or Mutel and Emerick's *From Grassland to Glacier, the Natural History of Colorado*.

Within the broad altitudinal zones, local conditions dictate development of a diversity of habitats, which we may call biotic community-types. Recognition and description of biotic community-types helps to

Subalpine forest, Kawuneeche Valley. *National Park Service*

point out the diversity of mammalian habitats in Rocky Mountain National Park. The list here is not exhaustive. It simply includes those sorts of communities that are most important from the standpoint of mammalian distribution. Under that criterion, nine community-types seem worthy of brief description. Let us consider each of these in turn, listing a few of the mammalian species characteristic of each.

Montane forest is the relatively open forest of moderate elevations in the Park, dominated by ponderosa pine (*Pinus ponderosa*) on drier, more exposed sites, and by Douglas-fir (*Pseudotsuga menziesii*) in moister locations. As the name implies, this is the forest community of the montane zone. In favorably moist areas, blue spruce (*Picea pungens*) may occur. In general, we may consider the montane forest to be a ponderosa

Krummholz. *National Park Service*

Lodgepole pine forest. *David M. Armstrong*

Montane meadow. *David M. Armstrong*

Streamside habitat. *David M. Armstrong*

24

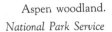

Aspen woodland.
National Park Service

pine woodland with local variations depending on soil moisture and microclimate. In some parts of Colorado it is appropriate to separate ponderosa pine woodland and the more complex montane forest as distinct community-types, but in our area such distinction is difficult and not very useful. Montane forest occurs along the western edge of Estes Park. Most of the private resort development in the vicinity is in this community-type, as is the National Park Headquarters and Visitor's Center southwest of Estes Park. Typical mammals of the community-type include such bats as the long-eared myotis (*Myotis evotis*) and the long-legged myotis (*Myotis volans*), and Abert's squirrel (*Sciurus aberti*).

Willow thicket. *David M. Armstrong*

Subalpine forest constitutes a relatively closed stand composed chiefly of Engelmann spruce (*Picea engelmannii*) and subalpine fir (*Abies lasiocarpa*). Limber pine (*Pinus flexilis*) occurs locally. The forest frequently is interrupted by bogs, ponds, and stands of quaking aspen. Tree species of the subalpine forest are stunted at high elevations to form an elfin woodland or krummholz, familiar to the traveler on Trail Ridge Road or the higher hiking trails of the Park. The upper limit of subalpine forest is treeline. Few mammals are restricted to subalpine forest. The snowshoe hare (*Lepus americanus*) and two species perhaps extirpated from the Park, the wolverine (*Gulo gulo*) and the lynx (*Lynx lynx*), would be characteristic of such forests. Other species of the abundant fauna of subalpine forest are more typical of adjacent communities.

Stands of *lodgepole pine* are found in the Park mostly on flat to gently rolling sites with well-drained soils. Often lodgepole pine stands have a history of fire. The trees form nearly pure stands, and a young forest presents an almost impenetrable maze of trees. From a mammal's-eye-view, this is an unimportant community-type. Because the heavy growth of trees prevents much light from reaching the forest floor, growth of herbs is minimal. Most of the community's resources are tied up in trees. Among herbivorous mammals, only chickarees (*Tamiasciurus hudsonicus*) are found in any numbers. Southern red-backed voles (*Clethrionomys gapperi*) may be associated with chickaree middens and martens (*Martes americana*) feed extensively on chickarees.

Throughout Rocky Mountain National Park are openings in the forest where *montane* and *subalpine meadows* have developed. Such meadows often are called "parks" locally, and when sufficiently large may be dignified with proper names—Estes Park, Hollowell Park, Tuxedo Park, Moraine Park, Horseshoe Park. Many of these larger parks (and some lesser meadows as well) develop in areas of fine-grained (poorly drained) soils and high water tables. Herbs (including both grasses and forbs) are sufficiently well established that the access of trees to the areas is precluded or slowed to an imperceptible pace. The consequences of these meadows for mammals are immense. For one thing, meadows provide optimal range for grazing mammals. For many years, elk competed with cattle for dominance in the major parks. Earlier, bison utilized mountain parks as prime summer range. For another thing, meadows break up the continuity of forests. There is a tendency for an increase in the diversity of species and in biotic productivity at the interface between adjacent communities. This is termed the "edge effect." The edge effect is due in part to the juxtaposition of the protective cover of forest and the greater productivity of the well-lighted meadow. By increasing the "edge" in the mountain ecosystem, meadows increase local diversity, productivity, and interest to people.

Species of mountain meadows include the Wyoming ground squirrel (*Spermophilus elegans*), the northern pocket gopher (*Thomomys talpoides*), and the long-tailed vole (*Microtus longicaudus*). In tall-grass meadows, the western jumping mouse (*Zapus princeps*) is common. Species of the forest edge include the yellow-bellied marmot (*Marmota flaviventris*), the golden-mantled ground squirrel (*Spermophilus lateralis*), Nuttall's cottontail (*Sylvilagus nuttallii*), the least chipmunk (*Tamias minimus*), and—at higher elevations—the Uinta chipmunk (*Tamias umbrinus*). Generally speaking, montane parks are drier than subalpine meadows and have a less extensive fauna. When adequately moist, however, montane meadows have essentially the same fauna as their subalpine counterpart.

Treeline. *David M. Armstrong*

Tundra above Forest Canyon. *National Park Service*

Fellfield, Trail Ridge. *David M. Armstrong*

Aspen woodland, dominated by *Populus tremuloides*, occurs through-out the Park, usually as small- to moderate-sized stands in relatively moist areas. Aspen woodland is an important stage in reforestation after fire on many sites. The dappled shade and moist soil of an aspen wood-land encourage the development of a luxuriant understory of herbs. This provides excellent habitat for such species as the montane vole (*Microtus montanus*) and the western jumping mouse (*Zapus princeps*). There are many similarities between the fauna of the aspen woodland and that of streambank and shoreline communities.

Streambank and shoreline communities develop along streams and about ponds and lakes, and in them occurs a typical mammalian fauna. Beaver (*Castor canadensis*) feed on willows, alder, and aspen near the water's edge. Marshy grasslands are inhabited by shrews (*Sorex cinereus, S. monticolus*), the muskrat (*Ondatra zibethicus*), and the western jumping mouse (*Zapus princeps*). Water shrews (*Sorex palustris*) occur about stream-side rocks and fallen timber. Such communities are found through much of the Park, from canyon-bound streams of lower elevations, to quiet ponds of the high forests, to snow-fed rivulets above timberline.

Alpine meadows and fellfield occupy much of the area above timberline. Within this community-type, which corresponds to the alpine zone, is a complex array of habitats. Alpine meadows consist of mats of low grasses, sedges, and forbs overlying a thin soil. On well-watered sites, thickets of dwarf willows prevail. Fellfield is a common term derived from the German word for rock (*Fels*) and refers to boulderfields, stabilized talus slopes, and any other very rocky terrain. Alpine habitats in the Park are quite accessible to the casual visitor along Trail Ridge Road. The more serious student of the alpine zone may follow such communities virtually uninterrupted along the Continental Divide the entire length of the Park.

No mammalian species is restricted to the alpine zone, although the pika (*Ochotona princeps*) may find optimal conditions there, and white-tailed jackrabbits (*Lepus townsendii*), marmots (*Marmota flaviventris*), and northern pocket gophers (*Thomomys talpoides*) are abundant. The community provides summer range for large grazers, including elk, deer, and bighorn sheep.

"Saxicoline" means "rock-inhabiting" and *saxicoline brush* refers to a community developed on broken, rocky terrain. Bitterbrush (*Purshia tridentata*) is perhaps the most important shrub in this community in our area of interest; to the east and north, mountain mahogany (*Cercocarpus montanus*) is important. A widespread community-type in Colorado, saxicoline brush is best developed in the Park at lower elevations on the Eastern Slope, in particular on the western edge of Estes Park. It is also prevalent in the canyons leading to the Park from the east and in the lower, rougher, more exposed parts of the foothills. Mammals typical of saxicoline brush include the dwarf shrew (*Sorex nanus*), the small-footed myotis (*Myotis leibii*), the Colorado chipmunk (*Tamias quadrivittatus*), the rock squirrel (*Spermophilus variegatus*), the rock mouse (*Peromyscus difficilis*), the Mexican woodrat (*Neotoma mexicana*), the spotted skunk (*Spilogale gracilis*), and the gray fox (*Urocyon cinereoargenteus*).

Sagebrush communities are characterized by shrubs of the genus *Artemisia*. Sagebrush occurs as small stands at widely scattered localities in the Park. However, extensive sagebrush communities occur only at lower elevations in Arapaho National Recreation Area. Such communities appear as broad expanses of grayish green shrubs, often with a generous

Saxicoline brush. *David M. Armstrong*

cover of low herbs beneath. Sagebrush communities are generally continuous from our area westward into Middle Park and other open country in the upper Colorado drainage. Mammals that typify the sagebrush community include the Wyoming ground squirrel (*Spermophilus elegans*) and the pronghorn (*Antilocarpa americana*). Farther west, the white-tailed prairie dog (*Cynomys leucurus*) is important and conspicuous.

Faunal Relationships of Rocky Mountain National Park. – Zoogeography is the study of the distribution of animals. Zoogeographic studies provide clues to the character of ecosystems of the past. Often, species are not continuously distributed, but occur as a patchwork or mosaic. Areas of habitat suitable for a given kind of animal may be separated from each other by tracts of unsuitable country.

In general terms, the closest faunal relationships of the mammals of Rocky Mountain National Park are to the north. A broad band of coniferous forest—sometimes called by its Russian name, "taiga"—stretches across North America and Asia. The mammals of the taiga

Sagebrush. *David M. Armstrong*

often are circumboreal (also termed holarctic); that is, they occur in both the New and Old worlds. The grizzly bear, gray wolf, lynx, wolverine, short-tailed weasel, and elk all are circumboreal species. In other cases, closely related species occupy similar niches in the taiga of Eurasia and North America. For example, there are species of red-backed voles in both Eurasia and North America. Southward, taiga is increasingly restricted to areas of high elevation. Temperature decreases with increasing elevation so that in many respects habitats of high elevation are comparable to those of high latitudes. At medium elevations in the Colorado Rockies, a zone of taiga occurs. Above timberline, habitats are somewhat comparable to those of the Arctic tundra. The farther south one proceeds, the higher one must go to reach conditions suitable for the development of taiga or tundra. In Colorado the taiga is more or less continuous along the main ranges of the Rockies. Continuity is interrupted for only short distances at major passes or breaks in the mountain chain. Alpine tundra, however, occurs only on high mountains. Patches of tundra are well isolated from one another, forming a chain of "islands." Farther south, taiga also becomes slightly discontinuous.

Although the taiga in Colorado is essentially continuous, it is separated from similar habitats in areas adjacent to the north (such as northern Utah and northwestern Wyoming) by appreciable ecological barriers. How did mountain mammals get to the forested "island" of the Colorado Rockies?

The Cenozoic era—the past 70 million years of geological time—has been marked by major changes in world climate. Throughout most of the era there has been a gradual cooling trend over the Earth. The most recent episode in this history is the so-called Quaternary period. The Quaternary period comprises the past 2 million years (more or less) and includes the Pleistocene epoch, or "Ice Age," and Recent or Holocene times. The Pleistocene was characterized by the recurrence of glacial advances both at middle and high latitudes and at high elevations. Glacial intervals were separated by interglacial periods in which de-glaciation was complete. For all we know, the present might simply be an interglacial interval.

The continental ice sheets which scoured much of Canada and the northern United States did not reach Colorado. There were, however, recurrent episodes of alpine glaciation. Glaciation and accompanying erosion carved the spectacular alpine scenery of Rocky Mountain National Park. Indeed, the physical landscape as we know it throughout much of North America is primarily a product of the Pleistocene epoch.

During the Pleistocene, valley glaciers occurred as low as about 2100 meters (7000 feet) in Colorado. At high elevations, valley glaciers sometimes coalesced to form cap ice. The effects of glaciation on the distribution of biotic communities were immense. In particular, cooling allowed an increase in effective precipitation. With moister conditions, forest communities typical of the mountains today could have occurred at lower elevations. The biotic zonation so readily observed in mountainous areas apparently was depressed, perhaps by as much as 1000 to 1200 meters (3000 to 4000 feet). With a depression of biotic zones, forest was continuous (at least intermittently) across areas that are not forested today. It was during the glacial stages that forest-adapted mammals made their way to and from Colorado.

Selected References.—Armstrong (1972); Cary (1911); Mutel and Emerick (1984).

IV. HOW TO OBSERVE MAMMALS

WILD MAMMALS CAN be difficult to observe. Perhaps that is why we hear more about bird watchers than we do about "mammal watchers." Most mammals could be described as "shy" or "retiring." Of course those are human terms describing human traits. Non-human animals have non-human adaptations, but their habits earn them anthropomorphic descriptions. Mammals are seldom "shy" when facing their environments on their own terms. They are simply hungry or they are not. Under usual conditions, many species are quite "curious" and the successful mammal watcher uses this fact to advantage.

A majority of mammals are active at night (nocturnal) or during the twilight hours (crepuscular). The squirrels, which are active by day (diurnal), are the principal exceptions to this rule in northern latitudes. Squirrels are interesting and entertaining subjects, a good group on which aspiring mammal watchers can sharpen their skills.

Select a comfortable spot at the edge of a meadow. If you remain quiet, the squirrels in the neighborhood soon will resume their normal activity. Wyoming ground squirrels scurry about in open, grassy areas. From beneath a boulder or fallen log, marmots venture forth to feed on leaves or sun themselves on warm rocks. Least chipmunks dart about, busily

Muskrat lodge. *David M. Armstrong*

Beaver lodge. *National Park Service*

Wyoming ground squirrel burrow. *David M. Armstrong*

seeking seeds or insects to eat. In the forest, chickarees bark their excited alarm, and then accept your presence and go about their daily round of activities. With practice, you will come to recognize individuals by distinctive scars, molt patterns, or behavioral peculiarities. Soon the complexities of social life will begin to be familiar. The most useful tool for the mammal watcher is patience. For observing marmots and tree squirrels, field glasses may be useful, but chipmunks are mostly too small and they move too rapidly to follow easily with binoculars.

Evening is the best time to observe the mammals of Rocky Mountain National Park. A beaver pond may appear lifeless during the day, save for the ripple of an occasional trout, or the splash of a startled leopard frog, or the whispering sound of a garter snake moving through a shoreline marsh. But return to the pond at dusk. Wear a warm jacket and insect repellent so that you can sit quietly and watch the pond. Soon beaver will begin to ply the pond, moving silently from lodge to shore to dam, feeding, repairing the dam, or storing winter food. Musk-

Aspen scraped by wapiti, or elk, Roaring River. *David M. Armstrong*

rats are also more active at dusk, usually using beaver ponds in the mountains.

Stay alert for mule deer or elk coming to the pond to drink. At lower elevations you may see raccoons beginning their nocturnal rounds. Overhead, bats flutter about taking their evening's toll of insects. The bats of the Park can often be distinguished by their typical patterns in flight and characteristic times of emergence. A musty smell in the willows near the water's edge may tell of a wet porcupine.

A handy device for the mammal watcher is a flashlight or battery lantern fitted with a red filter. Red plastic, cellophane, or even a coat of nail polish will do. Many nocturnal mammals are not at all disturbed by the red light, and this technique allows observation of species seldom seen otherwise. A good place to try your red light is in an unoccupied cabin or around a pile of rocks. During the day, note the sign of wood-rats or deer mice—droppings or nesting materials identify their hide-outs. Then return after dark and quietly await their appearance. With

Porcupine damage, ponderosa pine. *David M. Armstrong*

your red light you can observe their interesting – and often highly entertaining – activities without interfering with normal activity.

The sign of mammals – tracks, droppings (scat), nests, trails – provides
unmistakable evidence of a species' occurrence even though the animal
itself may never be seen. The observant naturalist can piece together
an image of mammalian activity in a community without ever seeing
the animals themselves.

Nearly everyone recognizes an aspen or willow gnawed by a beaver.
Claw marks on tree trunks are evidence of the black bear. Bark removed
from high on the trunk of a ponderosa pine tells of porcupines in the
neighborhood. Chickarees make their presence known by leaving piles
of unopened spruce, fir, or lodgepole pine cones neatly cut from the
branches and by accumulating middens of cone scales and other debris.
Abert's squirrels clip and drop bundles of needles from ponderosa pines.
In moist meadows, look for tunnels in the grass, the runways of the
montane vole. Often, short, neatly cut pieces of grass litter the trails

Chickaree midden. *David M. Armstrong*

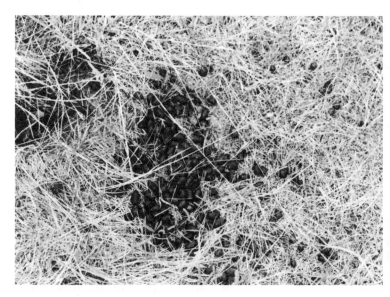

Elk droppings, Horseshoe Park. *David M. Armstrong*

of these mice. Old runways may be used by other small mammals, especially deer mice and shrews. The presence of grass from which the seeds have been stripped points to the activity of jumping mice. Look for small trees and shrubs from which the tender young branches have been removed. This may be the work of deer or may point to browsing by rabbits. At higher elevations, grasses and forbs are harvested by pikas and piled in "haystacks" to serve as winter food.

Scat, or droppings, is another kind of useful mammalian sign. The round fecal pellets of rabbits are familiar to most people as are the larger, elliptical droppings of deer. The minute scat of shrews frequently is deposited on conspicuous (from the shrew's point of view!) objects in the environment such as the tops of fallen leaves or a negligent visitor's paper plate. Coyote droppings are abundant in many habitats and frequently contain feathers or bits of broken bone.

Owls regurgitate pellets of fur, bone, and other undigestible materials. At first, these may be confused with the scat of a mammal, but owl pellets are far looser in their construction and they often contain unbroken bones, including intact skulls. Owl pellets are an excellent source of evidence of the small mammals of an area. Frequently owls are "the better mousetrap," providing evidence of the occurrence of secretive small mammals that would not be obvious otherwise.

Tracks are perhaps the most commonly observed sign of mammals. With practice, one can read detailed stories of the intricacies of mammalian activities and interactions simply by careful observation of tracks. You may see tracks of a coyote, for example, superimposed upon those of a rabbit. The evidence should tell you at what point the rabbit sensed the presence of the coyote, where instinct and experience told the rabbit to take flight, and whether the coyote captured the rabbit or turned elsewhere for dinner. Tracks of deer tell not only that deer are present, but how many have passed by, which direction they went, and how fast they were going.

For most would-be mammal watchers the best place to look for tracks is in the firm mud around a pond or along a streambank. Dusty trails and rocky areas are more difficult to work and tracks are less obvious. The best place of all is in fresh, wet snow. Here tracks of the larger, more familiar species are readily seen. In addition, however, the tracks of smaller mammals—a scurrying mouse and a bounding weasel—are preserved. The sight of myriad mammal trails on fresh snow is just one

Weasel tracks in snow. *National Park Service*

of the rewards reserved for those who venture out to observe the mountain world in winter on skis or snowshoes.

Making casts of tracks is an excellent way to "collect" mammals in the National Park, where all species enjoy well-deserved protection. Plaster of Paris (available at paint and hardware stores) is the commonest and most practical material for making casts of tracks. A form or collar of sheet metal or cardboard (sections of paper milk cartons are excellent) is placed firmly in the mud around the track. A thick (but fluid) paste of plaster and water is poured into the form. Gentle stirring will remove bubbles and fill in details with plaster. In a few minutes the plaster will set sufficiently to allow the cast to be removed. In a few hours it will have cured and any attached mud or soil can be gently brushed away.

Photography is the other method of choice for "collecting" mammals in the National Parks. At its best, of course, wildlife photography is a highly sophisticated art form, but that fact should not prevent the amateur from trying. The rewards are great long before any pictures are developed. The simplest camera will capture the larger mammals, although a "fast" film will be needed at dusk when such animals are usually observed. For detailed photos of smaller species, a telephoto lens may be necessary. For nocturnal species, elaborate setups may be employed which trick an unsuspecting mammal into taking its own picture. Like any art, wildlife photography is learned only by doing it (preferably alongside an experienced artist), is fun because it is creative, and is to be entered upon only with due trepidation, for it may become an irrational passion!

Selected References. — Murie (1954); Halfpenny (1986).

Water Shrew.

V. *Order* INSECTIVORA

Insectivores

THE ORDER INSECTIVORA—"insect eaters"—occurs throughout most of the world except Australia. The order includes the shrews, smallest of mammals. The pygmy shrew and the dwarf shrew, both of which doubtless occur in Rocky Mountain National Park, are among the smallest of the shrews. Other well known temperate zone insectivores are the moles (none of which occurs in the mountains of Colorado) and the hedgehogs of the Old World. All told, there are eight living families in the order and some 400 species. All insectivores in the mountains of Colorado are members of the family Soricidae.

FAMILY SORICIDAE—SHREWS

Five or six kinds of shrews occur in Rocky Mountain National Park. Shrews in general are readily recognizable by their very small size and their relatively long, pointed snouts. Particular species of shrews may be difficult to identify in hand in the museum, let alone in the field. This is the most diverse family of insectivores, with nearly 300 species. Nine kinds of shrews occur in Colorado and about 30 species inhabit North America north of México.

Masked Shrew
Sorex cinereus

Description. —The masked shrew is of medium size, slightly smaller than the wandering shrew but larger than the dwarf shrew. Adults range in total length from 90 to 105 mm; the tail is about 37 to 45 mm long. Weights typically are 3 to 5 grams. The color is grayish to medium brown above, slightly paler below. The sparsely haired tail is typically unicolored to obscurely bicolored. *Field Recognition.* —Medium-sized, brownish shrew. In the field, the masked shrew is hardly distinguishable from the wandering shrew. For comparison of the two species, see the account of the wandering shrew.

Distribution and Habitat. —The masked shrew, sometimes called the "common shrew," occurs widely in continental North America, from the Arctic Slope of Alaska and Canada southward to the north-central United States, and in mountainous regions to southern Utah, central New Mexico, North Carolina, and Tennessee.

This is a common mammal in moist habitats throughout the Colorado Rockies. Typically, individuals occur in moist meadows, bogs, about springs, and along the shores of ponds, lakes, and streams. No differences have been reported between the habitats of masked and wandering shrews, although the animals occur together over wide areas in the West. It is a canon of ecology (to which no substantial exception has been demonstrated) that two species cannot occupy the same ecological niche simultaneously. Eventually competition forces the exclusion of one or the other. Perhaps slight differences in size reduce the overlap of niches in this case. The two species may occur in a mosaic pattern, one species occurring in a given patch of habitat to the exclusion of the other. Whatever the underlying mechanism, these two shrews manage to share an apparently common habitat in our area.

Natural History. —The masked shrew, like other shrews, is highly active throughout the year. It forages with rapid, darting movements for invertebrates and other prey, relying mostly on touch and smell to locate food. Probably the tiny eyes can sense differences between dark and light. The animals forage above ground or beneath the surface of loose litter, either in burrows of their own making, or in those of other animals. The masked shrew has a voracious appetite.

Animals as small as shrews are prey for almost any meat-eating animal, although they provide a staple for none. Frogs, fish, and snakes all have been reported to eat shrews of one kind or another. Probably the most effective predators on shrews are hawks and owls. Weasels also take a toll. Other carnivores catch and kill shrews, but many (including house cats) will not eat them. Presumably they are unpalatable because of the strong scent from the flank glands and other secretions of the skin.

Female masked shrews are polyestrous, bearing and rearing several litters of four to ten young through the warmer months of spring and summer. Some females apparently breed late their first summer, although this has not been observed in Colorado. Young are born blind and helpless, are well-furred in about 10 days, and leave the nest, completely self-sufficient, at three to four weeks of age. They over-winter as young adults, and breed the following summer. Few individuals survive a second winter.

Selected References.—Brown (1967a); Forsyth (1976); Spencer and Pettus (1966).

Pygmy Shrew
Sorex hoyi

Description.—The pygmy shrew vies with the dwarf shrew for the distinction of being the smallest mammal in the Southern Rocky Mountains. The total length of the pygmy shrew (75 to 85 mm) is shorter than that of the dwarf shrew, but the tail (26 to 29 mm) is relatively much shorter, so that the body of the pygmy shrew is somewhat longer than that of the dwarf shrew. Adult pygmy shrews in reproductive condition weigh less than 4 grams. The animals generally are dark brown in color, darker than the other brownish shrews in the region. *Field Recognition.*—Small size with relatively short tail; dark brown color.

Distinguishing species of shrews in the museum is tricky enough, even for the experienced mammalogist; identification in the field may be impossible. If circumstances permit close examination, however, the teeth of each species clearly are distinctive. In the case of the pygmy shrew, the third and fifth unicuspid teeth are small, barely (if at all) visible when viewed from the side.

Distribution and Habitat.—The pygmy shrew occurs in the taiga of Alaska, Canada, and the north-central and northeastern United States. In the East, the animals follow the Appalachian Mountains southward to North Carolina. In the West, the species occurs—apparently as disjunct, isolated, relict populations – in the Rocky Mountains as far south as central Colorado. Definite records of the pygmy shrew in Rocky Mountain National Park are lacking, but the species is to be expected there in suitable habitat; records are available from near Cameron Pass, just north of the Park, and from Rabbit Ears Pass, west of the Park in Grand County.

The animals seem to favor drier upland forests over boggy situations, perhaps moving from wet areas to dry ones seasonally. With regard to moisture requirements, the species seems to be intermediate between the masked and wandering shrews (which apparently require a moist habitat) and the dwarf shrew (which may occupy dry brushy areas well away from water). In view of its seemingly adaptive nature and relatively broad tolerances, it seems peculiar that the pygmy shrew has so narrow a range in our area. Perhaps this anomaly will one day be found to be an artifact of our meager knowledge of our surroundings, and no fault of the shrew's!

Natural History. – Like most of its relatives, the pygmy shrew is a highly active mammal, foraging day and night the year around. The diet is mostly of insects, but includes virtually anything that moves and is small enough to apprehend and swallow. Captives have been reported to consume quantities of food in excess of twice their own weight each day. Such tremendous amounts of food are necessary because of their high rate of metabolism and the high ratio of radiative surface to heat-producing volume. The movements of this and other shrews are rapid and erratic. The appearance of nervousness is heightened by a constant twitching of the snout, with its ample touch-sensitive whiskers. Probably smell and touch are the keenest senses, but hearing may also be acute. Foraging activities may be interrupted suddenly by brief periods of deep sleep.

A thorough study of the biology of *Sorex hoyi* has yet to be made, and there is disagreement as to whether females produce one or several litters of young. The animals breed during the warmer months. Five or six young comprise a typical litter, with a maximum of seven reported.

Selected References. – Long (1974); Spencer and Pettus (1966). The pygmy shrew often is placed in the genus *Microsorex*.

Montane Shrew
Sorex monticolus

Description. – This is the largest brown-colored shrew in the Park.

Adults range in total length from 95 to 115 mm, and the tail ranges from 42 to 48 mm long. Weights of breeding animals range around 7 grams, and non-breeding adults are about 2 grams lighter. The animals are medium to dark brown in color above, paling to drab or pale brown below; the tail is obscurely bicolored. *Field Recognition.* – Medium-sized, brownish shrew. The montane shrew is easily confused in the field with the masked shrew, with which it apparently shares its habitat. The wandering shrew averages somewhat darker in color than the masked shrew and is heavier-bodied, but only by examining the teeth can certain identification be made. Merriam's shrews may be as large as wandering shrews, but they are consistently paler in color and occupy pronouncedly drier, upland habitats. Here again, dental characteristics (as outlined in the key to insectivores, Appendix I) allow certain identification.

Distribution and Habitat. – The montane shrew occurs in western North America, from northern Alaska southward at increasingly high elevations to central México and from Colorado to the eastern foothills of the Sierra Nevada. It was only recently that this species was demonstrated to be distinct from the wandering, or vagrant shrew, *Sorex vagrans*; much of the literature on the montane shrew in Colorado will be found under the latter name. Montane shrews occur in mountainous parts of Colorado at elevations to above 3350 meters (11,000 feet). The animals occur in suitable habitat throughout Rocky Mountain National Park. This is an animal typical of moist habitats in forested country. One may encounter the animals or their sign (tracks or minute brownish scat) in marshes, bogs, the edges of swamps, or around springs. The wandering shrew also occupies moist microhabitats in the forest proper, especially the rich accumulations of humus around fallen trees or piles of debris. In Colorado, the species is known to follow riparian communities into the foothills as low as 5300 feet. They also occur beneath dwarf willows above timberline.

Natural History. – The montane shrew is a rather abundant animal over much of its range, and (relative to other shrews) has been studied extensively. Individuals may be active at any time, day or night, throughout the year. The shrews may move about over light snow, but when deep snows form a continuous blanket, they forage in the litter beneath the snow, protected from harsh winds and severe temperatures. During the winter, the diet consists mostly of resting stages of insects (adults, larvae, eggs), worms, and spiders. Plant material is found commonly in stomach analyses, but this may be taken unintentionally, simply ingested along with animal matter. Vertebrates are not a mainstay of the shrew's diet, but captives will eat mice and—under crowded conditions—will even attack and eat other shrews.

A voracious, meat-eating animal like a shrew needs a fairly large foraging area. The home range of individual montane shrews is only about 0.04 hectare (0.1 acre). Spacing is promoted by mutual avoidance and nest defense. Actual combat is "expensive" in terms of energy demand, and is avoided by behavioral rituals in this and many other species of mammals. The social life of these animals apparently is limited to brief contacts of mother and offspring. Immatures seek contact with each other and with the mother to an age of six or seven weeks; then the juvenile behavior ceases and the young disperse.

There are distinct winter (darker) and summer (paler) pelages, with spring and fall molts. The spring molt occurs from April to June and the fall molt takes place in September and October. Molt is patterned; that is, replacement of hair is gradual and sequential over the body and does not occur all over at the same time. Molting individuals exhibit a pronounced molt line between new and old pelage.

Montane shrews are reproductively active in spring and summer, but whether individual females are polyestrous is not known. In Colorado most breeding appears to be in the period from June through mid-August. Males become sexually active in February and March.

The gestation period is about 20 days. The young are born blind and naked. A female carries two to nine (average 6.4 in Montana) embryos, and the size of litters doubtless is somewhat smaller, perhaps about five. The young develop rapidly, sheltered in a ball-shaped nest of grass and debris. Females apparently do not breed until their second summer. Very few individuals survive a second winter; 15 months marks old age for a shrew. Occasionally one finds an animal that obviously is very old—the teeth are worn to the gums and the pelage is ragged and patchy. Such aged animals most often are males. Flank glands, which seem to function in sexual attraction, are well-developed in males, more so during the breeding season. The glands are less conspicuous in females and immature animals.

Selected References.—Brown (1967a); Spencer and Pettus (1966)—as *Sorex vagrans*; Hennings and Hoffmann (1977).

Dwarf Shrew
Sorex nanus

Description. –This is the smallest of mammals in the Southern Rockies and one of the smallest anywhere in the world. The pygmy shrew may be shorter overall, but it has a longer body than does the dwarf shrew. These two species compete only with the lesser shrew (*Sorex minutus*) of Europe for the distinction of being the smallest mammal known. Adult dwarf shrews range in total length from 90 to 100 mm, and the tail is 39 to 42 mm long. Weights vary from 2.5 to 3.5 grams, about the weight of a copper penny. The dorsal color is medium brown, paling slightly beneath. The relatively long tail is bicolored. The teeth are arranged as in the montane shrew – the third unicuspid is markedly smaller than the fourth – but the dentition is much less robust. Also, the dwarf shrew inhabits drier habitats than does any other local shrew except Merriam's shrew, a relatively large, pale-colored species. *Field Recognition.* – Small size and relatively long tail.

Distribution and Habitat. –The dwarf shrew occurs in the western United States – in and near the Central and Southern Rocky Mountains – from Montana southward to New Mexico and Arizona, and eastward to western South Dakota. In Colorado, the species is known from the mountains and foothills of central and southwestern parts of the state and it may be expected in suitable habitat throughout Rocky Mountain National Park. The species is known from a variety of ecological situations and apparently has a wider range of tolerance than do its larger relatives. In Colorado and southern Wyoming the animals are known to inhabit forests (both unbroken and partially cleared), open woodland, rocky, shrubby foothills slopes, and alpine and subalpine rockslides. The elevational range of specimens in our area is from 1675 to 3050 meters (5500 to 10,000 feet).

Natural History. –The dwarf shrew has the dubious distinction of being the least known of our mammals – not only locally, but over its range. No real study of the species has been made; the meager available data are derived from incidental notes of collectors. A study conducted in Larimer County, Colorado, just north of Rocky Mountain National Park, indicated that numbers of dwarf shrews peaked in mid-August, suggesting that this is the time that the young begin to forage about on their own, adding to the trappable population. There is some evidence that females are polyestrous and have post-partum estrus. Breeding takes place during the warmer months, with the first litter produced about the end of July and second litters born a month later. Published embryo counts range from six to eight.

The type locality of *Sorex nanus* is Estes Park. (The type locality is the place where the holotype was collected. The holotype is the particular specimen on which the original description and scientific name of a species or subspecies is based.)

Selected References. – Armstrong et al. (1973); Brown (1967a); Hoffmann and Owen (1980); Spencer and Pettus (1966).

Water Shrew
Sorex palustris

Description. – The water shrew is the largest and most strikingly colored shrew in Rocky Mountain National Park, and that most readily seen by visitors. Adults range in total length from about 150 to 170 mm. The tail is approximately the same length as the head and body. Adults weigh from 12 to 18 grams. The upper parts are a rich, velvety, grayish black and the belly is silvery gray to white. The tail has a distinct black stripe above and is grayish white below. The relatively large hind feet (about 20 mm in length) are fringed with stiff hairs. *Field Recognition.* – Pond or streamside habitat; relatively large size for shrew; dark color; hind foot fringed with stiff hairs.

Distribution and Habitat. – The water shrew occurs in the coniferous forests of North America, from southern Alaska and British Columbia eastward to Labrador and Nova Scotia. The species ranges southward in forested mountains to central California, Arizona, and New Mexico in the West, and to Tennessee in the East. In Colorado and adjacent states, the water shrew is confined to the mountains where it occurs along streambanks, the margins of lakes and ponds, and in marshes. They frequently are seen around exposed roots of streamside trees or shrubs, or under cover of rocks or overhanging banks.

Natural History. – Like other kinds of shrews, water shrews are voracious eaters. Captives have been reported to consume a quantity of food equal to their own weight each day. In the wild, water shrews feed mostly on insects, both aquatic and terrestrial. In addition, some small fish are captured, and carrion is eaten when available. The vegetable matter seen in stomachs of some specimens may be taken inadvertently along with more typical animal food. Water shrews are active at any time of the day or night, foraging excitedly for short periods and suddenly dropping off to sleep. The eyes of water shrews are poorly developed, but the senses of touch, hearing, and smell apparently are acute.

Water shrews are excellent swimmers. Skimming across the water on fringed feet, they sometimes appear to run on the surface and, in fact, do so for short distances. These animals also swim beneath the water or actually scramble along the bottom, clinging to rocks. The velvety fur holds bubbles of air and thus resists wetting. This gives shrews swimming under water a striking, silvery appearance. Activity continues throughout the year. Water levels of mountain streams frequently fall in winter, and the water shrew is able to forage along streambanks beneath a cover of ice, yet above the winter waterline.

The water shrew undergoes two molts annually. The spring molt begins in late winter or early spring and is complete by June. The autumnal molt takes place in late July or August. In common with many small mammals, water shrews are short-lived. In natural populations, few individuals survive their second winter.

Male water shrews become sexually active in about January and breeding continues until August. As in other species of the genus *Sorex*, breeding males have glands on the sides, midway between the front and hind legs. The hairs over the glands are oily and matted. Presumably, the flank glands produce a substance that attracts the female. Ovulation is induced by copulation. The gestation period of the water shrew is not known with certainty, but probably it is between two and three weeks. Litter size varies from four to eight, the usual number being six. Pregnancy may recur while a female is nursing a litter, but such pregnancies seldom reach term. Nonetheless, several litters may be reared successfully by a female over the relatively long breeding season. Growth of the young is rapid; females born early in the season sometimes breed late in the same season, although most do not breed until the following spring.

Selected References. —Conaway (1952); Jones et al. (1983); Sorensen (1962).

Little Brown Bat.

VI. *Order* CHIROPTERA

Bats

BATS ARE THE only mammals capable of true flight. The "flying" squirrels and the "flying" lemurs of Indo-Malaysia are highly efficient gliders, but they cannot actually fly. As fliers, bats are members of an elite group: only four groups of animals have successfully evolved aerial niches. Many insects can fly, of course, and once there were flying reptiles (including the well-known pterodactyl). Birds evolved flight independently of flying reptiles. And bats represent the fourth independent line of flying animals, having evolved from primitive shrew-like mammals. Like pterodactyl—and unlike the birds—bats have wings formed by a membrane stretched between greatly elongate finger bones. The principal flight surface of a bird, on the other hand, is formed by feathers attached to the arm.

The earliest fossils of bats have been collected from shales of Eocene age (some 50 million years old) in southwestern Wyoming. The earliest known bats were already perfectly good fliers, and in many respects resemble groups now living. Intermediate stages between ground-dwelling insectivores and flying bats are unknown. There are about 900 living species of bats arrayed in 17 families, making this the second most diverse order of mammals.

For a number of reasons, bats have fascinated mankind down through the ages. In the early days, men shared their homes with bats. Bat bugs and bed bugs (Family Cimicidae—Order Hemiptera) are hardly distinguishable, and this common ectoparasite of bats and people is probably traceable to a former common cave-dwelling. Early in human cultural evolution, bats became the subject of myth and superstition. Misinformation about bats continues to the present day, even among otherwise enlightened peoples. Bats are mostly secretive and nocturnal. They can navigate with unerring accuracy in tight, dark places. To us this is remarkable, even though we know they navigate by echolocation—a natural "sonar"; to our ancestors it must have seemed supernatural.

Recently there has been a great deal of scientific research on bats. Much has been learned about echolocation and the role of bats as vectors of disease. The physics and physiology of flight have been studied in a number of species. Despite this new information, much remains to be learned. For example, many kinds of bats are migratory. A given species may occur in abundance in a locality in summer but be absent in winter. But no one knows where they have gone. In other cases, maternity colonies are well-studied, but the whereabouts of males remains a mystery. These and other basic questions about the biology of bats remain unanswered. Table 3 summarizes some natural history information on local bats.

Many kinds of bats form large colonies, either throughout the year, during the breeding season, or during hibernation. Often these aggregations are in places readily accessible to people—occupied or abandoned buildings, mines, or caves. In such places, roosting bats are often molested wantonly. Such molestation is to be strongly deplored. As active and voracious predators on insects, bats are firm allies of humans. The reproductive potential of most kinds of bats is low. Females of most species produce just one young per year. Once decimated, colonies may takes years to reestablish themselves, if they ever recover. If bats are roosting in large numbers in an occupied building, they may become a nuisance, of course. Under these circumstances one would be wise to notify the biology department of a nearby college or university. Inquiry will eventually lead to a specialist on bats who can suggest a solution to a specific problem that will spare the bat colony. In the long run, extermination by a commercial pest control service will probably be more harmful than beneficial.

Selected References.—Allen (1939); Barbour and Davis (1969); Hill and

Smith (1985); Humphrey (*in* Chapman and Feldhamer, 1982); Kunz (1982*b*); Ross (1967); Scott et al. (1984).

FAMILY VESPERTILIONIDAE—"COMMON BATS"

Probably eight species of vespertilionid bats occur in Rocky Mountain National Park, and an additional eight or more species occur elsewhere in Colorado. In the continental United States, the family is represented by about 30 species. This is the only family of bats with representatives in the Park, and—with over 300 species in over 30 genera—vespertilionids comprise the bulk of the bat fauna throughout the North Temperate Zone, both in North America and Eurasia.

Selected References.—Fenton and Barclay (1980).

Long-eared Myotis
Myotis evotis

Description.—This species has the longest ears (about 25 mm) of any North American myotis. The ears, wings, and interfemoral membrane are black, contrasting sharply with the medium brown fur of the dorsum. The underparts are tan. Total length ranges from 88 to 95 mm, length of tail from 42 to 46 mm, and the forearm from 37 to 40 mm. Adults weigh about 5 to 7 grams. *Field Recognition.*—Medium brown color with long, black ears.

Distribution and Habitat.—The long-eared myotis is a bat of western North America, ranging from British Columbia southward to Arizona, New Mexico, and Baja California. In Colorado, the species occurs in wooded areas in the western three-fifths of the state, and at moderate elevations throughout Rocky Mountain National Park on either side of the Continental Divide. They may roost by day in buildings or tree hollows, and caves and tunnels are used as night roosts. They forage in woodlands, frequently over ponds.

Natural History.—Little has been recorded about the habits of this pretty bat, despite the fact that the animals are widespread and not uncommon in the West. They emerge late in the evening to feed, after full darkness. In such areas as Hallowell Park and Moraine Park the species forages in the company of the hoary bat, the silver-haired bat, and the big brown bat—all of which are larger animals. The little brown bat and the long-legged myotis may also share such a communal feeding ground.

Table 3. Comparative summary of natural history characteristics of bats of Rocky Mountain National Park and vicinity.

	Day Roost	Night Roost	Foraging Habitat	Foraging Style	Foraging Height (m)
Myotis evotis—Long-eared Myotis	under bark, mines, buildings		near trees over water	gleaner	
Myotis leibii—Small-footed Myotis	buildings, mines, crevices		among boulders, shrubs	maneuverable pursuit	
Myotis lucifugus—Little Brown Bat	attics, mines	tree hollows, buildings	over water	erratic pursuit on repeated circuit	3–6
Myotis volans—Long-legged Myotis	rock fissures, under bark, buildings	caves, mines	over ponds, streams	relaxed foraging flight	3–4
Lasionycteris noctivagans—Silver-haired Bat	mostly trees, also open caves	open buildings	over clearings	repeated circuit	
Eptesicus fuscus—Big Brown Bat	buildings, caves, crevices	buildings	open areas	strong, straight	6–10
Lasiurus cinereus—Hoary Bat	trees	trees	openings in forest	fast, direct	
Plecotus townsendii—Townsend's Big-eared Bat	mines, caves, structures		near vegetation	gleaner	

	Foraging Time	Food	General Habitat	Hibernal Activity
Myotis evotis – Long-eared Myotis	after dark	moths, flies, spiders, beetles	coniferous woodland	unknown
Myotis leibii – Small-footed Myotis	early, still light	flying insects	shrubs, woodland	hibernates locally in mines, tunnels, caves
Myotis lucifugus – Little Brown Bat	dusk	aquatic insects, moths, flies	riparian woodland	locally migratory to mines, caves?
Myotis volans – Long-legged Myotis	early, still light	moths	woodland	locally migratory to caves, mines?
Lasionycteris noctivagans – Silver-haired Bat	late, full dark	moths, flies	forest	migratory, winter range unknown
Eptesicus fuscus – Big Brown Bat	dusk	insects, especially flying beetles	riparian woodland, urban	sedentary, hibernates in caves, mines, tunnels, buildings
Lasiurus cinereus – Hoary Bat	late, full dark	moths, beetles, grasshoppers, small bats	forest, woodland	migratory, winter range unknown
Plecotus townsendii – Townsend's Big-eared Bat	late, full dark	moths, beetles, flies	broken, rocky country	sedentary, hibernates locally in mines, tunnels

There is a single annual molt in mid-summer (July–August). As is usual among mammals with a cyclic molting schedule, males molt before females that have borne young.

No detailed study has ever been made of reproduction in this species. Small maternity colonies apparently form in buildings. A single young is born, probably in early July. The gestation period is undocumented, but probably is seven to eight weeks.

Selected References. – Barbour and Davis (1969); Black (1974); Husar (1976).

Small-footed Myotis
Myotis leibii

Description. – The small-footed myotis is the smallest bat in the Park. Total length ranges from 76 to 88 mm, and the tail from 35 to 39 mm. The forearm ranges in length from about 31 to 34 mm. The hind foot (7 to 8 mm long) is noticeably smaller than that of other local bats. This is the palest of the brown bats in our area. Although the color is variable, the dorsal hairs are predominantly pale to medium brown, the venter tan to nearly white. The ears are black and the wings and membranes are dark brown, presenting a strong contrast with the pale fur. The tips of the dorsal hairs are burnished, lending the pelage a metallic sheen. *Field Recognition.* – Small size; low, fluttering flight pattern.

Distribution and Habitat. – The small-footed myotis is fairly common in western North America, ranging from southern Canada to northern México. Eastward, the species is distributed erratically to the Atlantic seaboard from Maine to Virginia. These bats apparently occur statewide in Colorado in suitable situations at lower to moderate elevations. Whereas no specimens of the small-footed myotis are available from the Park, the species doubtless occurs in rocky areas at lower elevations, and probably also west of the Continental Divide in Arapaho National Recreation Area. Rocky, broken country provides habitat for the small-footed myotis. Locally, the bats are commonest in the foothills, but they occur in the mountains to about 2450 meters (8000 feet). To the east of the Rockies, the small-footed myotis occurs locally near rocky breaks in the otherwise featureless terrain of the Great Plains. Pawnee Buttes in northeastern Colorado is one such locality. This bat roosts in and around buildings, and in caves, mines, and fissures—in short, in just about any sheltered place.

Natural History.—Despite its diminutive size, the small-footed myotis is the hardiest species of *Myotis* in our area, and apparently the only one that over-winters here. In late fall, after most bats have left the area, the animals enter hibernation, hanging singly in caves, mines, and tunnels. Often such shelters are shared with the big-eared bat (*Plecotus townsendii*) and the big brown bat (*Eptesicus fuscus*). The latter species are more than twice the size of the small-footed myotis. How tiny *Myotis leibii*—with its small heat-producing volume and relatively great radiative surface—survives the hostile, cold and dry conditions of its hibernacula is not known.

These bats forage, generally near or over water, in a slow, fluttering movement. Slow flight is atypical of bats of such small size. No detailed study of food habits of the small-footed myotis has been made, although, like other vespertilionids, they are insectivorous.

Reproductive data are few for the small-footed myotis. Small nursery colonies (to about two dozen individuals) are formed. Single births are the rule, and the gestation period is about two months. In north-central Colorado, the young are born in July.

Selected References.—Turner (1974); Tuttle and Heaney (1974). In some older literature this species was called *Myotis subulatus*.

Little Brown Bat
Myotis lucifugus

Description.—*Myotis lucifugus* is of medium size for members of the genus. The total length of females is about 90 to 100 mm, and the length of the tail is 37 to 44 mm. The forearm is 37 to 42 mm in length. The color is variable, from medium to dark brown above and paler below. The hairs of the upper parts are usually glossy or even metallic in appearance. The dark brown ears are relatively short (14 to 16 mm) and have rounded tips; the rather blunt tragus is less than half the length of the ear. (In a sense, the little brown bat is rather nondescript; perhaps it is best identified by a process of eliminating those more distinctive species it is not!) *Field Recognition.*—Dark, metallic color; erratic flight for medium-sized bat.

Distribution and Habitat.—The little brown bat occupies a wide range in North America, from central Alaska eastward across Canada to Newfoundland, southward in the West to Chihuahua and in the East to Georgia. Over parts of its range, this is the commonest bat. In Colorado, the species is common in forested areas and woodlands at moderate elevations in and near the mountains, and is known from elevations to 3350 meters (11,000 feet). The little brown bat probably ranges throughout the Park and adjacent areas in suitable habitat. Our population is migratory, but the winter range is unknown. Nursery colonies of little brown bats roost in buildings, especially warm attics. Single males will roost in almost any sheltered place, including crevices in buildings and holes in trees. They generally forage over water, street lights or high yard lights in resort villages such as Estes Park, Allenspark, Glen Haven, or Grand Lake.

Natural History.—*Myotis lucifugus* is a common bat (perhaps the reason for the rather unimaginative vernacular name). Because of its abundance around major population centers (hence, around major universities) the biology of this species is as well known as that of any bat in the world. For example, many of the early studies of echolocation apply to the little brown bat.

Like other species of the genus *Myotis*, the little brown bat feeds primarily on flying insects. Prey in the size range from 3 to 10 mm is most common, and aquatic flies are frequently a staple, especially when insects congregate in mating swarms. The animals begin to forage at about dark and continue to feed intermittently until dawn. While feeding, the bats remain 3 to 6 meters above the ground, and an individual usually follows the same zig-zag path through the feeding area night after night.

The animals locate their prey by sonar, then scoop the insect with the wing into a "basket" formed by curling forward the tail and uropatagium (or interfemoral membrane—the membrane extending between the hind limbs and including the tail). The insect thus netted is then taken into the mouth.

The little brown bat mates in the fall on the winter range. Sperm are stored through the hibernation period in the uterus of the female. Actual fertilization of the egg cell occurs upon emergence from hibernation in the spring. Returning to the summer range, pregnant females establish nursery colonies which may include several hundred individuals (although in Colorado, colonies of a few dozen are more common). After a gestation period which varies with environmental temperature from 50 to 60 days, the naked, blind young are born in late

June or early July. A single young is the rule. To give birth, the female hangs with the head up (upside-down for a roosting bat!). The uropatagium is extended to form a basket to catch the young; parturition occurs in the space of a half hour. The newborn bats weigh 1.5 to 2.0 grams, nearly one-fourth the weight of the mother. When disturbed, the female will fly with the newborn young clinging to the nipple. The young learn to fly and forage beginning at about three weeks of age. These bats are long-lived for so small an animal. Ages in excess of 30 years have been reported, and reports of ages over 10 years are common. However, given mortality from predation, wanton molestation, and the stress of hibernation, average longevity is probably between one and three years.

Selected References. – Fenton and Barclay (1980).

Long-legged Myotis
Myotis volans

Description. – The long-legged myotis is slightly larger in size than other species of *Myotis* in the Park. Adults range from 96 to 106 mm in total length, and the tail is 38 to 46 mm long. The forearm is about 37 to 40 mm in length. Adults weigh 8 to 12 grams. As in many other kinds of bats, females average slightly larger than males. The upper parts are medium to dark brown in color, the underparts somewhat paler.

Even when close at hand, this bat might be confused at first glance with *Myotis lucifugus*, the little brown bat. The long-legged myotis differs in its slightly larger size, in its broader, more rounded ears, its less glossy pelage, keeled calcar, and in the fact that the fur of the belly extends on the underside of the wing to the level of the elbow. The last-mentioned character allows certain identification of an animal in hand. *Field Recognition.* – Short, rounded ears; "relaxed" flight pattern.

Distribution and Habitat. – Like the long-eared myotis, the long-legged myotis is a species of western North America, ranging from extreme southeastern Alaska southward to central México and reaching the eastern limits of its range in western parts of Texas, Nebraska, and the Dakotas. In Colorado, the species occurs in summer in suitable habitat in the mountainous western three-fifths of the state. The winter range of our population is unknown. The long-legged myotis occurs primarily in wooded areas, and may be expected throughout forested parts of the Park. The highest record of occurrence of the species in Colorado is at about 3500 meters (11,500 feet) on the Pikes Peak massif.

Natural History. — As is the case with many of our bats, the habits of this species are little known. The long-legged myotis emerges to feed well before full darkness, the first of the species of *Myotis* to appear. The flight pattern is more "relaxed" — slower and more erratic — than that of the little brown bat.

By day, the species roosts in trees, buildings, or crevices. Maternity colonies form in similar situations, commonly beneath the loose bark of trees. Tunnels or caves are used as night roosts. The foraging habitat is similar to that of the little brown bat and the long-eared myotis. Feeding flights are over woodland ponds or small openings in the trees. Activity peaks three to four hours after sunset. Moths are the principal food, but insects of many other groups are also taken. The long-legged myotis captures its prey in rapid, direct pursuit.

No thorough study of reproduction in this species has been made, but apparently the timing of parturition is highly variable geographically — in New Mexico the single young is born in early June, in northern Colorado in early August. The timing of birth may be related to latitude or altitude (or both), or may stem from characteristics of the winter range that are unknown. Nursery colonies may consist of hundreds of individuals, but the whereabouts of these animals after the breakup of the colonies remains to be learned. Maximum reported longevity is in excess of 20 years.

Selected References. — Scott et al. (1985); Turner (1974); Warner and Czaplewski (1984).

Silver-haired Bat
Lasionycteris noctivagans

Description. — The silver-haired bat is a medium-sized species, about the size of a large myotis. Total length ranges from about 95 to 105 mm, the tail from 36 to 40 mm, and the forearm from about 39 to 43 mm. Adults weigh 9 to 13 grams. The fur is black as are the ears and membranes. The hairs of the back are tipped with silver or white, making this one of our most strikingly colored bats.

In the hand, there is no mistaking this species. Only one other bat in our area, the hoary bat (*Lasiurus cinereus*), has white dorsal hairs. Hoary bats are large (forearm 50 to 56 mm), and have short, rounded, black-rimmed ears, and an interfemoral membrane that is heavily furred.

Field Recognition. —Silver-tipped pelage; very slow flight, usually only a few feet above the ground.

Distribution and Habitat. —The silver-haired bat is a widespread species, present either as residents or migrants from southern Alaska, across southern Canada and throughout the conterminous United States (except peninsular Florida). In Colorado the species may be expected statewide as migrants, and males are summer residents in the mountains. The silver-haired bat is a forest-dwelling species. The animals are rarely found in open country, although they do pass over such areas as migrants. Preferred foraging habitat is streams, ponds, or woodland clearings. In Colorado, records range to over 3050 meters (10,000 feet) in elevation, and this bat may be encountered in wooded areas throughout the Park on either side of the Continental Divide.

Natural History. —Resident silver-haired bats roost primarily in trees— beneath loose bark, in rotting snags and wind-throws, in tree-holes, and even in birds' nests. During migration, the animals will occupy virtually any kind of shelter, including buildings, trees in riverbank woodlands, and even woodpiles.

Silver-haired bats migrate in spring and fall. Most of Colorado apparently lies on the migratory path. The domestic arrangement is an enviable one in some respects: males summer in the mountains of Colorado, arriving in early spring; females generally migrate farther north along the Rockies to bear and rear the young. An individual was captured at Boulder on 21 March 1914, in "zero weather." The latest records of the species in this area in autumn are from early October. The winter range of our population is unknown, and general patterns of migration are poorly understood.

The silver-haired bat emerges relatively late in the evening to commence its slow, low-flying foraging pattern. Usually the animals feed over water, but clearings are also exploited as feeding areas. Campers frequently see these animals as they come to feed on insects attracted to the light of a campfire. The animals are mostly solitary while foraging. Food habits are apparently variable. Moths have been shown to be prominent in several studies, but a wide range of flying insects is taken. By day the silver-haired bat apparently roosts in trees, and they are rarely seen.

Contrary to the usual situation in bats, twin births are the rule in this species. Young silver-haired bats are born on the northern summer range in late June or early July, weighing about 2 grams. Fertilization occurs in the spring, accomplished by sperm stored over the winter in the reproductive tract of the female after a pre-hibernation breeding season in August and September. Gestation takes 7 to 8 weeks. Most young mature sexually their first summer. Nursery colonies may be formed, but evidence for them is equivocal and the breeding habits of this species are poorly known.

Selected References. — Kunz (1982a).

Big Brown Bat
Eptesicus fuscus

Description. — The big brown bat is the largest of the several brown-colored bats in the Park. Total length ranges from 105 to 125 mm, length of tail from 40 to 52 mm, and length of the forearm from 45 to 50 mm. Adults weigh 14 to 20 grams. Save for its size, the big brown bat is rather nondescript. Our population varies in color from pale grayish brown to nearly russet. The round-tipped tragus is less than half the length of the ear. The dark-colored wings are relatively broader than those of the much smaller *Myotis* species. The large size of this species makes it readily distinguishable from other brown-colored bats. *Field Recognition.* — Large size, brown color with black membranes; leisurely wing-beats.

Distribution and Habitat. — The big brown bat is a widespread species with broad ecological tolerance, ranging from the forests of central and southern Canada southward through Panamá and the Caribbean into South America. In Colorado, the species is distributed essentially state-wide from the eastern plains to elevations above 3350 meters (11,000 feet) in the mountains, and may be expected widely in the Park. Big brown bats are as nearly ubiquitous as any kind of bat. They may be encountered in rural or urban areas, in open country or woodlands, in deserts or riparian forest. The foraging habitat is comparably diverse and may be over water, above open vegetation, or along a lighted street.

Natural History. — They may not be the commonest bats in North America (certain cave bats form immense, local colonies), but big brown bats are probably those seen most often by man. This is because they readily roost in occupied buildings. Attics and lofts may be preferred, but any protective crevice may be utilized. The bats may also roost in hollow trees, caves, mines, tunnels, beneath bridges, and in storm sewers.

The big brown bat feeds on flying insects. Limited studies in the eastern United States suggest that beetles (Order Coleoptera), flying ants and wasps (Order Hymenoptera), and flies (Order Diptera) make up the bulk of the diet; moths are not used to any great extent. Experienced animals can fill the stomach within an hour; the inexperienced young animals have more difficulty detecting and catching flying insects and may take far longer to gather a full meal. In captivity, big brown bats will eat a variety of prepared foods including ground beef and canned pet food. Obviously, their prey need not be flying.

These bats emerge to feed at dusk. They may share a common feeding ground with other species; of the latter, only the hoary bat (*Lasiurus cinereus*) is obviously larger. The hoary bat begins to feed later than the big brown bat, after full darkness, and flies much more swiftly. Porches, eaves, and similar relatively exposed roosts are used intermittently by foraging big brown bats.

Apparently big brown bats are sedentary, although the whereabouts of many individuals in winter is unknown. Winter generally is passed in a shelter near the summer roost. A site is selected which remains cool but does not freeze. The hibernaculum must remain cool so that the bats can remain torpid. Winter activity places great demands on energy reserves, reserves that cannot be replaced because insects are unavailable in winter. In our area, the animals hibernate in mines, caves, tunnels, and cellars. If the temperature in the hibernaculum dips below freezing, the bats arouse, shivering and moving about, burning stored fat to maintain the body temperature at a tolerable level. Like many other bats, the big brown bat may be long-lived, the known age record being 18 years.

Mating takes place in the winter roost, between October or November and March. Sperm is stored by the female until the time of ovulation in April. The gestation period is about 60 days, and the young are born in late June. The young weigh about 4 grams at birth, and gain at the rate of 0.5 grams per day. Development is rapid, and juveniles are able to fly within a month. In the West, a single young is the rule, but in the East, twinning is the mode. Western mothers often carry their single offspring when foraging, but eastern mothers leave the young in the roost.

Selected References. — Barbour and Davis (1969); Kunz (1974).

Hoary Bat

Lasiurus cinereus

Description. –This is the largest of our local bats. Adults measure 120 to 145 mm in total length, and the tail is 50 to 60 mm long. The forearm is 50 to 56 mm in length. Adults weigh 24 to 32 grams. In flight, the hoary bat is recognizable by its fast, straight-line foraging pattern and large size (the wingspread is about 400 mm). The fur is dark reddish brown, mostly tipped with white, giving the animals their unique "hoary," or frosted, appearance. The dorsal surface of the interfemoral membrane is densely furred, as are the short, rounded, black-rimmed ears. *Field Recognition.* – Large size; white-tipped hairs; fast flight pattern.

Distribution and Habitat. –The hoary bat is the most widespread American bat, ranging from the islands of Hudson's Bay southward to Argentina and Chile. These bats are strong fliers and are the only non-marine mammals native to the Hawaiian Islands. In Colorado, the animals occur statewide as migrants, and are summer residents in the mountains, including places at moderate elevations in Rocky Mountain National Park on either side of the Continental Divide, to elevations of about 2900 meters (9500 feet). Hoary bats live in wooded areas, roosting in trees. Migratory individuals sometimes are captured in riparian woodlands on the plains of eastern Colorado.

Natural History. – Little is known of the natural history of this beautiful mammal, perhaps because it roosts singly in trees and thus is usually observed only by accident. The animals are mostly insectivorous, feeding largely on moths, although there is some indication that they occasionally feed on smaller bats. By day, the animals hang under cover of leaves, usually in deciduous trees, 3 to 5 meters above the ground. They emerge to feed, often over water, only well after dark. Among local bats only the big brown bat and the hoary bat make distinctly audible chirps in flight. The flight sounds of other species are mostly above the range of human hearing.

Obviously the hoary bat is migratory, but the winter range of our animals is uncertain. Probably it is in the southwestern United States and Mexico, but routes of migration have not been discovered. Migrating hoary bats seem to move in flocks of from several dozen to several hundred individuals. Flight is swift and strong. The animals arrive in our area about May and leave in late August or September.

Breeding habits of this species are largely unknown. Mating probably occurs on the winter range, with fertilization or implantation delayed until spring. Most records indicate that females bear and rear the young in Canada and the northeastern and north-central United States. A few females do bear young in Colorado, but most summer residents are males. The young are born in June. Twins seem to be the norm, but litters of one to four young have been reported. Until a week old, the young may be carried by the mother in flight, but older offspring are left hanging in a tree as the mother feeds. Older suckling young are so heavy that the mother cannot get airborne with them clinging to her teats. Not infrequently, a helpless mother with her large young is found beneath a tree from which she has been dislodged.

Selected References. – Shump and Shump (1982). Sometimes this species is placed in the genus *Nycteris.*

Townsend's Big-Eared Bat
Plecotus townsendii

Description. –The western big-eared bat is of small size – about 82 to 102 mm in total length, with the tail 35 to 50 mm long, and the forearm 39 to 45 mm in length. Adults weigh 9 to 14 grams. The color is brown, varying from grayish through medium to dark brown in our area. The venter is slightly paler than the dorsum. The snout bears a pair of rather prominent, rounded lumps above the nostrils. The magnificent ears save the species from being just another small, nondescript, brown-colored bat. There are prominent transverse ridges on the backs of the ears. When the animal is at rest, the ears are folded back. When the bat is aroused from torpor, the ears unfold, often one at a time, and move about semaphore-style, allowing the animal to orient to its acoustic environment. *Field Recognition.* – Long ears; irregular pursuit flights in full darkness.

Distribution and Habitat. –The western big-eared bat occurs in western North America, from southern British Columbia southward to southern México. East of the Rockies, distribution is disjunct and localized in areas with caves, eastward through the Arkansas and Ohio valleys to West Virginia. In Colorado, the species inhabits the rough, broken country of the western, central, and southeastern parts of the state. In the Park, this bat occurs at lower to moderate elevations. *Plecotus townsendii* is an animal of rough broken country, where caves, mines, and fissures provide suitable roosting sites. Vegetation on such terrain typically is brush or open woodland. Night roosts may be in buildings. The highest elevation in Colorado from which records are available is 2900 meters (9500 feet); in Rocky Mountain National Park, the animals may be expected in open woodland at moderate elevations on either side of the Continental Divide.

Natural History. –The western big-eared bat apparently feeds mostly on moths. The bats are excellent echolocators and (like their prey) have highly maneuverable flight, perhaps more so than any other local species. They emerge late, only in full darkness, often foraging over water.

This is primarily a cave bat. In our area, mines and tunnels are used as day roosts in summer and as hibernacula in winter. Buildings may be utilized as night roosts, for rest between feeding flights, but heated structures are too warm (and unheated buildings too cold) to be suitable for hibernation. Males are mostly solitary, but females form nursery colonies in summer. A single, overall molt occurs annually in about August.

Mating takes place in the hibernaculum, beginning in October and lasting intermittently through the winter months. Sperm are stored until the onset of ovulation in spring. Gestation is highly variable, depending on roost temperature, among other things, and ranges from 50 to 100 days, with an average of about 73 days. Young are born in early summer. Nursery colonies consist of 10 to a few hundred females with young. When foraging, females leave their single offspring hanging in a cluster. Upon her return to the colony, the mother locates the proper infant in the cluster. The young bat clings to the mother during the day. The young reach full size at about one month of age, fly at about three weeks, and are weaned by six weeks of age.

Selected References. –Humphrey and Kunz (1976); Kunz and Martin (1982).

Native Americans.

VII. *Order* PRIMATES

Monkeys, Apes, and Allies

THE PRIMATES CONSTITUTE a group of rather generalized mammals descended from an early, primitive insectivore stock. Early in their history, competition with rodents seems to have been keen. However, the groups diverged and both prevail today (although in terms of diversity and numbers, the rodents are by far the more successful). Recent Primates are arranged in 10 families, including over 150 species, mostly tropical or subtropical in distribution.

FAMILY HOMINIDAE — PEOPLE

The family Hominidae includes a single living member, the human species. *Homo sapiens* is the most widespread biological species, permanently inhabiting all continents save Antarctica.

People
Homo sapiens

Mankind needs no description. All of us recognize each other as comprising a single, diverse species. In fact, why mention us at all? There is a single, but compelling, reason: humans are a part of the native mammalian fauna, probably established locally as long as any species, and longer than many. Nearly everyone knows, of course, that we people are mammals, strangely "naked apes." But too often our relationship to the rest of the fauna is forgotten, our place in ecosystems (upon which we are utterly dependent) poorly understood. We allow the egocentric pressures of a burdensome humanity to obscure our basic "animality." Recognizing our fundamental animality makes us no less unique—each biological species is unique. It does, however, re-emphasize an important and immutable fact—we are a part of nature, not apart from it.

When human beings first came to the area now known as Rocky Mountain National Park is not known. Paleoindians occupied the margin of the plains to the east during the last glacial period ten millenia ago. Parts of the Park bear evidence of Indian occupation a thousand years ago. More recently, the Utes—a mountain tribe—hunted over the area, to be replaced by the plains-dwelling Arapahoe in the nineteenth century. Amerindian cultures left their mark on the landscape—fire-scars, camp circles, artifacts—but in many respects their long-term effects are less obvious than those of the beaver, the porcupine, the ponderosa pine bark beetle, or the spruce budworm. They lived as nomadic, opportunistic omnivores, emphasizing hunting. Local populations adjusted to the resources of the region. Imports and exports of materials and energy were minimal.

The first Europeans to visit the region were fur-trappers, the legendary "mountain men." Rufus Sage may have been the earliest of them; he described a place in 1840 that could very well have been Wild Basin. Enos Mills believed that Kit Carson entered the Park in 1841. In 1860, Joel Estes brought his family to the park that bears his name, and stayed for six years. The area finally passed to the Earl of Dunraven, a wealthy British nobleman. Mining opened the area west of the Continental Divide, spawning towns such as Teller, Lulu City, and Grand Lake in the 1870s. The pioneer economy of the entire region was extractive, exploitative—trapping, mining, market-hunting, and grazing. Biological production and physical resources were exported from the area. Fortunately for us, the mines played out and the Earl of Dunraven guarded his domain like a medieval manor. In January of 1915, through the persistent efforts of naturalist-writer Enos Mills and numerous others, Rocky Mountain National Park was established to preserve the region's most precious and fragile resource: a breathtakingly scenic landscape, a monumental mosaic of ecosystems, each with uniquely co-evolved communities of plants and animals linked by endless cycles of resources and a ceaseless flow of energy. The objective of management here is to minimize the effect of mankind on native ecosystems. This goal should be a personal commitment on the part of each visitor.

Selected References. – Buchholtz (1983); Estes (1939); Mills (1914); Trimble (1984).

Molting Snowshoe Hare.

VIII. *Order* LAGOMORPHA
Rabbits and Allies

FOUR KINDS OF lagomorphs occur in Rocky Mountain National Park. An additional three species occur elsewhere in Colorado. Lagomorphs were long considered to be rodents, but now it is realized that, although superficially similar in their dental adaptations for gnawing plant material, the orders have independent evolutionary histories, and may even have arisen independently from ancestral, primitive mammals. Lagomorphs are native to all continents except Australia (where they have been introduced, much to the detriment of natural biotic communities). There are approximately 65 species of living lagomorphs, arranged in two families (both of which occur in the Park).

FAMILY OCHOTONIDAE—PIKAS

The family Ochotonidae includes a single genus, *Ochotona*. The genus is holarctic in distribution and includes two closely related North American species and a dozen or more Asian species with a wide variety of lifestyles.

Pika
Ochotona princeps

Description. —The pika looks more like a grayish guinea pig than like its cousins the rabbits and hares. The ears are short and rounded and the tail is a mere vestige, so short it is lost in the fur. The animals range in total length from about 175 to 200 mm, and range about 200 grams in weight. The color is highly variable, often approaching the color of the rock in a given mountain range. In the Park, most are dirty gray, sometimes washed lightly with buff, paling to grayish white below. Molting individuals may appear to be darker because the lead-gray bases of the hairs are exposed. The pika can be confused with no other mammal, although the casual observer may mistake it for a rock. *Field Recognition.*—Diurnal habit; habitat in talus slides; metallic, nasal call note.

Distribution and Habitat.—The pika occurs in western North America, from central British Columbia southward to California, Utah, and northern New Mexico. The closely related collared pika (*Ochotona collaris*) occurs in southern Alaska and adjacent Canada. North American pikas are rather narrowly restricted to mountainous areas where talus slopes provide suitable cover. Locally, pikas live from above timberline down into the subalpine forest to elevations as low as about 2590 meters (about 8500 feet) where suitable rock slides exist. Occasional exceptional animals are found living under piles of boards or timbers or in burrows (probably made by other mammals), but broken rock (including mine tailings) is the usual habitat. Not just any rock pile will suffice—the rock must be sufficiently large that the spaces between provide corridors for movement, the slide must be of sufficiently recent origin that the spaces have not filled with debris from higher ground, and in the best habitat the talus is interspersed with meadow vegetation. There are innumerable patches of habitat in the Park suitable for pikas, and all but the most hurried visitor should expect to see them (or at least hear them), either along Trail Ridge Road, or on any of the high-country trails.

Natural History.—The pika (pronounced "pee-kuh" by purists—the name is taken from a Siberian dialect) has an intriguing variety of common names: little chief hare, rock rabbit, calling hare, cony, and "cooney" to list a sampling. Remarkably little is known of the biology of this fascinating little mammal, perhaps because its haunts are largely inaccessible through much of the year. Its best known habitat is the gathering of vegetation into "haypiles." These rounded stacks usually contain about a bushel of "hay," but they may be twice that size. In our area, building of haypiles begins in mid-July and continues in earnest for the remainder of the short growing season. Haypiles often are built under at least partial shelter of overhanging rocks. Presumably the animals are active through the winter beneath the snow using stored hay as food, but direct observations in winter are meager.

Pikas eat a wide variety of plant material depending on local abundance. Typically foliage makes up the bulk of the diet, although seeds are eaten in season. Forbs usually are more important in the diet than are grasses, and twigs, leaves, or bark of trees and shrubs may be eaten. The animals seem to have little (if any) need for free water, presumably meeting their requirements by eating succulent foliage. The urine is highly concentrated and viscous, frequently staining the rocks a chalky white to brown.

Like other lagomorphs, pikas produce two kinds of feces. True feces are round, fibrous, and hard, like those of rabbits but much smaller. A second kind of feces appears as an amorphous, elongate mass, and is termed "soft feces." The hard fecal pellets actually are waste matter; soft feces, by contrast, are not waste. They are high in protein and energy and perhaps vitamins. As much as one-fourth of such soft feces is reingested; that is, swallowed and passed through the digestive tract a second time.

Pikas are diurnal and readily observed. An hour of pika-watching is an hour well spent, for these are interesting and highly entertaining animals. One is first made aware of their presence by the characteristic metallic call. Several calls are produced. They may function as alarm-notes as well as signals to neighbors approaching the territory. There is also a distinct mating call. Scent-marking also is practiced. Scents are placed on rocks by rubbing with chin glands, and also with characteristic piles of feces and deposits of urine. Females are more likely to mate with familiar males, and familiarity appears to be a function of odor. Territories are closely guarded. Spacing is maintained mostly by vocalization, but intruders are also chased. Territories average about 400 square meters in extent, but the normal foraging range is somewhat smaller. When undisturbed, pikas spend their time in summer basking on the rocks (where they may be difficult to spot) or scampering about feeding. The animals are remarkably quick and agile but seldom jump. Toward fall the haypile becomes the overriding concern.

In early summer the animals undergo a conspicuous patterned molt, beginning on the head and progressing backwards. The summer pelage is much shorter and less lax than the winter coat. Summer pelage is worn for only about two months and then the fall molt begins. In any population during the warmer months some individuals are sure to be undergoing one of these seasonal molts.

Predation on pikas is poorly documented, but weasels (both the long-tailed and short-tailed weasel, or ermine) have been observed to capture pikas. Martens also prey on them, as do some of the larger carnivores—such as coyotes—that venture high into the mountains. Birds of prey, especially hawks, also must take a toll.

The breeding season begins in late March or April, and the last young are born in August. After a gestation period of a bit over 30 days, two to four (usually three) young, weighing about 10 grams, are born. The young are reared in a nest under cover of rocks, and are weaned at about 60 grams. Immediately after giving birth the female comes into heat (post-partum estrus). Two litters per season seem to be the maximum, but a single litter may be more common here. Environmental conditions affect survival and reproduction. There is evidence to indicate that in severe winters with late-lying snowpack and a late growing season, survival and reproductive success are lower than in other years. Maximum longevity has been reported from four to seven years.

Selected References.—Johnson (1967); Meaney (1983); Smith (1975, 1978); Southwick et al. (1986); Svendsen (1979).

FAMILY LEPORIDAE—RABBITS AND HARES

The Family Leporidae includes the rabbits and hares. Of about fifty species of leporids, six occur in Colorado, and three of these occupy various habitats in Rocky Mountain National Park.

Nuttall's Cottontail
Sylvilagus nuttallii

Description.—Nuttall's cottontail is a rather small rabbit, ranging in total length from about 380 to 410 mm, of which 35 to 50 mm is tail. The ears are densely haired inside, and short for a rabbit, 55 to 65 mm long. Weights range around 1 kilogram. This is the most richly colored lagomorph in the Park. From a distance, the upper parts appear to be dark brown, but closer at hand the hairs are seen to be reddish, mostly tipped with black. The nape is rusty red and the underparts and tail are white. Nuttall's cottontail cannot be confused easily with other lagomorphs in Rocky Mountain National Park, but nearby two closely related species occur. The desert cottontail (*Sylvilagus audubonii*) is about the same size as Nuttall's cottontail, but it has longer, sparsely-haired ears and is considerably paler in color. Another confusingly similar nearby species is the eastern cottontail (*Sylvilagus floridanus*). This species is somewhat larger than Nuttall's cottontail, and the color is slightly darker. The best way to distinguish the cottontails in the field is probably habitat preference—Nuttall's cottontail occurs in forest-edge situations (and in sagebrush country in northwestern Colorado); the desert cottontail occurs in open, semiarid grassland, and in shrub communities in the foothills; the eastern cottontail occurs in deciduous, riparian woodland. Only Nuttall's cottontail is to be expected in our specific area of interest. *Field Recognition.* — Small size, short ears, dark dorsal color.

Distribution and Habitat. — Interior western North America is the range of Nuttall's cottontail, from the Rockies to the Sierra Nevada, and from southern Alberta and Saskatchewan to Arizona. In Colorado, the species occurs over most of the western three-fifths of the state. Nuttall's cottontail is a mammal of brushy, forest-edge situations in the Southern Rockies. Elsewhere in the West stands of sagebrush are occupied as well. The species occurs throughout the Park, from lowest elevations to about treeline.

Natural History. — No comprehensive study of the life history of Nuttall's cottontail has been made. The animals are largely nocturnal. During the day they huddle to rest in rather deep forms in dense shrubbery, or in other sheltered spots, such as hollow logs, piles of brush or logging slash, or burrows abandoned by other animals. When startled, the animals may leave the form during the day, but they quickly find alternative cover. Predators include coyotes, bobcats, foxes, weasels, and owls. Snakes take nestling young. Internal parasites include flatworms and roundworms, and the animals host fleas and ticks and are susceptible to tularemia. In the evening, cottontails begin to feed. They are active throughout the year, and the diet varies with availability of food. During the growing season, succulent grasses and forbs are preferred, but in winter dry grasses, twigs, and bark are eaten. As in other lagomorphs, the upper and lower molar teeth of cottontails do not occlude directly. Chewing is by a side-to-side motion of the jaws, unlike the grinding motion seen in other mammals.

Although direct data are few, probably Nuttall's cottontail is polyestrous, breeding throughout the warmer months. Four to eight (mode, four or five) young are born after a gestation period of about four weeks. As is true generally of rabbits, the young are altricial—born blind, naked, and highly dependent. Such offspring require more careful attention than do young hares. They are bedded in a nest in a burrow, hollow stump, or other protected place. The nest is lined with fine grasses, leaves, and hair which the mother has plucked from her belly and chest.

Selected References.—Chapman (1975); Chapman, Hockman, and Edwards (*in* Chapman and Feldhamer, 1982).

Snowshoe Hare
Lepus americanus

Description.—Snowshoe hares are of moderate size, somewhat larger than cottontails, but markedly smaller than the white-tailed jack rabbit. Total length ranges from 400 to 450 mm, the tail from 30 to 60 mm. The ear is relatively short for a hare, 65 to 70 mm, but the hind feet are relatively large (hence the common name), 140 to 155 mm in length. Adults weigh about a kilogram. In summer, snowshoe hares are rusty brown, darkest along the dorsal midline and grading to grayish brown along the sides. The chin and belly are white to grayish, and the nape is grayish brown. The tail is black above, white below. In winter the pelage is white except for black tips on the ears. *Field Recognition.*— Moderate size; combination of short ears and large feet; in winter, combination of white pelage and forested habitat.

Distribution and Habitat.—The snowshoe hare is a boreal mammal, occurring the breadth of North America, from New England and Maritime Canada to the Pacific Coast. The species occurs from north of the Arctic Circle southward through Canada and along the principal mountain ranges to California, New Mexico, and Tennessee. In Colorado, the snowshoe hare is confined to the mountains, and it occurs throughout the Park in suitable habitat. These are animals of dense forests in Colorado, and are commonest where an understory of brush or shrubs is present. When a tract of forest has burned, shrubs soon invade, and such areas provide ideal habitat for local snowshoe hares. The altitudinal range in our area is from about 2450 to 3350 meters (8000 to 11,000 feet).

Natural History.—The snowshoe hare is sometimes called a "rabbit," but it is a true hare. Rabbits bear altricial young—naked, blind, highly dependent. Young hares, however, are precocial—furred, alert, and able to move about soon after birth.

Snowshoe hares are largely nocturnal. During the day they rest in "forms," unlined depressions under cover of shrubbery and they move only if disturbed. At night they move away from the form over well-worn paths to feed or to dust themselves for ectoparasites in communal dustbaths.

The diet consists largely of grasses and forbs when available, but in winter the bark and young twigs of woody plants are eaten. Winter feeding by snowshoe hares leaves many saplings stripped of bark at snowline. Such saplings cannot survive if girdling is complete, because nutrients cannot move from the leaves downward to nourish the roots. Although seemingly destructive, the hares actually may help the forest by removing occasional young trees, thus thinning the stand and improving conditions for the survivors. Unlike most other lagomorphs, snowshoe hares are known to eat carrion occasionally. Reingestion of soft feces occurs, as is true in other lagomorphs in the Park. Water needs seem to be met by the moisture in the food and the lapping of dew. Snowshoe hares also eat snow.

The snowshoe hare, as an herbivore, is an important link in the food web, converting vegetation into food for coyotes, bobcats, and the larger birds of prey. Weasels prey on the young. Farther north, the lynx is highly dependent upon snowshoe hares for food. Populations of hares are subject to wide fluctuation with about ten years between "crashes," and the lynx is subject to a closely related cycle of abundance. In Colorado, populations of snowshoe hares seem to fluctuate also, but this has not been studied in any detail.

Adult snowshoe hares are solitary animals. Aggression among them is reported frequently. During the reproductive season, males fight among themselves, and pregnant females are actively hostile toward males. Only on choice dusting spots does there appear to be any mutual tolerance.

The molt of snowshoe hares from "brush brown" to "snow white" is well known. The autumnal molt begins in September and takes two to three months to complete. Timing is controlled (in part at least) by day length. Molt begins on the appendages, then progresses to the dorsum, and occurs last on the shoulders and crown. The short underfur is not molted. In March or April, prevernal molt begins, with a pattern opposite that seen in autumn. In years with early or late snowfall, the pelage may be out of phase with the background, leaving brown animals conspicuous against the snow, or white animals obvious among dry, brown leaves. The timing of molt is adapted to average regional climate, and for the most part cryptic coloration must be adequate insurance against over-predation. In addition to color change, winter pelage has much better insulation value.

Snowshoe hares are polyestrous and exhibit post-partum heat. Breeding occurs from March to August, and females may bear one to three litters, with two being the most common number in Colorado. Litters of one to seven (average about three) precocial young are born — well-furred, the eyes open — after a gestation period of some thirty-eight days. The young huddle together in the unlined form, but by the second day they can move well if disturbed. Growth is rapid. Birth weights double in eight days, and when the young are weaned at about one month they have been eating some vegetation for at least two weeks, and birth weights have increased nine times. By three to five months of age the animals reach adult weight. Young of the year do not breed, however.

Selected References. — Bittner and Rongstad (*in* Chapman and Feldhamer, 1982).

White-tailed Jack Rabbit
Lepus townsendii

Description. —The white-tailed jack rabbit is by far the largest lagomorph in the Park. Adults are about 550 to 600 mm long, of which the tail comprises 75 to 85 mm. Females are somewhat larger than males. The ear is long, 90 to 115 mm from notch to tip. The hind foot is about 140 to 165 mm long, only slightly longer than that of the much smaller snowshoe hare. Weights range to a maximum of 5 kilograms, but 2 to 4 kilograms is more usual.

In summer, the white-tailed jack rabbit is pale buffy gray above, pale gray to white below. The tail is white, but may be marked with an obscure gray or black line. (This character is highly variable in our area.) The ears are white behind and tipped with black. In winter, most individuals don a white pelage, although the extremities and face often have a buffy tinge and the tips of the ears remain black. *Field Recognition.* — Large size, long ears; habitat in relatively open country.

Distribution and Habitat. —The white-tailed jack rabbit is a mammal of the Great Basin and the central and northern Great Plains, ranging from Alberta to New Mexico and from California to Iowa. This hare occurs almost statewide in Colorado, and throughout Rocky Mountain National Park. White-tailed jack rabbits occupy open grasslands in summer and tend to move into shrubby country in winter. In Colorado, these animals have as wide an elevational range as any mammal, from below 1220 meters (4000 feet) on the eastern plains to over 4270 meters (14,000 feet) in the alpine tundra. Because of their habitat preferences, white-tailed jack rabbits probably are more abundant at lower elevations in Arapaho National Recreation Area than elsewhere locally, but they range throughout the Park in suitable habitat.

Natural History. — Jack rabbits are not rabbits; they are hares, giving birth to precocial young. These are large lagomorphs, adapted to life in open habitats. Speed is useful insurance in such situations, and when pursued white-tailed jack rabbits may cover short distances at 65 kilometers (40 miles) per hour. The animals rely on cryptic coloration for concealment in their forms, however, and often can be approached quite closely before they flush.

Like the preferred habitat, diet changes with season. In summer, herbs (mostly forbs) compose up to 90 percent of the diet, but in winter three-fourths of the diet is shrubs. As in other lagomorphs, reingestion of soft feces occurs. The pellets are produced during the day (while the animals are resting) and are taken from the anus and swallowed. Reingestion allows the extraction of additional energy from the vegetable diet. The pellets also contain protein, as well as B-vitamins, probably produced in the intestine by bacteria, but not absorbable there.

Jack rabbits are mostly crepuscular, being active in early morning, and again in late afternoon and evening. Young jack rabbits are preyed upon by coyotes, foxes, weasels, and birds of prey. The larger carnivorous mammals and birds also surprise and capture adults, but perhaps disease, parasites, and destruction of habitat by humans are more important enemies.

The breeding season lasts from about March through August. Groups of three or four males may follow a female in heat. Gestation takes about six weeks. There is a post-partum estrus, but — in southern Colorado at any rate — a single litter of about five young (range, one to 11) seems to be the rule. The young are precocial and are reared in a simple form or in a burrow abandoned by another animal. Growth is rapid, and the mother's milk is quickly supplemented by vegetation.

Selected References. — Bear and Hansen (1966); Dunn, Chapman, and Marsh (*in* Chapman and Feldhamer, 1982); Hansen and Flinders (1969).

Bushy-tailed Woodrat.

IX. *Order* RODENTIA

Rodents

ABOUT 25 SPECIES of rodents occur in Rocky Mountain National Park, or sufficiently near the Park that their occurrence is considered likely. These species represent six families and utilize a broad range of habitats—in the trees, in the water, among the rocks, above and below ground. Rodents exceed all other mammals in the Park in terms of numbers of species and numbers of individuals, and the same may be said of most terrestrial ecosystems throughout the world. The Order Rodentia includes about one-third of living mammals (some 1700 species), arranged in over 30 families. The incisors of rodents grow in length throughout life, and are continually worn down by incessant gnawing on coarse plant materials. Because the face is hard enamel and the rear is softer dentine, the continual wear of upper and lower incisors against each other sharpens them.

FAMILY SCIURIDAE—SQUIRRELS

All squirrels in Rocky Mountain National Park are diurnal; hence, they are among the best known (and most appreciated) of rodents. There are about 260 species of squirrels in the world arranged in some 50 genera. Of the 17 species of squirrels that occur in Colorado, nine live in or near the Park.

Selected References. – MacClintock (1970).

Least Chipmunk
Tamias minimus

Description. –The least chipmunk is aptly named; it is our smallest squirrel. Adults range in total length from 190 to 215 mm, with a rather narrow tail 80 to 100 mm long. The hind foot is 29 to 32 mm long, and weights range from 40 to 60 grams.

The color of least chipmunks in our area is variable, because the Park is a zone of integration between a brightly colored eastern subspecies and a dusky, less reddish western one. The back is marked with well-defined black and white stripes, and stripes also mark the face. The tail is clothed with black-tipped hairs with reddish bases. The sides are reddish brown to brown and the underparts are grayish buff to white.

Species of chipmunks are not easy to distinguish in the museum and they are difficult or impossible to identify in the field. For starters, however, be sure that the "chipmunk" has stripes on its face; if it does not, it is not a chipmunk at all, but a golden-mantled ground squirrel. Next, look at its size. A decidedly small, retiring chipmunk probably is the least chipmunk. Both the Uinta and Colorado chipmunks are larger and somewhat bolder and more deliberate in their movements.

The Uinta and Colorado chipmunks are even trickier to distinguish. There are subtle differences in color, the proportions of the skull are different, and the bacula differ in shape, but overall the species are remarkably similar. In our area, the best criterion for identification may be habitat. The Colorado chipmunk occurs in rocky areas with shrubby vegetation or sparse woodland, mostly below 2300 meters (7500 feet) in elevation. The Uinta chipmunk occupies openings in the better developed forest of higher elevations, generally above 2450 meters (8000 feet). A warning: in intermediate areas, don't agonize over the specific identity of a chipmunk. I don't, for fear of losing perspective and my enthusiasm for squirrel-watching. The important thing is that the chipmunks can tell themselves apart (by inscrutable means of their own). *Field Recognition.* – Small size, bright color; rapid, nervous movements; habitat mostly in openings in wooded country.

Distribution and Habitat. –The least chipmunk is a widespread species, occurring from the Yukon eastward to Wisconsin, Upper Michigan, and western Quebec, and southward—especially in mountainous areas—to southern New Mexico. The species lives throughout central and western Colorado and is an abundant and conspicuous mammal through most of Rocky Mountain National Park. The least chipmunk has the broadest ecological tolerance of our chipmunks and ranges virtually throughout the Park, from the lowest elevations to timberline and above. Elsewhere, these animals occupy a diversity of habitats—shrub deserts, badlands, openings in damp coniferous forests. One seldom sees a chipmunk in unbroken forest, but any opening will support a few, and greatest numbers are found in the forest edge, the ecotone between forest and meadow or mountain park.

Natural History.—This is one of the most familiar small mammals in the Park, but surprisingly little is known of its natural history. Perhaps the difficulty of identifying species has made naturalists wary of chipmunks as subjects for field study; many older published observations cannot be attributed with certainty to any of the species presently recognized by taxonomists. A thorough study of the natural history of the least chipmunk in the Southern Rockies remains to be done.

Like most squirrels, this is a diurnal mammal. Least chipmunks are more nervous and animated than our other chipmunks and less easily approached. When startled they dart beneath the nearest rock or into their burrows. Sometimes they climb trees to avoid danger and they seem to climb better and more readily than our other chipmunks.

Chipmunks are adapted to a diet of seeds, but this and other species have rather catholic diets overall. Seeds—especially those of the aster family—form the bulk of the diet in season and they are stored in the burrow for winter, but other plant material, insects, and some carrion also are eaten. In the Park, the animals eat table scraps but they are by no means as proficient at panhandling as are the larger chipmunks or the golden-mantled ground squirrel. A study of the least chipmunk at Rainbow Curves found densities of least chipmunks seven times greater than more natural populations reported in the literature. Also, home ranges were smaller in the "provisioned" population. Artificial feeding of chipmunks and other wildlife is rightly discouraged for the sake of the animals' health and that of visitors as well.

Least chipmunks burrow beneath rocks, logs, shrubs, and other such shelters. Abandoned burrows of larger squirrels or pocket gophers may also be used. At the end of the complex tunnel is a nest chamber, used at night and through the long winter. With the first heavy snows, the animals go into torpor in October or early November and they remain below ground through the winter over much of the Park. The winter sleep is not true hibernation, however, for the animals arouse periodically to feed on stored food. At lower elevations they may emerge from the burrow during warm spells for brief periods.

Males emerge in spring in breeding condition, and females come into estrus in about a week. Thus, the timing of reproduction varies widely, depending (in part at least) on the timing of snowmelt and the availability of fresh food resources. Breeding in our area takes place from May to early June, and the young are born by early July after a gestation period of four to five weeks. Five or six young comprise a typical litter, with extremes of three to eight reported locally. The young are highly altricial and do not leave the nest until about four weeks of age. In our area, at any rate, females are monoestrous and young of the year do not breed.

Selected References.—Carleton (1966); Friedrichsen (1977); Skryja (1974); Telleen (1978); Vaughan (1969).

Colorado Chipmunk
Tamias quadrivittatus

Description.—The Colorado chipmunk is of moderate size, larger than the least chipmunk and of slightly stockier build than the Uinta chipmunk. Total length ranges from about 210 to 240 mm, the tail is 90 to 110 mm long, and the hind foot is 33 to 36 mm in length. Weights range around 70 grams.

The color is brighter overall than is that of the Uinta chipmunk, and thus is very similar to that of the least chipmunk. The black and white stripes of the dorsum and head are well-defined, and the sides are reddish, grading to buff. For comments on distinguishing chipmunks in our area, see the account of the least chipmunk. *Field Recognition.*— Large size, bright color; habitat in rocky country, generally below 2290 meters (7500 feet).

Distribution and Habitat.—The Colorado chipmunk is aptly named, for it occurs only in Colorado and neighboring parts of Utah, Arizona, and New Mexico. The species is not documented from Rocky Mountain National Park, but may be expected at lower elevations about Estes Park. In northern Colorado it occurs mostly in the foothills, in the lower canyons leading to the Park from the east. Here the Colorado chipmunk is a mammal of rocky areas, finding suitable cover beneath rocks and shrubs and about the bases of scattered conifers. Records in our area are all from below 2450 meters (8000 feet), roughly the elevation at which open woodland "closes up" into true forest.

Natural History. – Most of the meager information published under the name "Colorado chipmunk" for our immediate area probably pertains instead to the Uinta chipmunk. It was not until 1953 that the two species were recognized as distinct here. The Colorado chipmunk has a restricted distribution in northern Colorado. Along with the rock squirrel, the Mexican woodrat, and the rock mouse, it occurs in a narrow band along the foothills, entering the mountains proper only along sheltered canyons.

Like other chipmunks, this species prefers seeds and berries, but it eats a variety of plant materials as available and takes occasional insects as well. Burrows are excavated beneath rocks, shrubs, or the exposed roots of trees.

Mating occurs in late April or May. Gestation takes about 30 days and there is one litter of about five young per year. Newborns are altricial and weigh only about 3 grams, gaining about 0.5 grams per day for the first three months of life. The ears unfold after two or three days and the eyes open after about four weeks. Newborn chipmunks are hairless except for facial vibrissae ("whiskers"), but body hair appears quickly, and the dorsal stripes are evident in 10 days. The dentition is complete at about five weeks, and the young are weaned at six to seven weeks of age. Young animals commonly appear above ground in August.

Selected References. –Wadsworth (1969); White (1953).

Uinta Chipmunk
Tamias umbrinus

Description. –This is a moderate-sized chipmunk, obviously larger than the least chipmunk, with a slightly fuller tail, but not as heavy-bodied as the Colorado chipmunk. The color is hardly distinctive, but generally the Uinta chipmunk has the dullest dorsal color and the least distinct lateral stripes of our chipmunks. Often the hindquarters are grayish, with the stripes obscure. For further comparisons, see the account of the least chipmunk. Adults range in total length from 215 to 235 mm, and the tail is 90 to 110 mm long. The hind foot measures 33 to 35 mm. Weights range around 65 grams. *Field Recognition.* — Relatively large size (hind foot 33 mm or more), dusky color often with poorly defined stripes; habitat forest edge situations, generally above 2450 meters (8000 feet).

Distribution and Habitat. —The Uinta chipmunk has an erratic distribution in mountainous parts of the western United States, with disjunct populations in Colorado, northwestern Wyoming, Utah, and Nevada. The Coloradan population occurs in the north-central and northwestern parts of the state, and is not known to overlap with the Colorado chipmunk. I know of no obvious differences in habitat between the Uinta and least chipmunks. However, of the two, the Uinta chipmunk has the narrower altitudinal range (from about 2450 meters to timberline or slightly above) and seems to be more closely restricted to rocky areas (although less so than the Colorado chipmunk). Like the least chipmunk, this is mostly an animal of forest-edge habitat in the Park. Especially look for them in rocky openings in lodgepole pine forests.

Natural History. — Like other chipmunks, these animals excavate burrows beneath rocks or shrubs. At the end of the tunnel is a nest chamber. During summer, individuals feed on seeds and berries, supplementing the diet with other plant material and insects. Birds' eggs and carrion are eaten occasionally, but these items are hardly staples. In autumn, seeds and berries are stored in the burrow. Uinta chipmunks in the Park clean up after careless visitors. Often they bury a crust of bread or some other delicate morsel beneath a thin layer of soil near the source of supply and then sally forth for more booty, which is carried in capacious cheekpouches. While more tame than least chipmunks, they are less brazen than the larger golden-mantled ground squirrel.

In winter the animals are dormant in the burrow under a protective blanket of snow. Their habitat is such that it usually holds snow through the winter, but occasionally animals on favorably warm slopes arouse during warm, snow-free periods and appear above ground. Others arouse and feed on stored food but to not leave the burrow.

Watching chipmunks, one sees considerable social interaction between individuals. Apparently a dominance hierarchy exists, and one animal may drive another from a bit of food without any show of physical force. There is a repertoire of several calls, but this has not been studied in any detail. The calls of the Uinta chipmunk are typically higher in pitch than those of the least chipmunk.

The presence in the same area of two species of chipmunks and the golden-mantled ground squirrel may puzzle amateur naturalists, because they look very much alike. In fact, professional naturalists are puzzled as well. No trenchant differences are known in the ecological needs of these squirrels, yet a fundamental rule of ecology is that two species cannot coexist indefinitely in the same niche. How such similar species manage to live in such close proximity is unknown, but I suspect that one day we will learn that available resources are neatly, if subtly, partitioned, just as they have been demonstrated to be in the better-studied ecosystems on this well-ordered globe, by the firmest of arbiters, the process of natural selection.

Soon after the animals emerge in spring there is a flurry of activity, so seemingly irresponsible that it can only be associated with mating. Males drop all caution and pretense and chase females with abandon. I have seen animals dash through a campsite without regard for human observers, leap to a boulder, and—misjudging the distance to the next rock—land upside-down in a currant bush. These, recall, are the antics of males intent on becoming grandfathers! Somehow it works. Although not documented, gestation probably lasts about 30 days. Four or five offspring comprise a typical litter. The young are weaned and are foraging on their own in mid-July or August.

Selected References.—Telleen (1978); White (1953).

Yellow-bellied Marmot
Marmota flaviventris

Description.—The yellow-bellied marmot is the largest and stockiest of local squirrels and that with the relatively shortest tail. Adults range in total length from about 600 to 680 mm, of which the tail comprises less than one-third, 175 to 205 mm. Weights range from 2.5 to 5 kilograms or more, with heaviest weights in late summer when the animals have fattened for hibernation. As is typical of polygynous mammals, males average larger than females. Marmots (also called "woodchucks," "rockchucks," "whistle pigs," or "groundhogs") are quite variable in dorsal color, the abundant pelage ranging from yellowish brown through reddish brown nearly to black. The underfur is soft, dense, and grayish brown in color. The tail is colored like the back. The face, like the feet, is covered with short hairs, usually black in color, with irregular white markings about the mouth and chin. The underparts are rather thinly covered with yellowish (to reddish brown) hairs, hence the preferred common name. *Field Recognition.* – Large size, short tail; habitat about boulders; whistling call.

Distribution and Habitat. – The yellow-bellied marmot is an inhabitant of mountainous parts of western North America, from southern British Columbia to California and New Mexico, eastward to the Black Hills of South Dakota. Several closely related species, including the hoary marmot and the woodchuck, complement this range so that species of *Marmota* occupy much of North America north of México. In Colorado, the marmot occurs widely in the western three-fifths of the state, and throughout Rocky Mountain National Park.

For marmots, suitable habitat has two requisites: boulders (or a reasonable substitute) for cover and lush herbage for food. They are probably most abundant in the rockpiles about subalpine meadows, but they range from the foothills to well above timberline, mostly in open situations. They may burrow beneath woodpiles or cabins, and sometimes they live in dry culverts, road fill, or other man-made shelter.

Natural History. – The yellow-bellied marmot is a familiar animal in the Park and it is readily observed. The daily round of activity is rather stereotyped. Up with the sun, the marmot forages along well-worn paths for the green vegetation that comprises nearly all of its diet (although seeds are also eaten when available). Mid-morning is a time for basking in the sun. About noon, the animals retire to the burrow. After the usual brief afternoon rain shower, the marmot reappears to bask again, atop a boulder or other prominence. In late afternoon, foraging begins again in earnest. Within a few minutes after sundown, all will have retired to their burrows for the night. Basically, the program is that of tourists on well-earned vacations: marmots are gourmands and heliophiles – they eat or they sunbathe, and then they sleep.

Close watch of a colony of marmots reveals other sorts of behavior. Burrowing occupies a good part of the time. Burrows usually begin beneath a boulder and they may be extensive. Typically they are on a hillside, which prevents flooding. The burrow is the center of activity. The young are reared there and there the animals spend the mid-day period, the night, and the long winter. The burrow also provides protection from enemies and from inclement summer weather. In the main chamber a nest is built of grasses and other fibrous materials.

A resting marmot may seem complacent, but be assured that it is alert. The colony has no single sentry. Any animal sensing danger whistles and stands on the alert. Others nearby immediately become alert as well. If danger is imminent, the animals retreat to the burrow, either quietly or with a "scream" or squeal. In addition to the squeal, six different whistles have been identified. A given whistle seems to have no specific meaning; rather, "alert" or "alarm" are communicated by a whistle accompanied by visual cues. There is no "all-clear" signal; resumption of activity indicates that. Much marmot communication seems to serve a defensive function. Also, agonistic communication helps to maintain spacing between colonies.

The marmot colony consists of a single adult male, a "harem" of variable size, yearlings, and young of the year. Marmots meeting each other along a path may "greet" each other, sniffing about the cheeks. Spacing is maintained by mutual avoidance and "threat," which may be communicated by a peculiar whistle or by a loud chattering of the incisors. A dominance hierarchy exists within the colony, with priorities maintained by threats and submissive gestures. Yearlings are the most frequent objects of threatening behavior. After repeated harassment, the yearlings tend to move from the colony, sometimes for distances of 2 kilometers. Dispersal — movement from place of birth to place of reproduction — is an important feature of animal behavior. Dispersal removes offspring from potential competition with the parents.

The dispersing marmot is without the social protection afforded individuals in established colonies. The disperser has but two eyes to look for danger; colonial animals have the protection of many eyes. It is hardly surprising that dispersing marmots are especially susceptible to predation. These are not fast-moving animals, and coyotes and foxes have no trouble catching them. Colonial marmots are subject to predation by actively burrowing predators (especially badgers) and coyotes excavate a few. Weasels prey on the young in their nests. Outside the protective refuge of the National Park, marmots are subject to much wanton molestation by humans.

Marmots are hibernators. In late summer and early autumn they store large amounts of fat. The annual molt completed, they enter the burrow for the winter in September and early October, to emerge in spring in April or May. The length of the hibernation period varies widely with elevation.

Breeding occurs in spring soon after emergence from hibernation. Gestation takes four to five weeks, and three to eight (average four or five) young comprise a typical litter. Apparently there is some variation in the timing of the breeding season, because small animals some-times are seen in spring, suggesting that they are young of litters born late the previous season. The young are altricial and do not appear above ground for about a month. Once above ground, their growth is rapid; young of the year enter hibernation nearly as large as adults. The animals disperse as yearlings; all males move from the natal colony and many females do.

Selected References. – Frase and Hoffmann (1980).

Wyoming Ground Squirrel
Spermophilus elegans

Description. – This is a medium-sized ground squirrel. Adults range from 250 to 340 mm in total length, of which the tail comprises 60 to 100 mm. The ear is quite small, as is typical of burrowing rodents. Weights in early summer average about 325 grams for males, somewhat less for females. The color generally is brownish gray, but close examination reveals a dappled pattern of cinnamon and black. The belly is whitish to buff. *Field Recognition.* – Lean profile, upright alert posture, moderate size, grayish color.

Distribution and Habitat. – The range of the Wyoming ground squirrel consists of three disjunct segments, one in southwestern Montana and adjacent Idaho, another in northern Nevada and adjacent Idaho, and the third in southern Wyoming and adjacent Colorado. The range in Colorado apparently is actively expanding, and the animals have reached their present southern limits in the Gunnison Basin only in the last few years. Wyoming ground squirrels are abundant in the National Park in relatively open country where soils are sufficiently well-drained that burrows remain dry. Beyond that, Wyoming ground squirrels seem to have no real habitat preference. They often frequent parks, open valleys, and even small meadows surrounded by rather heavy timber. Elsewhere in Colorado, sagebrush stands and shortgrass prairie are also occupied. The species ranges in elevation from 1830 to 1660 meters (6000 to 12,000 feet).

Natural History. – The Wyoming ground squirrel – also known as "picket-pin," merely "ground squirrel," or (quite erroneously) "gopher" – is a highly competitive species. First reported from Horseshoe Park in 1911, the animals were regarded as common in Estes Park by 1915. Early reports suggested that the expansion of this species was partially at the expense of the golden-mantled ground squirrel, but ecological relationships of the two species never have been documented thoroughly.

In certain areas this is a very abundant mammal. A sunny slope with a good cover of herbaceous vegetation may support 20 animals per acre (50 per hectare), although densities are lower in areas with shrubby vegetation. Where they are abundant their extensive burrows perforate the soil. Typically, a rather substantial pile of debris litters the ground downslope from the entrance to the burrow. The golden-mantled ground squirrel does not leave such piles. Hence, the burrows of the two species can be distinguished rather easily. Dried grasses line the nest chamber. Picket-pins retire to the burrow at night and at midday on the warmest summer days. When the animals are above ground the burrow is still the center of activity.

Wyoming ground squirrels eat foliage for the most part, principally grasses, but also herbs and shrubs. Seemingly, they eat carrion more readily than other ground squirrels do, but the overall significance of carrion in the diet is not known. Wyoming ground squirrels frequently are seen on highways feeding on the remains of their brethren who have become traffic casualties. In mid-summer, the squirrels begin to convert food to fat for storage — mostly just beneath the skin — for the long winter. Accumulation of critical amounts of fat seems to trigger hibernation, which apparently occurs regardless of cues from the external environment. In the Park, these squirrels disappear below ground early, usually in August or early September. When they emerge in March, some fat usually remains. This extra fat is a safety margin. Animals that fail to store sufficient fat starve to death during hibernation. In spring, males emerge a few days ahead of females.

Like a number of other ground squirrels, the Wyoming ground squirrel has an upright alert posture; hence the name "picket-pin," alluding to the resemblance to the picket stake to which a horse is tied. In this posture, the squirrels remain motionless until danger has passed or until it is imminent. In the former instance, the alert posture gives way to resumed feeding or grooming. In the latter case, the animal vanishes instantly into its burrow. Raptorial birds and a variety of carnivorous mammals feed on these squirrels. Badgers often enlarge burrows of ground squirrels (and other rodents) and devour the occupants in their dens. A burrow that has been re-excavated by a badger is a remarkable mess; one wonders how a squirrel or two provides enough food energy to power such destruction. Coyotes and weasels also feed on ground squirrels, and a variety of parasites and diseases takes a toll. In this as in many other hibernators, a major control on numbers is the physiological stress of hibernation, from which many animals never recover.

In April, soon after emergence from hibernation, mating takes place. After a gestation period of a little over four weeks, the two to ten (usually five or six) altricial young are born. Neonates are hairless and toothless, and the eyes and ears are closed. Hair appears on the head at 10 days, vocalization begins at two weeks, and the eyes and ears open and the incisors erupt at about three weeks. Weaned at an age of five weeks, the young squirrels are above ground in early June.

Selected References. – Zegers (1984). (Early references to this species may appear under the generic name *Citellus*. Until quite recently, local populations were considered to be conspecific with Richardson's ground squirrel, *Spermophilus richardsoni*, a species of northern Montana and southern Canada.)

Golden-mantled Ground Squirrel
Spermophilus lateralis

Description. –The golden-mantled ground squirrel is a rather small but stocky ground squirrel, ranging from 245 to 295 mm in total length. The tail is moderately bushy and 75 to 115 mm long. Adults typically range in weight from 175 to 250 grams, but some of the over-nourished beggars in the National Park reach weights of 275 to 300 grams or more by early autumn.

This ground squirrel often is mistakenly called a "big chipmunk," and it does look much like its smaller cousins. Aside from larger size, the most obvious difference is that the ground squirrel has no stripes on the head. Also, the tail is relatively shorter. The ground color of the upper parts is golden to reddish buff, grading to whitish beneath. On the shoulders and neck is a russet to golden "mantle," the basis for the preferred (if rather cumbersome) common name. *Field Recognition.* – Dorsal stripes not continuing onto head; size large for striped squirrel.

Distribution and Habitat. –The golden-mantled ground squirrel ranges through the Mountain West, from central British Columbia and Alberta southward to Arizona and New Mexico, and from California eastward to Colorado and Wyoming. A closely related relict population occurs in Chihuahua, México. The golden-mantled ground squirrel occurs in suitable situations throughout Rocky Mountain National Park, from lowest elevations on either side of the Continental Divide to well above timberline. The animals occur in a variety of situations that are exposed to direct sun at some time during the day. In the Park they are found most commonly about rocks near the edge of forest of woodland. Rocky fill along roadsides shelters high populations, especially where a source of food is nearby. In southern Colorado and elsewhere, the animals also utilize mountain meadows extensively, but this is seldom so in the Park. Perhaps this is due to the presence of the Wyoming ground squirrel, which seems to displace its golden-mantled cousin where the two species come into contact.

Natural History. —The golden-mantled ground squirrel may be the most familiar small mammal in Rocky Mountain National Park. Certainly it is among the most beloved—its role as brazen pirate, mendicant, and Park-jester is well rehearsed. No campsite, picnic ground, or scenic over-look is without its resident troupe, begging peanuts and other morsels from visitors' larders. With their reliance on summer stock and the tourist tråde, one might question whether the animals have a "natural" history at all.

Away from tourist centers, these ground squirrels feed mostly on plant material, with morning being the most active period of feeding. Sharing their habitat with other squirrels (especially chipmunks), they feed on the stems and leaves of herbs, but seeds, berries, and fungi are eaten in quantity. Like other squirrels, they also eat some insects and carrion. On occasion they will eat eggs or kill and eat young birds. When two individuals converge on the same food item, a dominance hierarchy decides which will feed, precluding undue bickering. When crowded in captivity, one individual may kill and partially eat another, but this certainly is abnormal behavior. From an ecological and energetic standpoint, any actual physical strife within a species (let alone active and chronic cannibalism) is maladaptive behavior.

In late summer, heavy deposits of fat are stored on the back and sides, about the neck and shoulders, and over the lower abdomen. By mid-September they are set for the long winter, and in most parts of the Park they haven't long to wait. With the first snow and cold they enter a long period of deep winter sleep. The torpid ground squirrel rolls into a tight ball, exposing as little radiative surface as possible. During hibernation, metabolism is regulated to a minimum. Fat fuels a sort of metabolic "pilot light," and this activity accounts for a loss in body weight of about 0.2 percent per day. During warm spells, individuals at lower elevations may arouse for brief periods of activity above ground, but this does not usually happen in the Park, and few animals are seen in winter. After all, winter is far more hostile above the snow than beneath it. In spring, the squirrels emerge—sometimes burrowing through late-lying snowdrifts—to begin active foraging and to reproduce.

As with other hibernators, starvation is a common cause of mortality. Weasels take both adults and young, and hawks capture foraging animals. Rocky habitat protects these animals from badgers and diurnal activity precludes serious predation by nocturnal carnivores such as foxes and owls.

The burrow is similar to that of a chipmunk. The main entrance (there may be others) is hidden beneath a boulder or shrub, and usually it is not marked by excavated debris. A steep entrance tunnel leads to a more or less complex maze of tunnels 5 to 10 cm in diameter and about 30 cm beneath the surface. At the end of the tunnel is the nest chamber. The nest is built of dry grasses and other soft materials, including suitable items salvaged from negligent visitors—string, paper, and bits of cloth and plastic. Generally there is some fecal material in the nest along with the burrowing animals' usual cortege of parasitic and free-living insects and mites.

Upon emergence in spring, male ground squirrels are in breeding condition. Females come into estrus and mate about 2 weeks later. Gestation takes about four weeks, after which about five (range, two to eight) altricial young are born. A single litter is produced each year, and the animals first breed as yearlings. Neonates are naked (save for facial vibrissae and a patch of hairs on the head), pinkish in color, and weigh about 5 grams. At four days of age the lateral stripes are evident and the claws and external ears have begun to develop. At 15 days, the upper parts are well-haired and the front toes have separated; hind toes separate three days later. The eyes do not open until the young are over four weeks old. On a diet of milk, newborns gain about 1.2 grams per day; after weaning, they gain about 3.7 grams per day until nearly full grown.

Selected References.—Carleton (1966); Hatt (1927); McKeever (1964). Some older literature places this species in the genus *Callospermophilus*; that taxon usually is now treated as a subgenus.

Rock Squirrel
Spermophilus variegatus

Description. —The rock squirrel is the largest of the true ground squirrels in our area. In fact, one might mistake it at first glance for a tree squirrel, but no tree squirrel here shares its pale color or its rocky habitat. The animals are 450 to 500 mm in total length and the tail is 185 to 210 mm long. Adults may weigh upwards of a kilogram. The upper parts are a mottled blend of black, buff, and white, and the animals are reddish buff beneath. Prominent black cheek patches and a white eye-ring mark the face. The feet are buffy to reddish. The tail is full and flattened, black and buff edged with white. *Field Recognition.* —Large size, long flat tail, pale color; habitat in rocky, shrub-clad terrain.

Distribution and Habitat. —Rock squirrels are mammals of southern affinities which reach their northernmost limits in Colorado and Utah and range southward to the Mexican states of Puebla and Michoacan. They are restricted in our area to the narrow band of foothills along the Front Range, as are some other species, including the Colorado chipmunk, the Mexican woodrat, and the rock mouse.

Rock squirrels have not been documented in the Park, although their presence at the lowest elevations on the eastern boundary would come as no surprise. These large squirrels do occur sparingly in the canyons leading to the Park from the east, and the observant traveler coming from Lyons or Loveland might expect to see them.

The rock squirrel —as one might imagine— is an inhabitant of rocky country, where it burrows extensively beneath boulders and shrubs. In settled areas, they frequently occupy the coarse fill along canyon roads. Quarries and streamside thickets are also utilized as cover. In our area, they occur to about 2290 meters (7500 feet) in suitable habitat.

Natural History. —The rock squirrel is a bona fide ground squirrel but it does not hesitate to climb shrubs or low trees to reach preferred food—nuts, berries, and other fruit. They also eat seeds of herbaceous plants, foliage, and small quantities of insects. Food is cached in the burrow. Hibernation or dormancy doubtless occurs, but details are unavailable.

Remarkably little is known about the biology of this animal, perhaps because it is of little economic importance (although they can become pests in orchards). A closely related species, the California ground squirrel (*Spermophilus beecheyi*) is an important agricultural pest on the West Coast and it has been the subject of extensive study.

Rock squirrels breed once a year, in spring. Probably six or seven young are the mode, with eight being the maximum. Neonates are highly altricial and do not come above ground until nearly two months old.

Selected References. — Johnson (1981); Oaks *et al.* (1987).

Abert's Squirrel
Sciurus aberti

Description. — Abert's squirrel is a large, heavy-bodied rodent, of striking appearance because of conspicuous ear tufts and a long, full tail. Adults are 525 to 575 mm in total length and the tail is 240 to 300 mm long. Weights range around 700 grams. The local race of Abert's squirrel (*S. a. ferreus* — with type locality west of Loveland) occurs in three distinctive color phases. In the Park, a majority of individuals are dark gray dorsally, the banding of the hairs lending a "salt-and-pepper" pattern on close examination. There is a prominent black lateral line and the belly is white. There may be a mid-dorsal patch of brick-red hairs, but this is less common locally than in southwestern Colorado and adjacent parts of the Colorado Plateau. The grayish tail is prominently fringed with white hairs. Other animals in the Park have pure black pelage. Elsewhere in the mountains of Colorado's Eastern Slope, dark brown individuals are found. *Field Recognition.* — Large size, tufted ears, gray, black, or brown color.

Distribution and Habitat. — Abert's squirrel reaches its northern limit in extreme southern Wyoming, and is distributed southward in the lower mountains to New Mexico and Arizona, with relict, outlying populations in Chihuahua and Durango, México. This beautiful mammal occurs along the eastern margin of the Park at elevations to about 2600 meters (8500 feet). The principal habitat of Abert's squirrel is ponderosa pine woodlands, but the animals may range locally into other forest types.

Natural History. — Abert's squirrel is both larger and less boisterous than its contentious cousin, the chickaree. The visitor who chances to see this mammal ought to consider the day well spent. These are beautiful squirrels and they are sporadic in their distribution and are given to fluctuations in abundance.

Much of their diet is provided by the ponderosa pine—seeds, buds, inner bark, and young male cones are eaten. There is some evidence that feeding trees are selected on the basis of low levels of monoterpenes, the volatile chemicals that give pine trees their "turpentine" aroma. In addition, the squirrels feed on berries and other fruit, fungi, and some carrion as available. Like other rodents, they gnaw bones and antlers, presumably for their mineral content, sometimes carrying them to the nest. Food is not stored in appreciable amounts.

Nests are built of twigs in the crotch of a branch or in a "witch's broom"—a dense, pathologic growth of small branches stimulated by mistletoe infestation. In our area, most nests are at least 5 to 7 meters above ground in ponderosa pines of moderate size, trees averaging about a half meter in diameter. The nest chamber is about 15 cm in diameter, carpeted with soft plant materials or debris cast off by people. The animals retire to the nest at night and during harsh winter weather.

Abert's squirrel is not known to defend territories. The home range is rather large, averaging nearly 8 hectares (20 acres), some 10 times that of the chickaree (but recall that Abert's squirrel is a larger animal and that its resources are less concentrated). Intraspecific fighting is most common among males during the breeding season, and mating chases often are quite vigorous and vocal.

Perhaps hawks are the most important predator of Abert's squirrels. Terrestrial carnivores have difficulty preying on so arboreal a rodent to any significant extent, and martens usually do not range down into the open woodland frequented by the squirrels. The most important factors regulating populations (and their fluctuations) may be the availability of food. When cones are scarce, Abert's squirrels have been reported to take nearly three-quarters of the crop. Habitat has been influenced over much of the squirrel's range by the intervention of people in the ponderosa pine woodland. Also, the seed crop of the ponderosa pine is highly variable and could contribute to a pattern of cyclic abundance.

Abert's squirrels breed in spring—late March to May—and a litter of two to five (average about 3.5) young is born after a gestation period of approximately seven weeks. The newborn young are naked and blind and the ears are unopen. They are about 60 mm in length and weigh some 12 grams. At about seven weeks of age they are fully haired and venture from the nest for short periods of time. They are weaned at about 19 weeks of age and reach full adult size some six weeks later. There are two periods of molt each year, in spring and fall. Summer pelage is brighter and has more white hairs than does winter pelage.

Selected References. – Keith (1965); Farentinos (1972); Hoffmeister and Diersing (1978); Nash and Seaman (1977).

Red Squirrel, or Chickaree
Tamiasciurus hudsonicus

Description. – The chickaree – often called "pine squirrel" locally – is the smaller of our two tree squirrels. Total length ranges from 300 to 350 mm, and the bushy tail is 115 to 135 mm long. Adults weigh 195 to 200 grams. The ears are conspicuous but only slightly tufted. The textbook name for the animals – "red squirrel" – is inappropriate in our area (although descriptive over some parts of their broad range), because our animals are dark grayish brown in color, sometimes becoming slightly more reddish in summer pelage. In summer the venter is nearly white, and there is a distinctive black lateral line; in winter, underparts are grayish white and the black line is obscure. The tail is generally blackish brown bordered with a conspicuous fringe of white-tipped hairs.

Field Recognition. – Small size, ears without tassels; chattering alarm call; habitat mostly in dense forests of middle elevations; conspicuous middens of cone scales and cores.

Distribution and Habitat. – The chickaree is a boreal mammal, occurring from Alaska to Labrador and southward through the United States (at increasingly high elevations) to South Carolina, New Mexico, and Arizona. The chickaree does not occur in the Sierra Nevada and other far western mountain ranges, being replaced there by a closely related species, Douglas' squirrel. Chickarees occur in the heavy forests of middle elevation, preferring the cover of spruce-fir stands, Douglas-fir, or lodgepole pine to that of ponderosa pine woodland. Criteria for suitable habitat include conifers to provide cones for food and also sites suitably damp and cool for cone storage.

Natural History. – The scolding call of the chickaree is familiar to anyone who has wandered by day along the forest trails of the Park. There is something ventriloqual about the chickaree's voice and it may take some patience to locate the source of the mechanical chattering sound. But these are persistent alarmists and the din will continue until the intruder moves on. Listening closely for the raspy crackle of claws against spruce bark, one should be rewarded by the sight of this bold and hand-some defender of territorial rights. Chickarees reveal their presence not only by calls, but by leaving a copious and characteristic sign – a midden of scales and cores of conifer cones.

Chickarees are highly territorial mammals. A repertoire of distinctive calls warns the intruder against his trespass and challenges him to leave the vicinity. An additional call by the trespasser asks momentary peace of the trespassee. The territory ranges in size from about 0.4 to 1.2 hectares (1 to 3 acres), depending on the density of food resources. Territories may be defended by vigorous physical combat if the ritual vocalization fails. Males and females defend individual territories throughout the year, except when the female is in estrus. Then only does a female drop her defense, and males converge on her territory, calling and chasing each other and jousting for dominance and mating rights.

The chickaree midden is an obvious feature of the forest scene. The pile of litter may be 6 to 10 meters across and 30 cm or more deep, containing several cubic meters of debris. The largest middens represent the leavings of successive generations of squirrels over a score or more years. Often middens are between felled logs or alongside wind-thrown trees. The surface layer consists of a dry mulch but lower levels are in various stages of decay, leading to a rich humus. Abandoned middens are slowly succeeded by mosses, kinnikinnick, and other acid-loving plants, but active middens usually are devoid of vegetation. Most frequently, the midden is in a permanently moist, shady location. The dense cover of spruce forest is ideal because lower branches tend to lie at or near the ground, shielding the midden from drying. Cones are stashed up to 30 cm deep in pits dug in the midden. Several cones are deposited in each pit and then the cache is covered with litter. Cones also may be cached in bogs, pools, and springs. Cones of lodgepole pine, which remain closed even when dry, may be buried less deeply or simply stockpiled above ground.

In winter and spring the squirrels dig up cones – often burrowing through the snow to locate them – and carry them to a branch, rock, or other vantage point which serves as a feeding station. The seeds are removed and the inedible debris accrues to the midden. The principle is that of a person who builds a pantry and dining room out of cast-off tin cans, but the overall effect is rather more pleasant.

In summer, the diet is somewhat varied, including buds, fungi, berries, and other fruits, but the mainstay remains conifer seeds. Bark sometimes is stripped from small branches and eaten. The result of this activity looks like porcupine sign on a modest scale. As cones begin to mature, the early "milk" seeds are eaten. In August, seeds reach the "dough" stage and cone storage begins, continuing in earnest through October. On a productive tree, the chickaree works as a veritable cone-cutting machine, lopping off a green cone every 2 or 3 seconds. Cones of spruces are preferred, perhaps because of their large size and the fact that good cone crops occur two out of three seasons. Douglas-fir is a less reliable cone source, producing a large crop only one year in five. Lodgepole pine often is a staple because cones remain on the branches unopened and production is rather consistent from one year to the next.

Chickarees are active by day, especially in early morning. At night and during severe weather they retire to the nest, an informal globular affair 30 cm or more in diameter built of grasses and conifer needles and situated in a crotch 6 to 12 meters above ground. The nest chamber is 10 to 12 cm around and lined with mosses and shredded grass. Chickarees may also nest in tree-holes or hollow logs, and occasionally they nest in holes at ground level.

Chickarees spend a good deal of time on the ground where they are preyed upon by weasels, foxes, and coyotes. The classic enemy of the chickaree is the marten, a weasel-like arboreal carnivore. To escape danger in the trees, chickarees may jump 6 meters to the ground.

Chickarees mate once a year, usually in April. After a gestation period of about 40 days, one to six (average, four) young are born. The young are blind and hairless, but rather robust, with disproportionately large heads (as is typical of newborn mammals). Young squirrels are nursed until mid-July and do not leave the nest until one-third grown. If the nest is disturbed, the mother may carry the young in her mouth one-by-one to an alternate nest. Before the young leave the maternal territory to establish their own domains, there is a period of training in the arts of being a chickaree.

Selected References. — Finley (1969); Hatt (1943); Smith (1968).

FAMILY GEOMYIDAE — POCKET GOPHERS

Pocket gophers are a North American group, highly adapted to subterranean life. There are five living genera, with about 35 species. Three genera (including four species) occur in Colorado, but only one species lives in Rocky Mountain National Park.

Northern Pocket Gopher
Thomomys talpoides

Description. –The northern pocket gopher is a rather small, stocky animal, its architecture suiting its ecological role as a biological excavation service. Total length is 200 to 230 mm and the sparsely-haired tail is 50 to 70 mm long. Adults weigh about 120 to 150 grams. Males are somewhat larger than females, especially in cranial dimensions. In our area, northern pocket gophers are brownish in color, grayish to medium brown on the Eastern Slope and darker brown to nearly black west of the Continental Divide. The underparts and tail are paler in color than is the back and they are more sparsely furred. The most distinctive feature of the animals is their large, yellowish-orange incisors, always in view because the lips close behind them. The cheekpouches open externally, rather than into the mouth cavity, and they are lined with fur. The limbs are short and powerful and the forelimbs are strongly clawed. *Field Recognition.* –Moderate size, short tail; exposed incisors; shallow burrows marked with ridge of earth, and with conspicuous entrance mounds.

Distribution and Habitat. –The northern pocket gopher is a mammal of the Mountain West and the Northern Great Plains. In Colorado this is mostly an animal of the mountains; other species of pocket gophers inhabit western valleys and the eastern plains. Northern pocket gophers occur throughout Rocky Mountain National Park in open situations with well-drained soils. Pocket gophers inhabit all open habitat-types in the Park, but reach greatest abundance in meadows, where perennial forbs provide a rich food supply. In ranchlands adjacent to the Park, hayfields are favored habitat. Pocket gophers also occur in grassy parks and above timberline. Their burrows are conspicuous in the alpine tundra along Trail Ridge Road.

Natural History. –Northern pocket gophers, known simply as "gophers" or sometimes as "moles" (quite incorrectly, because moles are insectivores and do not occur in the mountains of Colorado), are the most highly evolved burrowers in our local fauna. Only rarely are they seen above ground. The external ears and the eyes are greatly reduced, further adaptations to their digging behavior. Seemingly, no soil is too rocky, or hard, or shallow for them. I have seen evidence of gophers burrowing beneath the thin subalpine sod covering a large, flat rock. The soil –probably trapped from the wind by pioneer plants –was less than 3 cm deep. The gopher simply pushed its way along between rock and sod, leaving an arch of turf overhead. As satisfactory a burrow might have been built between a livingroom floor and a carpet; the effect was much the same. The lips purse behind the incisors, so the mouth can be closed while rocks and soil are carried with the teeth. The burrow system of a pocket gopher may be over 150 meters in length, usually from 10 to 45 cm below the surface. This represents the excavation of nearly 3 tons of soil. Side tunnels and chambers are filled with food or feces or are used for nesting. Excess soil is thrown out in characteristic loose mounds. Only rarely does one find an obvious entrance, because openings are plugged when not in use. Abandoned burrows are preempted by a variety of animals, including other rodents, salamanders, toads, snakes, and insects.

The diet consists exclusively of plant material. During the spring and summer, foliage and stems are eaten, forbs more than grasses. Vegetation is clipped at night from around the mound, and it may be stored in subterranean chambers. During the winter, the animals subsist largely on roots, bulbs, or tubers. Some foraging occurs above ground in snow tunnels, either on the surface of the soil, or in the snowpack itself. In spring, nest chambers may be built high in the snowpack, because tunnels in the ground are saturated with melt-water. Snow tunnels are packed with soil brought up from below ground. After snowmelt in spring, these sinuous winter casts (sometimes called "gopher garlands" or "eskers")—which are 5 to 10 cm across and may be several meters in length—are conspicuous features of the mountain landscape. Their presence suppresses the growth of some plant species and thus influences plant succession.

Badgers and coyotes excavate pocket gophers and prey on them. Weasels also capture some and owls take a toll, especially dispersing young, which tend to move above ground. Ticks, mites, lice, and fleas affect pocket gophers as they do most mammals. Endoparasites include both roundworms and flatworms.

Under good conditions, populations may reach densities of 50 or more individuals per hectare (20 per acre). The soil in such situations may be so completely undermined that it gives away underfoot. Often it is impossible to say where one burrow stops and the next begins, although underground there is little or no overlap between adjacent gophers. On rangelands and in cultivated areas, especially where natural predators have been limited by humans, pocket gophers may be significant pests. Their mounds damage mowing equipment and livestock can be injured by stepping into burrows. Sometimes gophers burrow through ditchbanks, giving the rancher unsolicited assistance with the irrigation program. However, they are very important agents in the soil-building process. Fortunately, pocket gophers (and all other wildlife) have free rein in the National Park to perform their unique roles in the continual evolution of ecosystems.

Adult pocket gophers breed in the spring, beginning as yearlings. Mating occurs in April or May and three to ten (average, four to six) young are born in April or June. A single litter is produced each year. The young mature rapidly and are above ground as early as late June. From July to September the young leave the maternal burrow to establish residence on their own.

Selected References. – Hansen (1960); Hansen and Ward (1966).

FAMILY CASTORIDAE – BEAVERS

There are two living species of beavers, comprising a single Holarctic genus (*Castor*). The family is less diverse today than it once was; 14 extinct genera are known as fossils.

Beaver
Castor canadensis

Description. –The beaver is the largest rodent in Rocky Mountain National Park, and indeed, the largest in North America north of Panamá. Adults are about a meter in total length, of which the broad, flat tail comprises about one-third. Large old males may weigh over 25 kilograms. The animals are a rich brownish color above, paling somewhat to golden brown beneath. The dense underfur is grayish brown. The scaly, nearly naked tail and feet are black. *Field Recognition.* – Large size, flat tail; sign: dams, lodges, waterways, gnawed tree stumps.

Distribution and Habitat. –The beaver ranges throughout most of North America north of México, except for parts of the Arctic Slope, the Desert Southwest, and peninsular Florida. This is a familiar mammal throughout Rocky Mountain National Park, wherever permanent streams of moderate grade provide suitable habitat.

Natural History. – Certainly the beaver is among our most familiar and fascinating native mammals. The fur trade, with the beaver as a mainstay, was responsible for the early exploration of much of North America.

Beavers have had an important role in ecological as well as social history, however. They have a more profound and conspicuous effect on their immediate environment than any mammal other than humans. Major features of the landscape in the Park (Beaver Meadows and Horse-shoe Park, for example) owe their existence to the persistent work of innumerable generations of beavers over thousands of years.

The most far-reaching ecological effects are produced by the construction of dams. Barriers of logs, sticks, rocks, and mud are built across shallow streams. The dam may be 2 meters high and several hundred meters long (the record is 4.2 meters high and 1000 meters long). The pond impounded by the beaver dam protects the lodge from predators and assures a swimming area beneath the winter ice. As the catchment basin behind the dam fills, the surrounding soil becomes waterlogged. Many kinds of plants cannot survive in the saturated, oxygen-poor soils. They die and their demise allows the invasion of species adapted to permanently moist soil: alder, willows, cottonwood, aspen. The bark and twigs of these species are the staple foods of beavers. Thus, a beaver pond not only serves as an all-weather transportation route and a protective moat, but also favors a plant community dominated by preferred food species. Beavers are not just builders, they are farmers as well. And that's not all. They also are "inn-keepers," for the pond provides still water habitat for a variety of other wildlife—muskrats, fish, mink, ducks and shorebirds—that might not occupy the swiftly flowing waters of an unmodified mountain stream.

A stream not only carries water, it also carries a load of silt and organic debris. As streamflow is slowed, its load-bearing capacity diminishes. Silt falls to the bottom of the pond. The long-term fate of the beaver dam is no different than the fate of a man-made dam. Eventually (unless carried away by flood) the dam becomes a retaining wall at the lower end of a rich deposit of silt and organic detritus. The pond becomes a meadow and one day the meadow may become a forest. Beavers fascinate us with their industry. They can also help us to put our most colossal works in proper perspective—powerless against the obstinate and inexorable forces of ecological succession, ephemeral in the immensity of geological time.

Beavers build "houses" of various kinds. Dens may be built along streambanks, simple burrows or surface dens walled with sticks and mud and accessible by an underwater tunnel. Lodges are familiar and common. Unlike the bank den, a lodge is built in the open water of the pond. It may be 2 meters or more in height and up to 5 meters in diameter. The lodge is built in water 2 to 3 meters deep. The foundation has a doorway and the entire structure is hollow. Logs, limbs, and sod form the walls which narrow to enclose the top. Most of the house is plastered with mud and sod, although some open areas aid in ventilation. Inside, a floor is built a few centimeters above the high-water line. Here a nest chamber is built, lined with grass and shredded bark.

Systems of canals may be built to float logs and food materials to the pond, and the water level in canals may be maintained with a system of dams. The "engineering" ability of beavers is remarkable and has earned them a place in folklore and a reputation larger than life. We are inclined to ascribe their feats to superior intelligence, but in fact their "ingenuity" stems from a highly evolved program of innate behavior. One frequently hears, for example, that a beaver can fell a tree in any desired direction, such as toward the water. Actually, cut trees fall toward the water because trees grow toward the open space above the stream or pond where light is more intense. Thus, competition for light inclines trees in a fortuitous direction. Reports of beavers pinned beneath falling trees are sufficiently common to dispel some of the legends concerning their great skill and intelligence.

The diet consists exclusively of vegetable matter and varies in composition with the season. Grass and other herbage is eaten during the summer, and the consumption of bark during the growing season is largely incidental to preparing building material. Branches of conifers may be cut for construction material but they are eaten only rarely. Reingestion of soft feces has been reported.

Aquatic habits protect beavers from serious predation. Mink can enter the den to prey on the kits. Although wonderfully graceful in the water, on dry land beavers are rather clumsy and slow. When dispersing overland or attending to their needs for food and building materials, they may be surprised and killed by coyotes, bobcats, or mountain lions. When near the water, of course, they escape quickly from terrestrial predators, a quick slap of the tail warning the rest of the colony of danger. Tularemia and parasites exact a toll of beavers each year. Probably flood and drought were the most effective controls on populations before the arrival of European settlers. Over-trapping pushed the beaver to the verge of extinction in many areas, but now habitat modification by humans may be a more important factor in population control over most of the beaver's wide range.

Beavers are highly modified for aquatic life. The hind feet are webbed. The eyes are small and have a clear inner "lid" which allows the eyes to remain open under water. The ears are short and valvular – capable of being closed when the animal submerges. The nostrils also are valvular. The pelage is dense and heavy, with a sleek, waterproof coat of coarse guard hairs and a fine dense underfur. The body is very streamlined. The urogenital and digestive tracts empty into a single chamber, the cloaca, and hence have a common opening. (This feature makes the sexes virtually indistinguishable externally.) Due to special controls on heartrate and breathing, the animals routinely remain submerged for 4 to 5 minutes, with maximum dives of 15 minutes.

There is a single molt annually. The two inner toes of each hind foot are cleft and are used in grooming to maintain the pelage. Paired anal scent glands called "castors" are present in both sexes but are better developed in the male. Their secretions may have a function in courtship.

The social life of the beaver is based on a nuclear family – a pair of adults, the yearlings, and the kits. A large colony may consist of several families. When crowded, individuals disperse along streams or overland to found a new colony. In prime habitat in the National Park there may be a beaver colony per 3 or 4 kilometers of stream.

Beavers breed in January or February, and four or five (range one to nine) young are born in April or May after a gestation period of some 120 days. Females produce a single litter of young per year. Newborn beavers are small but are fully furred and have the eyes open. Females breed at two years of age, but full growth may not be achieved for several years. The young remain in the parental den as yearlings and then disperse. Beavers are long-lived rodents, the record being 19 years.

Selected References. – Hill (*in* Chapman and Feldhamer, 1982); Jenkins and Busher (1979); Neff (1959); Rue (1964*b*).

FAMILY CRICETIDAE – NATIVE RATS AND MICE

The cricetids comprise a diverse assemblage of rodents, including at least nine species in six genera locally. Some 25 species of cricetids occur in Colorado. Two common household pets, the hamster (*Cricetus*) and the gerbil (or jird – *Meriones*) are Old World representatives of this family which includes about 550 species in nearly 100 genera. There is no real consensus on the classification of these mammals. Some zoologists contend that the cricetids ought to be merged into a single family with the great group of Old World mice, the Muridae (a family which includes the all-too-familiar house mouse, *Mus musculus*, and the black and Norway rats, *Rattus*). Two distinctive subfamilies of the Cricetidae occur locally—the cricetines (mice and woodrats) and the microtines (voles and muskrat). The smaller members of these two groups are distinguished by many people as "field mice" and "meadow mice," respectively.

Rock Mouse
Peromyscus difficilis

Description.—This is a relatively large, long-tailed mouse. Adults are 170 to 200 mm in total length and the tail is 80 to 100 mm long. Weights range around 28 to 30 grams. Adults are grayish above, buffy on the sides, and dirty white beneath. The tail is bicolored (although sometimes obscurely so). Only the deer mouse could be confused with the rock mouse, and once one actually has seen a rock mouse, with its remarkably long (22 to 24 mm) ears, there can be no question about the distinction. *Field Recognition.*—Grayish color, large size, relatively long ears, and tail as long as body.

Distribution and Habitat.—The rock mouse is mostly a mammal of the Mexican Plateau, ranging from Oaxaca northward to Arizona, New Mexico, and Texas, and then occurring in a narrow band northward along the foothills of the Colorado Rockies nearly to the Wyoming boundary. This linear, "intrusive" distribution is shown also by the Mexican woodrat, the Colorado chipmunk, and the rock squirrel. The common name "rock mouse" is an appropriate one, for this is a species of broken foothills habitats. In our area the animals most often are associated with stands of mountain mahogany and bitterbrush, shrubs typical of rocky sites. Stands of ponderosa pine and Rocky Mountain juniper are also occupied. The elevational range of the species is rather narrow, from about 1675 to 2560 meters (5500 to 8400 feet), depending on local exposure and topography, and reaching highest elevations on south-facing canyon walls.

When this mouse first was discovered in Estes Park it was thought to be an unknown species and was named *Peromyscus nasutus*. More recently, the local population was discovered to be the same as mice to the south in Mexico, so animals from our area are now recognized as a subspecies of *Peromyscus difficilis*. The animals occur in Rocky Mountain National Park only along the eastern boundary, the western margin of Estes Park.

Natural History. –The rock mouse makes its home in rough, rocky terrain, and very little is known of its habits. Like other species of the genus, it is largely a seed-eater, feeding on seeds and fruits of a variety of plants, but taking insects as opportunity allows. The habitat is shared with the smaller, shorter-tailed deer mouse, and no study has been made of the means by which the species, both nocturnal, divide resources between themselves. One might suppose that, with its longer tail for balance, the rock mouse would be the more agile climber, better suited to clamber about shrubs and rocks in its foraging rounds.

Male rock mice are in breeding condition from about March or April through August. Females are polyestrous, with breeding beginning in April and continuing through July with the last young born in August. Two to six young are born after a gestation period of three to four weeks. Quite probably females born early in the season breed their first summer, but the extent to which this happens is unknown.

Selected References. –Cinq-Mars and Brown (1969); King (1968).

Deer Mouse
Peromyscus maniculatus

Description. –The deer mouse is highly variable in color and size in our area, because the eastern boundary of the Park lies in a zone of intergradation between a large, dark mountain race and a smaller, paler plains subspecies. Total length ranges from 145 to 180 mm, and the tail is 55 to 75 mm long. Weights range from about 18 to 30 grams. The grayish ears are conspicuous, but obviously shorter than those of the rock mouse. The color of the back varies from grayish tan to rich reddish brown. The belly and feet are white, although sometimes appearing grayish as the bases of the hairs sometimes show. The tail is black above, whitish below. The rock mouse is the only local species with which the deer mouse might be confused. The deer mouse is smaller in size than the rock mouse, has markedly shorter ears and tail, and adults are predominantly brownish in color rather than grayish. *Field Recognition.* – Small size, brownish color with white underparts; tail shorter than head and body and markedly bicolored.

Distribution and Habitat. –The deer mouse occurs from northern Canada to southern México and from coast to coast in the United States (including many off-shore islands), except in the Southeast. Virtually every terrestrial habitat in Rocky Mountain National Park supports a population of these ubiquitous little mice, although the animals are more common in upland habitats than in meadows and shoreline communities. Forest-edge situations and broken, shrubby terrain probably afford the best conditions and support highest populations. Areas disturbed by fire, mining, or settlement and overgrown by weedy vegetation support large numbers of deer mice. Weeds, by nature, are invasive plants that produce copious amounts of seed, thus providing abundant food for seed-eating rodents. Weedy plants are opportunistic invaders of ephemeral habitats. In a certain sense, so are deer mice, and it is rather useful to think of them as "animal weeds." It came as no surprise to learn that deer mice were the first small mammals to take up residence on the debris fan left by the Lawn Lake Flood. The elevational range is from the foothills to the tops of the highest peaks.

Natural History. –The deer mouse is our most common native mammal. Being nocturnal, they seldom are seen, and only an occasional nest or a trail of tiny, elongate droppings reveals their presence, but they are surely there. This is *the* mouse locally, and it is unfortunate that they are so secretive, for they are beautiful little mammals. Were they more widely known some of the popular misconceptions about mice might be dispelled, or at least momentarily forgotten. True, they can be pests, particularly if allowed the run of a pantry. They feed on virtually any vegetable matter and mankind's provisions are an irresistible lure. It is also true that they may set up housekeeping (and establish a very active nursery) among clothes in a neglected trunk, leaving a tattered shambles at the end of the season. But the motive is hunger, or cold, or curiosity – never malice.

Away from human settlement, deer mice live in nests of soft grasses beneath shrubs, rocks, logs, or debris, or in burrows abandoned by other animals, especially pocket gophers. Unlike voles, they do not make runways, but when foraging they do make use of those of other species. They are fairly agile climbers, foraging readily in low shrubbery, but they are far less arboreal than their long-tailed cousin the rock mouse. The diet consists of seeds, fungi, berries, and other fruits, with lesser amounts of green herbage. Insects are eaten when available and may comprise the bulk of the diet for some individuals in season. Food habits change with local and seasonal availability. In diet as in habitat selection, opportunism is the rule. Adaptability, coupled with a remarkable reproductive potential, is probably the key to their obvious success over a wide geographic and ecological range.

Home ranges seem to vary widely among individuals. Some mice are rather sedentary while others range over a quarter hectare or more. Generally, immature individuals seem to range more widely than do adults, and males wander farther than females do. Juvenile males were the most abundant mice on the debris fan left by the Lawn Lake Flood. There is no well-defined territory, although mutual avoidance may promote spacing. Unlike many rodents, deer mice can be crowded—even on short rations—and show no particular evidence of stress. A male may share a nest with a pregnant female, and a mother will tolerate the presence of weaned juveniles while she is nursing their younger siblings. Such tolerance is rather rare among small mammals.

In many situations, deer mice are the most abundant mammalian consumers. As a consequence they form an important link in the food web, bridging the energy gap between plants and flesh-eating animals. Coyotes, foxes, bobcats, weasels, skunks, owls, and snakes all feed on them. When pursued, the deer mouse follows an erratic zigzag course to the nearest cover and then becomes motionless. So stereotyped is this behavior that a mouse may hide its head and freeze, leaving the posterior wholly exposed to view. Like many other aspects of animal behavior, this pattern would seem to leave room for improvement. But over the long run, their behavior must work. These are successful animals by any criterion. The mice host a wide variety of external and internal parasites. Predation, parasites, a harsh environment, and the stress of almost continual reproduction contribute to a short life expectancy. A year-old mouse is old indeed; few survive a second winter.

Female deer mice are polyestrous and exhibit post-partum estrus. The average female stays pregnant almost continually throughout the warmer months of the year. In more hospitable climates, these animals breed year around, but here the reproductive season is about April to September. The gestation period varies from about 23 days to over 4 weeks, the longer extreme being more characteristic of lactating females.

The mother gives birth in the daytime (as is typical of nocturnal mammals). There are only six mammae, but litters of one to nine are known to be reared successfully. Females at higher elevations tend to have fewer, larger litters than do those lower down, perhaps because the breeding season is shorter.

The pinkish neonates are naked (except for facial vibrissae) and blind.

Chickaree. *Dennis M. Henry*

Abert's Squirrel. *Wendy Shattil and Robert Rozinski*

Golden-mantled Ground Squirrel. *Wendy Shattil and Robert Rozinski*

Least Chipmunk. *David W. Johnson*

Wyoming Ground Squirrel. *William Ervin*

Pika. *William Ervin*

Yellow-bellied Marmot. *Wendy Shattil and Robert Rozinski*

Beaver. *Wendy Shattil and Robert Rozinski*

River Otter. *Wendy Shattil and Robert Rozinski*

Ermine. *William Ervin*

Nuttall's Cottontail. *Wendy Shattil and Robert Rozinski*

Black Bear. *Wendy Shattil and Robert Rozinski*

Bobcat. *Wendy Shattil and Robert Rozinski*

Coyote. *Wendy Shattil and Robert Rozinski*

Bighorn ewes and lambs. *Wendy Shattil and Robert Rozinski*

Mule Deer. *Wendy Shattil and Robert Rozinski*

The ears are closed and the toes, although clawed, are not yet separated. Newborn young are about 45 mm long and weigh about 1.5 grams. The gray juvenal pelage develops the first week and the eyes open at the end of the second. The young are weaned abruptly at about 3½ weeks, when the mother gives birth to a new litter. By that time the young are quite agile and forage on their own. They molt to a grayish brown subadult pelage at about 6 weeks of age. By this time—or soon after—both males and females are reproductively mature (although only about half their eventual body weight), and—unless bad weather intervenes—they may breed, although full size and adult pelage are several weeks away.

Selected References.—Armstrong (1977); Douglas (1969); King (1968); Merritt and Merritt (1980).

Bushy-tailed Woodrat
Neotoma cinerea

Description.—Bushy-tailed woodrats are the largest of Coloradan woodrats. Adults range from 375 to 420 mm in total length, and the tail is 150 to 190 mm long; males average about 15 percent larger than females. Males weigh about 350 grams, females about 300. The pelage is long, dense, and remarkably soft. The upper parts are golden to orangish buff, becoming grayish when the pelage is worn, and the hairs of the underparts are white with grayish bases. As the common name suggests, the tail is bushy (especially pronounced in adult males), quite distinctive among Coloradan woodrats. The tail is pale gray above and white below.

Distribution and Habitat.—The bushy-tailed woodrat is a mammal of the Mountain West, ranging from Alaska southward to New Mexico and from the Pacific Coast to the badlands and scarps of the Dakotas and Nebraska. In Colorado, the animals occur through mountainous parts of the state and in the rough country along the rim of the High Plains in the northeast. They occur throughout Rocky Mountain National Park to elevations above timberline, and are especially abundant in talus slides and fractured cliff faces.

Natural History.—This is a "packrat's packrat." Few local rodents are the subject of more—or more amusing—folktales, and interestingly enough, much of the legend is true. There is a common misconception, however, that this is a thief with a conscience, that packrats—or "trade rats"—will not steal an object without leaving another in exchange. In fact, such "trades" do occur, but they stem from limited cargo capacity and not from some innate sense of fair play. The collecting instinct is so strong that one object is dropped to allow another to be picked up. To give an idea of the range of the animal's tastes, here is a partial catalog of the contents of some dens in Colorado: tarpaper, nails, rattlesnake carcass, peach pit, snakeskin, rope, leather glove, shotgun shell, coal, bolt (and spare nut), hacksaw blade, wire, porcelain insulator, sticks, stones, and dung. Bones are common in dens; they are used for construction material and gnawed for their mineral content.

These collected materials add to the bulk of the house, which protects these animals from perils both physical and biological. The den is built mostly of sticks from nearby trees and shrubs. It is usually situated in a vertical crack or on a shelf in a cave or building. Within the house, a cup-shaped nest is built of fibrous plant materials. A given den may contain more than one nest.

The diet of bushy-tailed woodrats is catholic. There is a predilection for foliage over other parts of plants, but virtually any plant species is suitable. Food may be eaten on the spot during the nocturnal foraging expedition, or it may be stored. Large quantities of leaves are stored in crevices in the rocks for winter use.

Like other mammals, these rats host a variety of parasites. Their predators include coyotes, bobcats, and raptorial birds (especially owls). Snakes and weasels take the young. In general, however, inaccessible habitat probably protects them from most predators.

The bushy-tailed woodrat typically has a single litter of young per year, but post-partum estrus does occur, and females pregnant while lactating have been reported. Females attain sexual maturity during their first winter and breed as yearlings. After a gestation period of about four weeks, one to six (mode, four) young are born.

Selected References.—Finley (1958).

Mexican Woodrat
Neotoma mexicana

Description.—This is the smaller of our two local woodrats. Adults range in total length from 300 to 360 mm, of which the tail comprises 130 to 170 mm. As is true of woodrats generally, males are larger than females. In color, the upper parts are grayish brown, with a heavy sprinkling of blackish guard hairs and a dirty yellow wash, especially noticeable on the sides. Beneath, the hairs are gray basally and white-tipped. The tail is covered with short hairs and markedly bicolored, with a black mid-dorsal stripe. *Field Recognition.* – Moderate size, short-haired tail; habitat in horizontal rock formations of foothills.

Distribution and Habitat. – The Mexican woodrat is a mammal of the southwestern United States and western México. The northern limits of the range are along the Front Range in northern Colorado and the species ranges southward to Honduras and El Salvador. In Colorado, the foothills provide the Mexican woodrat with suitable habitat. Broken exposures of sedimentary rock provide an abundance of horizontal cracks and overhangs, which are preferred denning sites. Typical vegetation on such outcrops consists of stands of shrubs with scattered junipers and ponderosa pines. Man-made structures, including mines, cabins, and outbuildings, may be occupied, but less extensively by this species than by bushy-tailed woodrats. In our area, the Mexican woodrat may occur at elevations in excess of 2440 meters (8000 feet), but is usually more common somewhat lower.

Natural History. – The den of a Mexican woodrat is mostly a deep rock shelter. A few sticks may mark the entrance, but most of the plant material present will have been gathered as food. The large piles of debris accumulated by bushy-tailed woodrats simply are not typical of the Mexican woodrat; the collecting instinct seems to be much weaker. The nest itself is cup-shaped, with or without a roof, and built of matted fibers and bark.

The diet consists largely of foliage from shrubs and forbs. Dry twigs of shrubs from which the leaves have been eaten compose the bulk of the house. Other parts of flowering plants – flowers, fruits, stems – are also eaten, and conifer needles are important in the diet locally. The composition of the diet depends more on availability than on preference for one species over another. Large quantities of food are stored in autumn for winter use. The animals are nocturnal and active throughout the year.

Mexican woodrats begin to breed in March. After a gestation period of about four weeks, two to five (mode, three) young are born in April. There apparently is a post-partum estrus in at least some individuals. At any rate, most females bear two litters of young in a summer. Some females born early in the year reproduce their first summer, but males

120

do not enter the reproductive population until they are yearlings.
Selected References. — Brown (1969); Finley (1958).

Southern Red-backed Vole
Clethrionomys gapperi

Description. — This is a beautiful little animal, 125 to 150 mm in total length, with a tail 33 to 44 mm long. Adults weigh 20 to 30 grams. A broad patch of rich reddish hairs extends from head to tail, contrasting rather strongly (unless badly worn) with the buffy sides. The belly is silvery white to buffy. *Field Recognition.* — Small size, fairly short tail; reddish back contrasting with buffy sides.

Distribution and Habitat. — The southern red-backed vole is actually a northern mammal, ranging from central Canada southward along mountain ranges to California, Arizona, and New Mexico, and North Carolina. The animal is "southern" only by comparison with a closely related mouse, the northern red-backed vole (*Clethrionomys rutilus*), which occurs in Alaska and northern Canada and ranges across boreal Eurasia. In Colorado, the southern red-backed vole ranges in the mountainous central part of the state, throughout forested parts of Rocky Mountain National Park. Spruce-fir and lodgepole pine forests at middle elevations present optimal habitat, but the animals also live in elfin woodland near timberline. Although frequenting moist areas in forests, red-backed voles are seldom found in wetlands.

Natural History. — Red-backed voles burrow to nest beneath logs or rocks, and tunnel beneath the duff that litters the forest floor. They are active throughout the year. Chickaree middens are a common habitat. The voles take some stored conifer seeds, but probably make greater use of the fungi that grow in the moist litter of cone scales deep in the midden. They also eat some herbage, berries, bark, and occasional insects. Unlike those of evolutionarily more advanced voles, the cheek-teeth are not ever-growing, and thus are poorly adapted to a steady diet of abrasive grasses. The animals may be active at any time, but are most active at night. Populations to 50 animals per hectare have been reported.

Like other small rodents, red-backed voles are preyed upon by a variety of carnivorous birds and mammals. In their forested habitat, perhaps weasels are the most important predators. Maximum longevity is about 20 months.

Breeding begins in March beneath the snowpack, continuing throughout the warmer months, until October or November. An average of six (range, two to eight) altricial young are born after a gestation period of about 18 days. Females show post-partum estrus. Eyes open at about 2 weeks and weaning is completed about day 18. The natal nest is a simple, orange-sized globe of plant fibers.

Selected References. – Merritt (1981).

Heather Vole
Phenacomys intermedius

Description. – This is a small vole, ranging from about 135 to 145 mm in total length, and from about 25 to 35 mm in length of tail. Weights from 30 to 40 grams. Externally, this is a rather nondescript species, grayish brown above, pale gray to white (or even slightly buffy) below. The fur is fluffy and soft. The tail is pale below, darker above, usually with enough white hairs to lend a salt-and-pepper appearance. Only by examining the teeth can one be absolutely certain of the identity of this mouse. Unlike other local voles, the inner angles of the lower molars (as viewed from above) are deeper than the outer angles. The species most readily confused with the heather vole is the larger montane vole, which is mostly a species of wetlands and an obligate runway builder. *Field Recognition.* – Small size, grayish color, with short, white-speckled tail.

Distribution and Habitat. – The heather vole has a range similar to that of the southern red-backed vole, but less extensive, occurring southward along the Sierras and the Rockies (to northern New Mexico), but being absent from the mountains of eastern United States. The species occurs – at least locally – throughout mountainous parts of Colorado and is known from a number of places in Rocky Mountain National Park. Streamside communities seem to be favored habitat, but a variety of situations are occupied, from open pine woodlands to dense subalpine forest and from shrubby burns to alpine tundra. The heather vole probably occurs throughout the Park except at highest elevations.

Natural History. – The heather vole is probably the least-known rodent in Rocky Mountain National Park. This dubious distinction stems from its apparent scarcity here (and elsewhere in Colorado); of course this "scarcity" may be no fault of the heather vole's, but merely an artifact of our crude techniques for studying small, secretive mammals. Heather voles nest in burrows in summer and at or near ground level in winter. They forage along the surface in well-concealed runways, best developed in the immediate vicinity of the nest. The animals are active throughout the year and (in summer at any rate) are mostly crepuscular and nocturnal.

The cheekteeth of heather voles are rooted, precluding a strict diet of grasses (which are abrasive and wear the dentition rapidly). Rather, a variety of plant foods (including herbage of forbs, berries, seeds, and fungi) is eaten. Bark is an important food item, especially in winter. Food is piled in caches near the nest throughout the year.

Predation on heather voles has not been studied in our area, but surely these animals — like other small rodents — figure in the food web from plant to carnivore and eventually to microbe, their importance limited only by their seemingly meager numbers.

The heather vole is polyestrous and undergoes post-partum heat. The animals breed throughout the warmer months, from June to August. Two to eight (average about five) young are born after a gestation period of about three weeks. Development is rapid and females of early litters mature sexually and breed their first summer. However, males apparently do not.

Selected References. — Armstrong (1972); Williams (1952).

Long-tailed Vole
Microtus longicaudus

Description. —The long-tailed vole (as both common and Latin names imply) has a relatively long tail; at 55 to 65 mm it comprises more than 30 percent of the total length of 175 to 195 mm. Weights range from 40 to 55 grams. The color is as the montane vole, grayish to grayish brown above and paler beneath, but the tail is distinctly bicolored and the upper parts may show a slight reddish tinge. *Field Recognition.* —Relatively long tail, runways poorly developed.

Distribution and Habitat. —The long-tailed vole is a mammal of the Mountain West, ranging from southern Alaska to southern Arizona and eastward to the Black Hills of Wyoming and South Dakota. The western three-fifths of Colorado is occupied, a range encompassing all of Rocky Mountain National Park. Long-tailed voles utilize a wide variety of habitats, tolerating a broader spectrum of conditions than do our other voles. They are found in moist situations such as stream side woodlands, aspen groves, and spruce-fir forest, and also in drier situations, including upland meadows, ponderosa pine woodland, and krummholz stands at treeline.

Natural History.—Runway building is less prevalent in long-tailed voles than in other local microtines. Hence, the animals range through habitats with little ground cover. Shallow burrows are dug among roots or beneath litter, and the nest is at or near ground level.

As in the montane vole, the cheekteeth are ever-growing. This is an adaptation to a diet of grasses, which contain an abundance of silica and hence are abrasive. As the teeth are worn off they are replaced continually from below. Bark, fungi, berries, and some seeds add variety to the diet. As herbivores, long-tailed voles are, in turn, food for carnivores and thus are an integral part of the food web in local biotic communities.

The older literature refers to this species as *Microtus mordax*, the "cantankerous vole," in reference to its reputed foul temper. I cannot say that these are actually less friendly than other microtines, however. None of the voles is particularly tolerant of either human intruders or other mice of the same species. Wounding by bites from other voles is common, and rates of wounding increase as populations grow more dense.

Like most other voles, this is a polyestrous species with a high rate of reproduction. The animals breed throughout the warmer months of the year and produce several litters of one to seven (average about four) young at approximately 21-day intervals. As is true of other mammals with short periods of gestation, the young are altricial. Growth is sufficiently rapid that females may reach reproductive maturity their first summer.

Selected References.—Smolen and Keller (1987); Stinson (1978).

Montane Vole
Microtus montanus

Description.—The montane vole is about 155 to 180 mm in total length, and the tail is usually less than one-third that long, 40 to 60 mm. Weights range from 35 to 55 grams. Above, the color is grayish to grayish brown, sometimes with a hint of a yellowish wash; the underparts are silvery gray. The tail is indistinctly bicolored. The montane vole is easily confused with other local microtine rodents. It differs from the long-tailed vole in relatively shorter and less distinctly bicolored tail. From the heather vole it differs in somewhat larger size and heavier body. At a quick glance (except for the red-backed vole), "a vole is a vole." Certain identification often depends on details of teeth and skull. To some extent, habitat differences separate the several species. *Field Recognition.* – Habitat mostly in wetlands; grass-roofed runways conspicuous.

Distribution and Habitat. – As its name implies, the montane vole is largely a mountain mammal. Ranging from southern British Columbia to Arizona and New Mexico, it occurs along the Sierra–Cascade and Rocky Mountain systems and on lesser ranges of the Great Basin between them. This mouse occupies higher parts of central and western Colorado, occurring throughout Rocky Mountain National Park in suitable habitat. Montane voles are especially abundant in moist meadowlands and bogs and in aspen woodlands. They may occur also in drier meadows and in sagebrush stands with a grassy understory, but they are not found in unbroken coniferous forest. These mice seem to be obligatory runway-builders and they need a dense cover of grasses. Such cover is seldom present beneath subalpine forest.

Natural History. – The montane vole has a well-developed runway-building instinct. In a moist meadow, remove the "thatch" from the surface of the ground and you will likely uncover a segment of a runway, a well-worn path about 3 cm wide. When populations of voles are high, such runways form an intricate network obvious to the most casual observer. The runway is a foraging path and active runways are littered with short (3 to 10 cm), neatly clipped bits of grass. Ball-shaped nests of grass fibers are built along the runway. The superficial root systems of aspens also provide an abundance of nesting holes. The montane vole is mostly nocturnal, but may be active by day as well, especially when populations are high. Hidden in a "subway tunnel" beneath the litter, however, they are seldom seen. The animals do not hibernate, but are active throughout the year.

The diet consists mostly of grasses. Like the long-tailed vole, the montane vole has ever-growing cheekteeth which suit it to eat abrasive foliage: as the teeth are worn off at the top they are replaced from the roots. A variety of other plant foods supplement the diet. Montane voles are preyed upon by virtually all local vertebrate carnivores – mammals, raptorial birds, and snakes.

Like a number of other microtine rodents, montane voles exhibit cycles of abundance. Local voles do not show the dramatic population explosions and crashes of their northern relatives, the lemmings, but there is nonetheless an obvious cycle of "boom and bust." Cycles have not been detailed in Colorado, but they do exist. Some years voles are virtually impossible to capture and other years they are so abundant that they are active by day and seldom out of sight. As in all populations, numbers increase if the birth rate exceeds the death rate, and because excessive births mean more reproductive individuals in the next generation, populations tend to increase in a "geometric" (or Malthusian) fashion.

A particular tract of habitat has only so much carrying capacity for a particular species. When that carrying capacity is reached or exceeded, something has to "give"—either input (birth and immigration) must be reduced, or outflow (death and emigration) must be increased. A species may solve its population problem by working with any of these variables. Lemmings rely on emigration (which ultimately increases the death rate as individuals move into unsuitable habitat). Montane voles decrease the birth rate somewhat as populations increase. Also, the incidence of fetal and nestling mortality increases markedly. The population of montane voles in spring is about constant from one year to the next, but differences in survivorship result in a peak population every three or four years.

Montane voles are polyestrous and breed throughout the warmer months of the year. Breeding begins in early spring and the first litter may be produced under the snowpack. A litter of two to ten (average, five or six) young is born after a gestation period of about three weeks. There is a post-partum estrus. The young are altricial, but development is rapid and females born early in the season may breed their first summer.

Selected References. — Armstrong (1977); Hoffmann (1958); Vaughan (1969, 1974).

Muskrat
Ondatra zibethicus

Description. —The muskrat (so-called because of the odor of secretions from perineal glands) is the largest of our cricetid rodents. Adults are 475 to 650 mm in total length, of which the scaly, laterally flattened tail comprises 225 to 230 mm. Weights range from 900 to 1200 grams. Males are larger than females. The sleek guard hairs are dark brown above (nearly black along the mid-line), paling on the belly. Beneath the guard hairs is a thick coat of silky brown underfur. The hind feet are considerably larger than the forefeet, are partially webbed, and are fringed with stiff hairs. The short ears are barely visible beneath the abundant pelage. *Field Recognition.* – Semi-aquatic habitat; conspicuous lodges and burrows; large size; laterally flattened tail.

Distribution and Habitat. –The muskrat is the most widespread of North American microtine rodents, ranging from Alaska, the Aleutians, and the southern shores of Hudson's Bay southward to the Gulf Coast and northern Baja California. The species has been introduced in Europe, where it has increased rapidly and expanded its range, becoming a nuisance in the process, as is all too typical of introduced species. In Colorado, muskrats occur essentially statewide. In Rocky Mountain National Park, their range is coextensive with (and to a considerable degree determined by) that of the beaver, being more common at lower elevations. They inhabit margins of ponds, lakes, and slow-moving streams on both sides of the Continental Divide.

Natural History. – Muskrats may be thought of as over-grown, subaquatic voles. In most respects, the animals are much like our other microtines, especially internally. Externally, however, major and minor details of structure adapt the animals strongly to life in the water. The sleek fur is virtually waterproof. The hind feet are partially webbed and fringed with stiff hairs. The ankles are twisted sideward, increasing their efficiency as paddles (but dictating an awkward, waddling gait on dry land). The tail is flattened from side to side; it serves as a rudder and provides some propulsive force while swimming.

Like proper voles, muskrats are active by day to some extent, although they are more active at night. Also, like some of their terrestrial kin, they make conspicuous runways through semiaquatic vegetation, including not only superficial tunnels, but slides as well.

Muskrats are less common in the National Park than on the plains to the east or in North and Middle parks. In fact, they occur in the mountains mostly as guests of the beaver. It is the beaver that dams streams, changing whitewater to flat water, providing a transportation artery beneath winter ice, and encouraging the growth of subaquatic vegetation. The animals do not compete directly for food and hence can coexist without difficulty. Indeed, an instance has been reported of a muskrat's building its den in the wall of an occupied beaver lodge.

The muskrat is far more imaginative in its dietary habits than is the beaver. Virtually any vegetable matter is eaten, including shoots and roots of grasses, sedges, rushes, horsetails, and forbs. Food habits change with seasonal availability. Food is stored in the burrow or den and, during the winter, parts of the lodge may be eaten. Muskrats also take some animal food as opportunity allows—fish, frogs, salamanders, and even birds (especially moribund individuals) and eggs, as well as some carrion—although neither the teeth nor the digestive tract is specialized to handle such food. Muskrats may build conspicuous dome-shaped houses, piles of reeds, rushes, and algae a meter or more high and to two meters in diameter. One or more underwater entrances leads to a central nest chamber a few centimeters above high-water line. Some animals live in burrows in the bank. At times these burrows may undermine levees or ditchbanks, causing appreciable damage.

Muskrats are preyed upon by mink and raccoons. In autumn, muskrats (especially younger individuals) wander widely in search of uninhabited waters suitable for colonization. At such times they are ready prey for coyotes, foxes, and other mammalian predators, as well as for the larger birds of prey.

Muskrats are mostly promiscuous and breed in spring and summer. The gestation period is three to four weeks. Nursing mothers carry subsequent litters longer than the first litter of the season. Post-partum estrus occurs and two or three litters are produced annually. The average litter contains perhaps six young, but the range is wide, from one to 10 or more.

The young are blind and nearly naked at birth and are about 100 mm long. The tail of neonates is round and the hind- and forefeet are about equal in size, so the young look very much like ordinary voles. Growth is rapid, however, and the animals are able to dive before the eyes open at about two weeks. During the third week, milk is supplemented with vegetable food and growth accelerates. At one month, the young are relatively independent, although full growth will not be attained until the following spring. In our area, the young do not breed during their first summer, although some females do so in areas of milder climate. In the wild a three-year-old muskrat is an old animal.

Selected References.—Errington (1963); Perry (*in* Chapman and Feldhamer, 1982).

FAMILY ZAPODIDAE—JUMPING MICE

Jumping mice are of wide distribution, occurring from central Europe and southern Scandinavia (birch mouse) to Mongolia and China. In

North America there are two genera, including four species, mostly of boreal distribution. Sometimes the jumping mice are placed as a subfamily in the family Dipodidae, an Old World group with strong evolutionary tendencies toward bipedalism.

Western Jumping Mouse
Zapus princeps

Description. – Jumping mice are unmistakable; no other local mouse has as long a tail or such over-sized hind feet. Adults are 220 to 250 mm long, have tails 130 to 150 mm in length, and weigh 20 to 30 grams. The upper parts are mostly blackish brown in color, flecked with yellow. On the sides, yellowish hairs form a narrow line, giving way to pure white beneath. The tail is dark above, pale below, and almost naked.
Field Recognition. – Tail much longer than head and body; bipedal jumping gait.

Distribution and Habitat. – The western jumping mouse is mostly a mammal of the Mountain West, ranging from the Yukon southward to the mountains of New Mexico and Arizona. On the Northern Great Plains, the species occurs eastward north of the Missouri River to the eastern Dakotas. In Colorado, this is mostly a mammal of the mountains. It lives in suitable habitat throughout Rocky Mountain National Park. Jumping mice frequent moist streamside willow thickets and they are also relatively common in the rank grasses about beaver ponds and beneath aspen groves. Sometimes they follow dwarf willows to above timberline. The elevational range is about 1830 to 3500 meters (6000 to 11,500 feet).

Natural History. – This is the only saltatory (jumping) mammal in the Park. In keeping with its habit, the hind feet are huge and the tail – of obvious use in balancing and steering when airborne – is elongate. Although mostly nocturnal, they are seen by day if the nest is disturbed. The summer nest is in tall grass. Teeth are adapted to a diet of seeds, but some foliage is eaten as are occasional insects.

In July and August, the animals store fat to provide energy for maintenance during the long period of hibernation. Individuals that store too little fat do not survive until spring. In September, the animals enter the hibernaculum, which is a hole beneath a stump, a log, or a clump of willows, as much as a meter deep. The winter nest – a sphere of grasses lined with soft plant fibers – must be below the frost line and it will be insulated with snow. Jumping mice emerge from hibernation in May or June – females about 10 days later than males – having lost about one-fifth of their body weight over the winter. Temperatures of about 10 degrees Celsius (50 degrees F.) seem to trigger arousal.

Western jumping mice are seldom found far from water. A study in southeastern Wyoming indicated that home ranges are linear areas 15 to 50 meters wide and 50 to 350 meters long, paralleling a stream. Females have smaller home ranges than males and tend to be more sedentary, cruising the same home range in successive seasons.

As mice go, western jumping mice are notably long-lived, some surviving four years or longer. Deer mice, by contrast, almost never survive two winters. Perhaps the hibernating habit of jumping mice has something to do with this. An animal that hibernates for eight or nine months of the year actually "lives" only about one-fourth to one-third of its life and "coasts" through the rest. Recall that our bats – which not only hibernate but also suspend thermoregulation while at rest during the day – are among the longest-lived of small mammals. During hibernation, the jumping mouse is also safe from the myriad predators which find it a worthy meal, although the stress of arousal from hibernation may be the most forceful check on populations. During the summer, the animals fall prey to foxes, coyotes, bobcats, weasels, garter snakes, and owls.

Males come into breeding condition soon after coming out of hibernation. Females breed their first week above ground. Gestation takes about eighteen days and five young (range, four to eight) compose a typical litter. The young are weaned at about one month of age. A single litter per year is the general rule. Additional litters of young (and their mothers) could hardly fatten for winter during the short season remaining above ground.

Selected References. – Brown (1967b, 1970).

FAMILY ERETHIZONTIDAE – NEW WORLD PORCUPINES

The four genera (ten species) of erethizontids occur only in the New World. A single species occurs in the United States and Canada and another, the coendou, ranges northward to México; all other species are South American. Old World porcupines (family Hystricidae) resemble New World porcupines in many ways, but there is as yet no strong consensus among mammalogists about their evolutionary relationships.

Porcupine
Erethizon dorsatum

Description. — Porcupines are second in size only to the beaver among local rodents. Adults range from 700 to 850 mm in total length, and the tail is 200 to 280 mm long. A large adult may weigh over 15 kilograms. The animals appear even larger and heavier than they actually are because of the abundant pelage. Three kinds of hairs are present. The underfur is soft, thick, and dark in color, blackish to grayish brown. Over the back, tail, and limbs, long (to 10 cm), coarse guard hairs are present. These are mostly yellow in local animals. On the belly the guard hairs are much shorter and brownish in color. Between the guard hairs and the underfur are the infamous quills, actually highly specialized hairs. The quills are hollow and may be 6 to 8 cm in length. The barbed tips are black and the waxy shaft is white to yellowish.

The overall color of a porcupine varies with the animal's attitude and the observer's vantage point. Resting calmly, porcupines viewed from the front appear to be black, with a yellowish cast lent by the guard hairs. More common, however, is a posterior view of an irate porcupine. With quills erect the color scheme is much paler, the shade of the exposed shafts of the quills. *Field Recognition.* — Large size; waddling gait with swaying of quills and coarse guard hairs.

Distribution and Habitat. —The porcupine occurs from Alaska and Canada southward to northern México. In the United States the animals are present in all forested regions except the southeast. The species is common in the mountains of Colorado and occurs in suitable habitat throughout the state. Porcupines probably are most abundant in the open ponderosa pine woodland of moderate elevations in the foothills and mountains. Along streams, they range into the broadleafed riparian woodlands of the plains and willow thickets provide shelter and food in the alpine zone. Visitors may expect to see porcupines at least occasionally in nearly all terrestrial habitat-types in Rocky Mountain National Park.

Natural History. —Porcupines are called by a variety of vernacular names, including "porky," "quillpig," and (quite erroneously) "hedgehog" (actually an Old World insectivore); more colorful (but less distinctive and less publishable) names have been applied when the animals have gnawed the handle of a favorite ax for its salt content or turned the muzzle of an over-zealous dog into a swollen pin-cushion. Porcupines are common animals in our area, and the observant visitor will likely see them.

On the ground, porcupines move with a heavy, lumbering gait, the waddle accentuated by the swaying motion and rustling sound of the quiver of quills. For all their apparent clumsiness on the ground, however, the animals are remarkably agile in the trees, climbing rapidly with strong, curved claws. The stout tail is used as a sort of fifth foot and once positioned in the crotch of a tree they are very difficult to dislodge. Frequently, porcupines spend the day in a thicket of streamside willows. When disturbed in such situations, they swim readily and well, buoyed high in the water by their hollow quills.

Porcupines typically are solitary, although in coldest weather two or more may share a den. Any sheltered spot will serve as a denning site; rocky overhangs, hollow logs, and willow thickets are used in the Park. No nest is built except in the nursery den, but their unimproved shelters are recognizable by a litter of crescent-shaped droppings. The animals are active throughout the year except in the most severe winter weather, wearing a path from the den to preferred feeding trees.

Food habits change with seasonal availability of plant materials. Herbs often provide the bulk of the summer diet; the bark of woody plants is used at other times of the year. The succulent inner bark (cambium) of conifers seems to be preferred, but bark, leaves, and twigs of broadleafed trees also are eaten. When porcupines are abundant their damage is quite conspicuous. Some trees may be protected by distasteful chemicals, but ponderosa pines are frequently top-killed in our area by porcupines. Trees are killed outright when they are girdled completely, preventing the flow of food molecules from leaves to roots. When bark is peeled from small branches, chickarees, and not porcupines, may be responsible.

The popular literature is replete with tales of mayhem wreaked by porcupines. They can damage stores and equipment in a poorly guarded camp, gnawing salt from sweat-seasoned tool handles and raiding cached provisions. These habits differ from those of mice only in degree, of course, but porcupines are large animals, and that degree of difference is quite significant.

Another legendary attribute of porcupines is an ability to shoot quills. Although widely denied, the tale enjoys equally wide credence. But it is not true. Still, the most superficial brush with one of these animals will leave one with a potentially painful souvenir. Quills are tipped with minute, imbricate (shingle-like) barbs. Left in place they readily work their way through clothing (even boot leather) or skin. When removing quills from oneself or a friend, give them a quick twist; drawn straight out they tend to bring along a painfully large piece of flesh.

When other food is scarce, any of the larger carnivores will prey on porcupines. Individual coyotes reportedly develop skill in killing porcupines by rolling them over quickly to expose the unarmed belly. In the boreal forest, fishers (robust arboreal weasels closely related to our pine marten) are habitual porcupine killers. Overall, however, predation is not a major problem for porcupines; many a naive, would-be predator has starved to death, incapacitated by a mouthful of quills from a porcupine that escaped largely unscathed. Parasites and diseases may be more of a problem than predators under natural conditions. In settled areas, vehicular traffic is probably the most important check on numbers. Like skunks, porcupines are adapted to be instructive rather than destructive; they are adapted to intelligent perils, other animals capable of learning from experience. Their passive defense is not at all effective against the ignorant machinery of civilization.

Breeding occurs in late autumn or early winter. As one might suppose, mating of animals so thoroughly armed is a precarious and complicated venture. After a gestation period of about 210 days (one of the longest of any rodent), a single, precocial, 500-gram young (rarely twins) is born in April or May. The eyes of neonates are open and the pelage is well-developed. The quills are soft at birth but they harden quickly when exposed to the air. Young gain at a rate of 450 grams per month. Maximum known longevity is 10 years, with usual old age at five to seven years of age.

Selected References. — Costello (1966); Dodge (*in* Chapman and Feldhamer, 1982); Woods (1973).

Mountain Lion.

X. *Order* CARNIVORA

Carnivores

THE CARNIVORES ARE native to all continents but Australia, and there they were introduced (in the form of the dingo) by early humans. The carnivores include both terrestrial representatives and an impressive array of marine species (the seals, sea lions, and walruses). There are about 270 species of carnivores in some 110 genera. A broad spectrum of the extant diversity of terrestrial carnivores occurs in Rocky Mountain National Park, where these mammals compose the "top layer" of the food web in most biotic communities. Three carnivores—the gray wolf, the grizzly bear, and the river otter—have been extirpated here since the advent of European civilization; river otters are being reintroduced. If the black-footed ferret ever occurred here it is gone now. The status here and elsewhere in Colorado of the wolverine and the lynx is poorly known. On the other hand, the raccoon has come to occur in the Park in rather recent years, and the ringtail is of possible occurrence. Hence, as many as 20 species of carnivores representing five families may have occurred in Rocky Mountain National Park in the past century.

FAMILY CANIDAE—DOGS AND ALLIES

The dog family is highly successful and widespread, with a range on land about as great as the entire Order Carnivora. There are 34 species of dogs, arrayed in a dozen genera. Four of the six canids that have lived in Colorado within historical times are known from Rocky Mountain National Park.

Coyote
Canis latrans

Description.—Coyotes are about as large as medium-sized shepherd dogs; total length is 100 to 120 cm, and the full tail is about 30 to 40 cm long. Males average larger than females. Adult males average about 11 kilograms in weight, females a kilogram lighter, but individuals in excess of 20 kilograms have been reported. The general color is buffy gray above, paling to nearly white below. The head, ears, and limbs are prominently marked with reddish hairs, and the full tail may be marked with black-tipped hairs. Both albinism and melanism have been reported, but neither condition is common. *Field Recognition.*—Tail black-tipped, directed downward when running.

Distribution and Habitat.—The coyote ranges from the Arctic Slope of Alaska southward to northern Costa Rica and from the Pacific Coast eastward to New England and Maritime Canada. In recent years the animals have expanded both in the Northeast (into the former range of the gray wolf) and Southeast (into the former range of the red wolf) in the United States. The animals occur throughout Colorado and are present in most habitat-types in Rocky Mountain National Park. Coyotes are highly adaptable animals and range through a wide variety of habitats in search of food and cover. They are more common in open, park-like situations, woodland, and rough, brush-clad country, than in closed forests.

Natural History.—The coyote—whose name is a corruption of the Aztec word *coyotl*—is certainly the most frequently encountered of local canids. Unlike its larger cousin, the gray wolf, the coyote has thrived over most of its range despite concerted human efforts to eradicate it. Indeed, the animals actually have expanded their range in the past few decades. Even those who fear economic impact from the coyote's alleged depredations on their livestock often admit a certain curious, albeit grudging, respect for their persistent adversary.

Part of the coyote's versatility is attributable to a catholic diet. Studies of scat from Moraine Park indicated that carrion of deer and elk was the principal food. In many areas, rabbits and hares are staples, especially during the warmer months. Mice, voles, woodrats, ground squirrels, beaver, porcupines, marmots, pocket gophers—in short, virtually all rodents—are eaten. Some birds, especially ground-nesters, are taken. Even other carnivorous vertebrates are eaten, despite their usually strong odors: weasels, shrews, snakes, and even skunks. Larger prey, such as deer, is taken on occasion, especially when snow or ice makes travel difficult for ungulates. Plant material may make up 10 to 20 percent of the diet.

Coyotes frequently hunt in pairs, sometimes displaying intricate patterns of teamwork. Unlike wolves and feral dogs, however, they do not typically hunt as packs. A habitual hunting trail is followed, often as much as 15 kilometers in length. The runway makes use of game or stock paths as well as roads and other man-made trails. The animals are not averse to swimming. A single trail may be used by a coyote throughout its life (to 10 years or more), as long as food remains available. Like many breeds of domestic dogs, coyotes follow a scent quickly until potential prey is sighted and then they "freeze" momentarily before pouncing on the quarry. Excess food is sometimes cached.

As is true of other canids, coyotes have anal scent glands. When individuals meet, mutual sniffing occurs. Scent varies with the individual and lends a distinctive odor to the urine, which is used to mark the boundaries of the animal's domain. The bark of the coyote—a series of "yips" or "yaps" and a trailing howl—is perhaps the most exciting vocal offering of our extant native fauna. The sound of this nocturnal serenade is a hopeful sign that at least part of the natural system remains intact. May it never vanish from the West.

Coyotes are susceptible to rabies and tularemia. Virtually any parasite found on domestic dogs also afflicts coyotes. Pronounced social tendencies help to foster a heavy load of ectoparasites—fleas, ticks, mites—and the notoriously uninhibited diet assures a wide range of internal parasites as well.

Coyotes breed first as yearlings from January to March. The animals seem not to mate for life, but pairs may remain together for several years. Packs of three or four (and sometimes to a dozen or more) individuals may run together before pairing begins. Females are monoestrous, becoming receptive in mid- to late winter. Gestation takes 60 to 63 days. Five to seven pups compose a typical litter. Occasionally two litters are found in a single den, suggesting that some males are polygynous. The young are born virtually hairless, and the eyes do not open for 9 to 14 days. The male forages to feed the nursing female. Hybridization between coyotes and domestic dogs is not uncommon.

The young are reared in a burrow, often the remodeled lair of a badger or other species. Dens are frequently found near water and they range from simple holes to extensive systems of tunnels with several entrances. The female may prepare a number of dens before whelping, moving the pups if disturbed. The male helps to provision the mother and their pups. The young emerge from the den at about three weeks of age. When pups are 8 to 10 weeks old, the den is abandoned, and the family forages as a group until fall, at which time the family unit disbands. Longevity in the wild usually is less than 10 years.

Selected References. – Bekoff (1977; *in* Chapman and Feldhamer, 1982); Bekoff and Wells (1980, 1986); Young and Jackson (1950).

Gray Wolf
Canis lupus

The wolf is gone from Colorado, the last meager remnant of the population eradicated in the southern part of the state in the 1940s. In our area they were gone even sooner. Merritt Cary, in his *Biological Survey of Colorado* (published in 1911), noted that wolves were common in North Park, and scarce but present in Middle Park. They were reported as abundant in the vicinity of Estes Park in 1894, but apparently they were gone before Rocky Mountain National Park was established in 1915. In the works of Enos Mills—pioneer naturalist and poet laureate of Longs Peak—I find no direct report of wolves in the immediate area, although in *The Rocky Mountain Wonderland* (1915), he mentioned wolves in North Park and later noted that a "scattering of wolves" remained in the area of the nascent National Park itself.

Wolves were trapped and poisoned because of transgressions against stockgrowers, but human extirpation of the bison and decimation of the wapiti must have been the ultimate reason for their demise. Wolves survive today in North America in parts of Alaska, Canada, and the Great Lakes states. The gray wolf is half again as large as a coyote, about the size of a large German shepherd, and the head is markedly broader and more massive. Running alone or in small packs, wolves hunt a circuitous route as much as 150 kilometers in length (but more commonly 30 to 100 kilometers long). It is unfortunate, but probably true, that there is not room for these animals in Rocky Mountain National Park today.

Selected References. – Mech (1974); Paradiso and Nowak (*in* Chapman and Feldhamer, 1982); Young and Goldman (1944).

Red Fox
Vulpes vulpes

Description. – Adult red foxes range from about 90 to 120 cm in total length, of which the long, full tail comprises about one-third, 30 to 40 cm. The abundant long pelage makes these slender animals appear larger and heavier than they really are; weights range from 3 to 6 kilograms, males averaging about one-quarter larger than females. In color, the red fox is unmistakably familiar – the upper parts are yellowish orange; the belly, chest, chin, and the tip of the tail are white; legs, muzzle, and backs of ears are black. Occasional individuals of black, "silver," or "cross" (brownish marked with black) phases occur with more typical litter mates. Foxes of non-red phases are not common in Colorado, and they have not been reported in the National Park. *Field Recognition.* – White-tipped tail; black feet.

Distribution and Habitat. – The red fox is a holarctic animal – it occurs across Eurasia and in North America, from Alaska southward through most of the United States except for the driest parts of the Great Plains and the Desert Southwest. Red foxes occur in suitable habitat throughout Colorado, and they are present locally in the Park on both sides of the Divide. These are mostly mammals of moist forest and wetlands, and in our area they are found most commonly in forest-edge situations, about beaver ponds, and in rank openings caused by fire or logging. Such situations provide an abundance of suitable food. Red foxes are never found far from water.

Natural History. – Red foxes are opportunistic feeders, although food habits have not been studied intensively in the West. In the East, however, cottontails are a staple, and mice and other rodents comprise about half the diet. Birds, reptiles, insects, amphibians, eggs, and fruit are eaten as opportunity allows. Some carrion is eaten, and plant material, especially fruit, is taken as available.

The animals hunt by smell, "following their noses" for a few dozen meters or so and then pausing to look around, often leaping to the top of a log or other vantage point. A hunting trail is worn by an individual, for the same route is followed night after night. Mostly nocturnal, the animals may also hunt at dawn and dusk. Every brushpile and thicket is investigated thoroughly. Burrowing mammals may be dug out, but foxes seldom chase prey for any great distance, relying on surprise more than speed to gain the advantage of the quarry. When food is abundant, it may be cached against the prospect of lean times ahead. Adult red foxes need about 2.25 kilograms of prey per week — the equivalent of perhaps 100 average mice. During the breeding season, foxes hunt in pairs. Typically the home range is 2 to 8 kilometers in diameter, depending on the density of food resources. As is true of most carnivores, the red fox is active throughout the year.

Dens are used as shelter during severe weather and when the pups are being reared. Usually the den is a renovated "hand-me-down" from some other animal, such as a beaver, a marmot, or a badger. Dens may be in banks, beneath roots or downed timber, or even in abandoned buildings, usually near permanent water. There may be several entrances 15 to 30 cm in diameter.

Once the pair-bond is formed, male and female are virtually inseparable, hunting and playing together. The same individuals may pair in successive seasons, but during the autumn all individuals are solitary. Foxes are monoestrous, breeding annually in winter. The gestation period is 52 days. Litters of one to 11 young have been reported, but four or five is the usual number. Born blind, the young are balls of dark grayish brown fur with white-tipped tails. The eyes open at about one week of age, but the pups remain in the den until they are about five weeks old. Then they begin to spend increasing amounts of time playing outside the den with each other and with "toys" — bits of bone, fur, or other refuse. The young are weaned at 2 months and begin to hunt with the parents, putting to productive use the skills developed in earlier play. The deciduous "milk teeth" are lost at four months and the glossy reddish subadult pelage is donned about two months later. In early autumn, the family disperses.

Enemies of the red fox include hawks, golden eagles, and such mammals as bobcats, all of which are known to prey on the pups. Fleas, ticks, roundworms, and tapeworms parasitize the animals. Some parasites are shared by red foxes and domestic dogs. Rabies is not uncommon in some parts of the country. Humans — with their vehicles, firearms, and traps—are the major enemy of the red fox today.

Small, paired, anal scent glands lend the animals a pungent "foxy" odor which allows humans (at close range) to identify foxes (or their dens) in general and presumably allows foxes to identify each other in particular. The bark is a short "yip," not unlike that of a terrier.

Selected References.—Rue (1969); Samuel and Nelson (*in* Chapman and Feldhamer, 1982).

Gray Fox
Urocyon cinereoargenteus

Description.—As in other foxes, the abundant pelage of the gray fox makes the animal appear larger than it really is. Males range in total length from about 90 to 100 cm; females are slightly smaller. The tail is long—about the length of the body (30 to 35 cm)—and full. Weights range from about 3.5 kilograms for small females to over 4.5 kilograms for large males. The overall color is grayish, but the back is marked with a grizzled, black medial stripe that continues posteriorly as a mane of black bristles atop the black-tipped tail. The white underparts are separated from the grayish back by a prominent line of reddish hairs that extends from the backs of the ears, down the sides of the neck, along the sides, to the underside of the tail. The limbs are also reddish, and the short muzzle is black. *Field Recognition.*—Black-tipped tail with dorsal mane of bristles; reddish lateral markings.

Distribution and Habitat.—The gray fox is a mammal of southern affinities, ranging northward through much of the United States (except for higher parts of the Mountain West) to extreme southern Canada, and southward into northern South America. Its occurrence is not documented in Rocky Mountain National Park, but records from Estes Park and near Lyons suggest its probable presence, at least occasionally, on the eastern edge of the National Park. It is unlikely west of the Continental Divide.

In the West, gray foxes live in rough, broken country covered with woodland and shrubs. In Colorado they are most common in the piñon-juniper country of the southern part of the state, but they do occur northward along the foothills in the ponderosa pine community.

Natural History.—Gray foxes are less conspicuous than red foxes, even in areas where both species are abundant. Gray foxes are more secretive and less tolerant of civilization, more tolerant of dry conditions, and they seem to prefer denser overhead cover. Although mostly nocturnal, they may be active at any time, often feeding at dawn and dusk. The call is a hoarse, broken bark, and there is much olfactory communication, scents being deposited as urine and feces.

Like other foxes, the gray fox spends part of its time in a den, but it seemingly is not very serious about what that den is like. The retreat may be a hollow log, beneath brushpiles or rubbish, under an abandoned building, or in a burrow excavated by some other animal. Sometimes—but apparently as a last resort—they may dig a burrow of their own. The den is usually within a kilometer of permanent water and it contains no formal nest. Reported home ranges vary widely, from about 100 to 1000 hectares.

Gray foxes are agile climbers, remarkably arboreal for canids. Trees are used as refuges from danger and sometimes as a foraging ground. The diet includes small rodents and rabbits, insects, some birds, reptiles, and amphibians. Considerable quantities of fruits and berries are eaten as available, as is carrion. In short, gray foxes are opportunistic feeders and the diet varies widely with season and geographic location.

Fleas, ticks, and roundworms parasitize gray foxes. Rabies sometimes takes a toll, and the young may fall prey to large raptors. Otherwise, as is true of most large mammals, the greatest danger is persecution, exploitation, and habitat modification by humans.

Gray foxes apparently are monogamous and they mate about February or March. A litter of one to seven (average about four) 90-gram young is born after a gestation period of about nine weeks, and reared in an unlined den. The male provisions the female when she is confined with nursing pups. The newborn young are blind but fully furred, development is rapid, and the juveniles forage with the parents by mid-summer. In autumn, the family unit disperses. Gray foxes generally breed first as yearlings. Maximum longevity is 14 to 15 years, but most animals in any population are less than two years old.

Selected References.—Fritzell and Haroldson (1982).

FAMILY URSIDAE—BEARS

Bears are closely related to dogs. They are mostly a northern group, although some species do occur in the Malayan Region, the Andes of South America, and the Atlas Mountains of North Africa. There are eight living species of bears, of which one occurs in Rocky Mountain National Park, and another occurred as recently as a half-century ago

Black Bear
Ursus americanus

Description. – Black bears are familiar to most people, if only from folk literature. A large male may be 175 cm long and weigh nearly 225 kilograms (about 500 pounds), although the average length is nearer 150 cm (including the stubby tail) and most males in good condition weigh less than 135 kilograms (300 pounds). Females are some 20 cm shorter than males and usually weigh 40 to 70 kilograms.

Locally, most black bears are truly blackish, or very dark brown – with a brownish muzzle and occasional white ventral markings – but cinnamon-colored bears are not rare. These color phases can both occur in the same litter, but early observers sometimes thought that cinnamon-colored bears were grizzlies, leading to a great deal of confusion in some of the early literature. The only species with which the black bear could be confused is the grizzly bear. For comparisons, see the account of the latter species. *Field Recognition.* – Large size, stubby tail, flat-footed gait.

Distribution and Habitat. – Black bears once ranged over most of North America, from the edge of the Arctic tundra southward to central México, save for parts of the Desert Southwest. Over much of that area, the species has been extirpated, but black bears occur in mountainous parts of Colorado and they persist in low numbers in Rocky Mountain National Park. In our area, the black bear inhabits forested country. Unlike its relative, the grizzly bear, it seems never to have frequented open parklands or alpine tundra to any extent.

Natural History. – Black bears are less typical of Rocky Mountain National Park than they are of Yellowstone or Yosemite, but they are still an integral part of the fauna. Fortunately, traffic-stopping "bear-jams" are rare, but visitors may see bears along roads or trails at middle elevations.

Black bears are infamous omnivores. They will eat virtually anything organic, most of it with seeming relish and in vast quantity, but they rarely kill animals of any great size for food. Insects (including bees, ants, and grubs), berries, nuts, and other fruit, leaves, flowers, roots, fish, small mammals, birds – all are taken as opportunity allows. Young deer or wapiti may be killed if stumbled upon. Carrion provides a major part of the diet in many areas. Garbage – thoroughly nutritious refuse of an affluent human society – is eaten whenever available. Careless handling of rubbish in bear country is an open invitation to serious problems. Bears are not malicious (although most adults might be labeled "grouchy"), but their peculiar combination of massive clumsiness and insatiable hunger may spell disaster in a camp kitchen. Essentially solitary, the communal feeding so common near resort villages is a rarity in the wild. As might be expected, given their dietary habits, black bears carry heavy loads of endoparasites such as flukes, roundworms, and tapeworms.

Black bears are plantigrade; that is, they walk "flat-footed," like we people do. The usual gait is a shuffling walk, but with provocation they can break into a rolling run and move quite rapidly. They swim well and are able tree-climbers. The usual reaction is to avoid humans, but some individuals learn readily to equate settlement with food (the handout may be intentional or not) and come to seem deceptively tame (sometimes attaining record-book weights in the process). Like many other mammals, bears "wallow" in mud or dust to cool themselves or to snuff pestering insects. They usually are silent, but growl when alarmed. Claw-marks sometimes are seen on trees, as high as a standing bear can reach (to near 3 meters). These form a denser pattern than the toothmarks of the wapiti, and have been interpreted as a sort of "patent," or "register" mark, identifying an area with a particular individual.

Black bears are not hibernators in the usual sense. Hibernating bats or ground squirrels regulate their body temperature to that of their surroundings, down to quite near the freezing point; the black bear, by contrast, maintains a temperature near the summer norm. The deep winter sleep of bears is best called dormancy. Dormancy is an evolutionary response to seasonal shortage of food as well as to cold weather; black bears in the southern United States become dormant in winter even though the temperature seldom remains below freezing for any extended period of time. Bears usually den individually, under rocks, fallen trees, or other natural shelter, sometimes under little more than a blanket of snow. From about December to early March the animals sleep, living on fat stored in late summer or autumn. When they awaken in spring, they often are quite thin, their gaunt appearance heightened by the unkempt look of the molting pelage.

Black bears mate in summer, June or July. Implantation is delayed until November. One to four (usually two or three) cubs are born in January while the female (or "sow") is dormant. Neonates are highly altricial, weighing about a kilogram, but they are mobile when the mother emerges from dormancy. The extent of the adults' winter fat is remarkable. Not only does it fuel the sow for three to four months, but it sustains the developing embryos and the suckling young as well. Cubs remain with the mother through the summer and autumn, playing among themselves and submitting to the rough counsel of their mother. They may den near the mother (or even with her) their first winter, but thereafter they are on their own, solitary wanderers except for brief intervals to breed. Sexual maturity is reached the third year. Females breed only in alternate years. A sow with cubs will not tolerate the presence of a mature male.

Selected References. – Pelton (*in* Chapman and Feldhamer, 1982); Van Wormer (1966).

Grizzly Bear
Ursus arctos

The grizzly (or "brown") bear averages larger than the black bear by about one-third; indeed, this is the largest of land-dwelling carnivorous animals. The present consensus is that the brown bears, including the grizzly bear, the Kodiak bear, and the Eurasian brown bears, comprise a single, holarctic species. In contrast to the black bear, the grizzly bear has prominently humped shoulders and a long, coarse pelage, forming a sort of mane on the upper back. The claws of the forepaws show in the track; they are about twice as long as the claws of the hindfoot. The face has a conspicuously concave ("dished in") profile.

The grizzly bear is so large that active hunting does not suffice to feed it, and the animals have turned to omnivory, eating virtually anything, animal or vegetable, alive or dead. It is hardly surprising that livestock sometimes is eaten. A corralled horse or a poorly guarded flock of sheep may be the easiest meal a grizzly bear encounters in a lifetime of voracious wandering. It is also hardly surprising that the grizzly bear now is gone not only from Rocky Mountain National Park, but from all of Colorado.

Merritt Cary reported the grizzly bear from our area in his *Biological Survey of Colorado* – near Grand Lake and on Baker Mountain in 1905 – but suggested that ". . . along the eastern slopes of the Front Range . . . it appears to be extremely rare or entirely absent." Estes Park is the type locality of one of the numerous nominal species of grizzly bears (*Ursus shoshone*).

Enos Mills was enamored of grizzly bears. In *The Spell of the Rockies*, he wrote of two cubs taken on Mount Meeker and kept as pets and he described reactions of grizzlies to a forest fire on the upper Grand River (now called the Colorado River even to its sources in Rocky Mountain National Park). In *The Rocky Mountain Wonderland*, Mills wrote that the grizzly nearly had been exterminated in the Park. He described an encounter with a grizzly bear in North Park, however, and told of another that had "hibernated" above timberline on Battle Mountain (just northeast of Longs Peak). In 1922, Mills published *Watched by Wild Animals*, including the tale of a three-legged grizzly sow and her cubs that ranged between Echo Mountain (the west end of Shadow Mountain) and Longs Peak. These animals seem to have wandered over much of the region—from Berthoud Pass and James Peak northward to Grand Lake, Wild Basin, and Longs Peak, an area in excess of 300 square kilometers (200 square miles). The "Echo Mountain grizzly" is the last Mills ever knew and the last reported from northern Colorado. The loss of the grizzly bear—like the loss of the gray wolf—leaves the wilderness ecosystems of the National Park incomplete from both scientific and esthetic standpoints. However, given the grizzly's unpredictable habits and prodigious resource needs, both food and room to roam, its reintroduction in the Park seems unwise and unlikely.

Selected References. —Craighead and Mitchell (*in* Chapman and Feldhamer, 1982); Schoonmaker (1968).

Family Procyonidae—Raccoons and Allies

The procyonids are mostly an American group; the lesser panda of Asia is the apparent exception. There are eighteen recent species in the family, including raccoons, ringtails, coatis, and the kinkajou. A single species, the raccoon, is known to occur in Rocky Mountain National Park, although a second, the ringtail, is of possible occurrence.

Raccoon
Procyon lotor

Description. —The raccoon figures so prominently in American folklore that it is familiar to nearly everyone. Adult males are 800 to 950 mm in total length, and females range about 50 mm shorter. The full, ringed tail comprises about one-third of the total length. Weights range from 6 to 10 kilograms (15 to 25 pounds) or more. Local raccoons are rather pale in color, buffy to silvery gray beneath and grizzled grayish yellow above, heavily overlain with black. The guard hairs of the back are long and tipped with black, forming a prominent mid-dorsal line. The face is marked with a conspicuous black mask. The tail is cylindrical (not at all flattened like the ringtail's), and the black rings are complete (although darker and wider above than below). The only species that might possibly be confused with the raccoon is the smaller, more slender, and paler ringtail. *Field Recognition.* – Black mask; completely ringed, bushy tail.

Distribution and Habitat. – Raccoons range through most of temperate and tropical North America, from northern Alberta to Panamá, except for the highest mountains and the driest desert basins. Raccoons apparently have become abundant in Rocky Mountain National Park only in rather recent years. They first were reported in the western part of the Park in 1957; in 1958, a raccoon was observed crossing Trail Ridge Road at Tundra Curve, above 3350 meters (11,500 feet). During the 1960s, the animals increased dramatically at lower elevations east of the Continental Divide. Raccoons inhabit moist situations, especially streambanks and shorelines, although they forage over a diversity of habitats. They prosper in close proximity to civilization, wherever humans are sufficiently generous or careless to contribute their garden produce or camp provisions (or garbage) to the raccoon's larder.

Natural History. – A great deal has been recorded about the habits of the raccoon, especially the animal as it occurs in the eastern part of the country – the source of much of our wildlife lore. True to legend (and true to their name – *lotor* means "washer" in Latin) the animals rinse their food, perhaps to aid the sense of smell. This is especially prevalent in captive animals, but it does occur in free-ranging raccoons as well. The animals are seldom found far from water, for they exploit the diverse food resources of streambanks and shorelines. Raccoons are omnivorous; availability is a far more important criterion of diet than is preference. In our area, small mammals, amphibians, fishes, various invertebrates, and native fruits probably constitute the bulk of the diet, which is supplemented by occasional birds, eggs, and carrion. Ranging here above the limit of kitchen-gardens and cornfields, raccoons often turn to garbage dumps to levy their tithe from civilization.

Foraging raccoons may follow a circuit several kilometers long over several nights' activities. During the day they seek shelter beneath boulders or logs, in tree holes, or in bank dens, shifting from one shelter to another almost nightly. Raccoons swim well, with a strong "dog-paddle," buoyed high in the water by their abundant fur coat. They also climb with agility. The well-developed grasping "hand" allows dextrous manipulation of objects and a tenacious grip.

Raccoons do not hibernate, and they may be active during severe winter cold. When snow covers the foraging trail, however, they often retreat to cover and spend the unfavorable period asleep, living on stored fat. Dormant raccoons—like dormant bears and unlike hibernating ground squirrels or hibernating bats—arouse readily when sufficiently disturbed. Mature animals den singly.

The mating system is promiscuous. Females are monoestrous, coming into heat in February or March. Males exhibit no obvious reproductive cycle; timing of breeding depends on the receptivity of females. Males—reproductively active their second winter—wander widely, whereas females in estrus tend to be more sedentary. Females may breed as yearlings. The gestation period is about 63 days and up to seven (usually three or four) young are born in April or May, well-furred but with the familiar mask and tail rings indicated only as pigmented skin. Eyes and ears are closed, opening during the third week. As in other promiscuous species, the mother alone cares for the young. Milk is the sole food until the young begin to forage for themselves at 8 to 12 weeks of age. They are weaned completely by early fall, but full growth takes about two years.

Adult raccoons are subject to few predators. They are not particularly fast, but they are agile and evasive. If all else fails, they stand and fight ably. Larger carnivores, like coyotes, take a toll of raccoons, but probably this predation is minimal on mature animals. Like other carnivores, raccoons support roundworms and tapeworms, ticks and lice, but parasitic disease seldom is fatal. On adequate range, protected from hunting and trapping, a two-year-old raccoon will have avoided all major perils except the automobile and may expect a lifespan of three to five years, occasional animals living twice that long.

Selected References. — Lotze and Anderson (1979); Kaufmann (*in* Chapman and Feldhamer, 1982); Rue (1964*a*).

Family Mustelidae — Weasels and Allies

At least eight species of mustelids have lived in Rocky Mountain National Park over the past century, of the eleven kinds known from Colorado. Altogether, the family includes some 65 species, most common in the Northern Hemisphere, but occurring in South America, Africa, and Southeast Asia as well.

Marten
Martes americana

Description. – Martens are medium-sized, arboreal carnivores, distinctly weasel-like in appearance and habits. Adult males average about 600 mm in total length, females about 550 mm. The full tail is 180 to 210 mm long. Weights range from about 650 grams for small females to over 1200 grams for large males. Dorsally the glossy fur is medium brown, the tail somewhat darker. The chin and belly are paler, ranging from buffy to almost orange. The ears are upright and rounded, sometimes marked with a buffy rim. As in other weasels, there are abdominal and anal scent glands. *Field Recognition.* – Medium size; pale venter, dark, solid-colored tail; arboreal habitat.

Distribution and Habitat. – The marten – or "pine marten," as it is often called locally – is mostly a boreal mammal, ranging across Alaska and Canada to Newfoundland and southward at increasingly high elevations along mountain ranges to California and New Mexico. In the East, its former southern limits were in Illinois and Ohio. Martens are most typical of subalpine spruce-fir forest, but their range of habitats in Colorado is fairly broad, including tundra rockpiles and talus slopes as well as montane woodland. The marten occurs in suitable habitat throughout Rocky Mountain National Park.

Natural History. – Martens are the most arboreal of local mustelids, sometimes moving great distances from tree to tree, never touching the ground. In the trees, martens prey on chickarees (especially in winter) and birds. They are also at home on the ground, where they hunt mice, chipmunks and ground squirrels, marmots, rabbits, and pikas. Insects and carrion may supplement the diet. Prey is killed by a bite to the neck or base of the skull. Martens usually take their prey to cover to eat it. Except for the largest prey items, the food is consumed completely. Thus, the feces contains an abundance of hair, feathers, and bits of bone. Martens are active throughout the year and are mostly nocturnal, showing peaks of activity just after dusk and just before dawn. Days – and the most severe winter weather – are passed in tree holes, abandoned squirrel nests, and similar shelter. It should be mentioned that martens seem to tell time with their stomachs and not with their eyes; they are not averse to foraging by day if appetite dictates. Minimum home range for males is 2 to 3 square kilometers, more than twice that of females.

There is a single, gradual molt annually in autumn, and the dense fur that insulates the feet in winter simply is worn away by summer. The animals have a charming tolerance of humans, often described as "curiosity," with good reason. Headlong retreat is the response to arch-enemies like eagles and owls, but the reaction to other animals — including people — is to select a comfortable spot to observe the observer, often hissing or growling mild disapproval from a branch or fallen log. Martens sometimes follow hikers for several minutes, remaining barely out of sight in the timber. They can become quite tame, taking table scraps or entering occupied cabins periodically to rid the premises of mice.

A variety of larger carnivorous mammals and birds have been reported to eat martens, but arboreal habits and general scarcity protect them from becoming staple fare for any predator. A number of diseases and parasites have been reported. Habitat destruction and trapping are the greatest perils over most of their range.

Martens are monoestrous. They mate in summer, but implantation is delayed for 6 to 8 months, and the one to five altricial young are not born until April, following an active pregnancy of fewer than 30 days. The young are blind at birth and barely furred, but — as is typical of members of the weasel family — development is rapid. The young are weaned at two months and leave the nursery nest. They breed first their second autumn.

Selected References. — Strickland *et al.* (*in* Chapman and Feldhamer, 1982).

Long-tailed Weasel
Mustela frenata

Description. — When full-grown, long-tailed weasels are 300 to 450 mm in total length, of which the tail comprises about one-third. The animals are of slender physique and weigh just 100 to 200 grams. Males average about 20 percent larger than females. In summer the animals are a rich brown above and sulfur-yellow to orangish below. In winter, however, the pelage is uniformly snow white except for the tip of the tail, which remains black throughout the year. By comparison, the marten is larger, heavier, and arboreal; the ermine is smaller and has a notably shorter tail. *Field Recognition.* – Small size, slender body with tail half as long as head and body; bounding, "inch-worm" gait.

Distribution and Habitat. – The long-tailed weasel occurs from coast to coast in the United States, except for the Desert Southwest, and from southern Canada southward to Bolivia. The range in Colorado is statewide and these opportunistic animals occupy a variety of habitats in the Park – from brushland to dense forests and from montane parks to alpine tundra. Perhaps they are most abundant along streamcourses and in rocky, brush-covered terrain, where the rodents which provide the bulk of their diet are most abundant.

Natural History. – The long-tailed weasel is probably more abundant and more nearly ubiquitous than any other carnivore in the Park, and – being partially diurnal – it is among the most frequently seen. We describe the many readily visible mammals, the squirrels for example, as "bold" or "curious." The long-tailed weasel is neither; it is oblivious. Often one can watch a long-tailed weasel for some time unnoticed because the animals are preoccupied with their more immediate concerns (more often meals than men). The bounding, "inch-worm" gait of weasels is peculiar. The back is arched so high that the hind feet come down nearly in the tracks left by the forefeet. Only when "puzzling" over a trail or entering a burrow does a weasel walk in any conventional sense. Long-tailed weasels are largely terrestrial, but they can climb and swim well if necessary.

Weasels are highly efficient predators. By reputation they are "vicious," but by nature they are merely hungry. The long, slender body means that there is an extensive radiative surface per unit of heat-producing volume. To maintain a high and constant body temperature in the face of this unfavorable surface:volume ratio, weasels consume one-fourth to one-third or more of their own weight in food each day. There is some basis in fact for the widespread belief that, when circumstances allow, weasels kill more prey than they can eat at a given time. In autumn, some provisioning may occur. Furthermore, a weasel frequently kills its prey, feeds on it until satiated, and then becomes drowsy. After an interval of sleep, the weasel then returns to its meal. Discovering a partially-eaten carcass, one might conclude that the killing had been "wanton," whereas in fact the weasel has simply stumbled off for a "mid-meal nap." The diet consists mostly of small mammals – mice and voles, chipmunks, ground squirrels, pocket gophers, and shrews, with occasional larger mammals such as woodrats and young rabbits. After a short chase, the prey is wrestled to the ground and dispatched with a strong bite to the base of the skull. The legs of the weasel are short, and the supple, sinuous body helps to grasp the prey. A slender build allows the weasel to follow many small mammals into their own burrows and to pursue winter meals beneath the snow. The diet is supplemented with small birds, amphibians, snakes, insects, and even occasional plant matter, especially berries.

When not foraging, weasels retire to a simple burrow system. Frequently a remodeled "hand-me-down" excavated originally by a ground squirrel or pocket gopher, the burrow commonly is 8 to 10 cm in diameter and about 30 cm deep. A "latrine" littered with droppings marks the entrance of the burrow. Often the scat consists mostly of matted hair.

Weasels occasionally are preyed upon by owls and other larger carnivorous vertebrates. No predator specializes in eating weasels (or other small carnivores), however, and predation is probably not an important check on populations. In the first place—like other mustelids—weasels have musk glands which give them a rather strong odor (and presumably an even stronger taste). Secondly, preying on carnivores is just poor economics. At best transfers of energy between levels of the terrestrial food web are only about 10 percent efficient. Hence, 100 grams of plant makes 10 grams of mouse makes 1 gram of weasel. Even if mouse and weasel tasted equally good (which I sincerely doubt), mouse is at least a 10-fold better investment from the viewpoint of ecological efficiency. Parasitism and disease may exact a toll, and many weasels are killed by automobiles (which are particularly undiscriminating "predators").

Two molts occur annually, allowing seasonal color change. Spring molt begins in March and may take two months to complete. Brown hairs begin to appear over the shoulders and head and then new hair appears progressively down the back and tail. The autumnal molt to snow-white pelage begins in October. The pattern is the reverse of that seen in spring.

Weasels mate in summer, from June through August. Ovulation is induced by copulation. Gestation takes about 280 days, but during most of that time the development of the embryos is suspended. Implantation of the early embryo (the blastula) is delayed until spring and the interval between actual implantation and parturition is only about 27 days. The four to nine young are born in April. They are sparsely haired and weigh only about 3 grams, but already they are "weasel-shaped." The young are reared in a nest-chamber lined with chopped grass and hair. There is some evidence that the male has a role in the care of the young, at least early in post-natal life. The eyes open at about five weeks of age and weaning begins soon thereafter. Ensuing development is rapid and females may breed their first summer (although implantation, development, and birth do not occur until the following spring).

Selected References.—Hall (1951); Svendsen (*in* Chapman and Feldhamer, 1982).

Ermine
Mustela erminea

Description.—The ermine, or short-tailed weasel, is the smallest carnivore in the Southern Rockies and one of the smallest anywhere in the world. Adults are from 200 to 250 mm in total length, males averaging considerably larger than females. The tail is about one-third the length of the head and body, 50 to 65 mm long. Weights range from 30 to 55 grams. In summer, the upper parts are brown, the belly and chin usually white. In winter, the animals are entirely white except for the tip of the tail, which remains black throughout the year. It is in this white pelage that short-tailed weasels most often are called (and marketed as) "ermine." Our local weasels are easily distinguished from each other if due attention is paid to size and relative length of tail. *Field Recognition.*—White venter and obviously small size distinguish the ermine from other local mustelids; tail short, about one-third length of head and body.

Distribution and Habitat.—The ermine has an holarctic distribution, occurring in both Eurasia and North America. On the latter continent, it ranges from the Arctic Islands, coastal Greenland, and Alaska, southward through the boreal forest of Canada, the forested mountains of the western United States, and in the eastern deciduous forest to Iowa and Maryland. The animals occur throughout Rocky Mountain National Park. In Colorado, typical habitat includes aspen woodland, subalpine forest, and talus slides.

Natural History.—Like its larger cousin, the long-tailed weasel, the ermine is a rather strict carnivore, feeding on mice, shrews, chipmunks, small woodrats, young rabbits, and pikas. Some birds are taken, as are occasional invertebrates. The prey may be much larger than the agile predator, which typically kills by a quick bite to the base of the skull. Populations never have been studied in Colorado, but in Minnesota ermines cycle in abundance with the voles upon which they feed. Population densities of about four individuals per square kilometer have been reported from Canada, but in Colorado the animals do not seem to be that abundant anywhere.

Ermines are mostly nocturnal and they are active throughout the year. In winter, they often forage beneath the snow. As with the long-tailed weasel, the gait is a bounding, "inch-worm" affair, with leaps to 2 meters in length. The hind feet land nearly in the tracks made by the forefeet. Enemies of the ermine include owls, eagles, and fur-trappers. Perhaps most individuals seen by people are those killed by automobiles.

A litter of four to eight young is born in April or May. The animals breed in May or June, thus exhibiting a total gestation period in excess of 10 months. However, development is not active for the entire period. Rather, development proceeds for about two months and then is suspended until implantation occurs in late winter. Ovulation is spontaneous. The altricial young are reared in a nest lined with fur and fine vegetation at the end of a burrow beneath a tree or boulder. Neonates are flesh-colored, scantily-haired (except for a conspicuous "mane" on the neck), and weigh less than 2 grams. The eyes open at about 35 days. The animals first breed as yearlings.

Selected References. — King (1983).

Mink
Mustela vison

Description. —The mink is a medium-sized, semi-aquatic carnivore, thick-set for a weasel, but still of slender build. Males are 500 to 600 mm in total length, with tails 150 to 200 mm long; females average about 50 mm shorter. Males may weigh 1.5 kilograms, but average weight is closer to 1 kilogram, and females weigh about 675 grams. The fur is mostly dark brown, grading to black toward the end of the tail. Variable white patches often mark the belly and chin. The outer hairs, long and shiny, overlie a dense, soft, gray-based underfur. The ears are short. The toes are webbed at their bases and weakly clawed. Field Recognition. —Brownish color above and below; semi-aquatic habit.

Distribution and Habitat. —The mink is a wide-ranging carnivore, living in Alaska, most of Canada, and throughout the United States except for the Desert Southwest. Although present statewide, the mink is more abundant in the mountains of Colorado than on the plains. These are semi-aquatic mammals, commonly occurring in marshes, about lakes and beaverponds, and along streams. Mink are not common in the Park, despite an abundance of seemingly suitable habitat. Occasional mink are observed in the Glacier Creek drainage, especially about Bear and Nymph lakes.

Natural History. –The mink is a secretive species, mostly nocturnal. Days are spent in dens beneath piles of brush or driftwood, beneath rocks, in hollow logs, or in houses or dens abandoned by beaver or muskrats. By night the animals forage.

The diet consists almost entirely of animal food. Fish and small mammals are staples, and frogs, insects, and birds are important components. Some carrion is eaten. The diet changes with seasonal abundance of prey. There is some evidence that preferred prey-size differs between sexes, which hardly is surprising, because males are nearly twice as heavy as females. In winter, excess food may be placed in "cold storage" in the den. Mink are excellent swimmers, easily capturing aquatic prey. On land, the gait is much like that of the true weasels, when due allowance is made for the mink's somewhat stockier build.

Except in severe cold, snowy weather, mink are active throughout the year. There is a tendency for males to wander widely, ranging along 2 to 5 kilometers of a stream, whereas females tend to remain near a single den and range over a smaller area.

Breeding is promiscuous, commencing in mid-winter. Females are polyestrous, coming into heat again if the first estrus does not result in pregnancy, but a single litter per year is the rule. Ovulation is induced by mating, and implantation is delayed. Gestation takes 40 to 75 days, depending upon when implantation occurs; active pregnancy lasts about four weeks. The litter of about four young (range, one to eight) is born in April or May. The young are altricial, weighing only about 10 grams. However, they develop very rapidly, attaining 40 percent of adult body weight by an age of seven weeks. They apparently breed their first year.

Numerous parasites are known to infest mink. Beyond that, direct and indirect human influences are the most important checks on numbers. Environmental pollutants such as mercury, PCBs, and chlorinated hydrocarbon biocides are documented hazards to these carnivores, owing to their partial dependence on fish as food. Outside the National

Park, trapping and destruction of habitat probably are the most effective mortality factors.

Selected References. – Linscombe, Kinler, and Aulerich (*in* Chapman and Feldhamer, 1982).

Wolverine
Gulo gulo

Description. – The wolverine is the largest terrestrial member of the weasel family, with a total length of 700 to 1050 mm. The short, full tail is 175 to 250 mm long. Females weigh to 11 kilograms (about 25 pounds), males to perhaps 18 kilograms (40 pounds). This is a large mustelid, and the abundant, coarse pelage makes the wolverine appear even larger than it actually is. Dorsally, the animals are dark brown. The sides are marked with a distinct, pale yellowish stripe, which begins over the shoulder, broadens posteriorly, and narrows to a "V" over the tail. The belly is pale brown. The face is dark brown to blackish, often with a paler "mask" about the eyes. *Field Recognition.* – Large size and obvious, pale lateral stripe.

Distribution and Habitat. – The wolverine is a holarctic mammal, occurring both in Eurasia and in boreal North America. It ranges southward from the Arctic Islands through the Colorado Rockies, but its present status at the southern limits of its range is quite uncertain. Perhaps extirpated from the Park, the wolverine once occurred at least sparingly. Abner E. Sprague saw a wolverine on the south side of Moraine Park in 1878, and pioneer trappers of wide experience and high credibility reported the animals from the mountains about North and Middle parks in the 1880s and 1890s. Occasional reports of tracks are still received from parts of northern Colorado, and nearly every summer brings reports of supposed wolverines from the higher parts of the Park. One must hesitate to dismiss from his armchair reports from observers in the field, but sight-records of wolverines – like those of other scarce and furtive species – should be subjected to the closest scrutiny. An account of the wolverine is included in this handbook in the hope that it will help to increase our knowledge of the distribution of this animal in the Southern Rockies. Wolverines are mostly mammals of heavy forest, but they may range past treeline into alpine or Arctic tundra.

Natural History. – Wolverines must rank among the least-known of our larger mammals. Not that there is any paucity of literature concerning the "glutton," but the ratio of verbiage to knowledge is frightfully high; wolverines have inspired a reputation larger than life. They have been cast as "devils of the North" since humans first ventured into the taiga. Old-timers in the High Sierra Nevada were convinced that any mammal would yield to the wolverine. Stories abound of wolverines killing lynx and cougars as well as deer, caribou, and even moose, of cabins torn apart with obvious malice, of trap-lines raided systematically for bait and for captive fur-bearers. At least some of this pervasive reputation must have some basis in reality. Part of the reality seems to be that, although not especially aggressive, wolverines are fiercely defensive and virtually fearless. They have no traditional enemies other than humans.

The animals are opportunistic feeders. They are solitary and neither fast nor agile—the gait is a rolling walk, midway between that of the weasel and that of a bear—and scavenging is more important than is active hunting. The powerful jaws crush bones easily. Wolverines are not truly fossorial, but they can excavate marmots and ground squirrels. They climb well, using the sharp front claws. Senses of hearing and smell are acute, but sight is less so. Mostly nocturnal, wolverines will hunt by day if need be. They are usually silent, but sometimes utter a low, hoarse growl or grunt.

Wolverines are active throughout the year. In winter the feet are fitted with "snowshoes"—coarse hairs between the toe-pads and around the margins of the foot. Much of the wolverine's reputation for ferocity may be founded on its hibernal exploits. Snowcover makes travel difficult for many larger animals. It buries browse and weakens herds. Under such circumstances, a healthy wolverine can readily overpower an ungulate ten times its size.

Females are monoestrous, breeding in summer. Implantation is delayed, however, until January, as in many other mustelids. Total gestation is about nine months, active gestation only about five weeks. Studies in Alaska indicate that one to four young are born about March and leave the nursery den in April or May.

Selected References.—Wilson (*in* Chapman and Feldhamer, 1982).

Badger
Taxidea taxus

Description.—Badgers are stocky, short-legged mustelids. Males are 650 to 750 mm long, the short tail comprising 110 to 150 mm of the total length. Females average about 50 mm shorter. Weights vary widely with season, to about 10 kilograms (average, 4.5 to 5 kilograms—10 to 12 pounds). The name "badger" apparently derives from the conspicuous "blaze" or "badge" of white on the forehead, which may extend well down the back. The face is black with pale (buffy to nearly white) markings. The pelage of the back is grizzled and highly variable in color, ranging from rich reddish brown to pale buff, variously overlaid with black-tipped hairs. In our area, paler animals predominate. The feet are blackish and the venter is buffy to white. *Field Recognition.*—Low, flat profile; waddling gait; white mid-dorsal stripe.

Distribution and Habitat.—The badger occupies a wide range in central and western North America, from California to the Great Lakes Region and from northern Alberta southward to central México. Badgers are mammals of open, upland situations, and they occur statewide in Colorado. In Rocky Mountain National Park they frequent all of the larger mountain parks and some smaller, isolated meadows as well. Often they occur above timberline.

Natural History.—The badger is the most fossorial of our mustelids, and it is highly adapted for its burrowing habit. The forefeet bear heavy, elongate claws, and the shoulder region is massively developed. The limbs are short and powerful, and the profile is remarkably flat. The tail is quite short for a weasel. Burrows are recognizable by their shape—20 to 30 cm across and broadly elliptical, with a flattened bottom—in short, badger-shaped in cross-section. Denning burrows most often are on open slopes, rather than in valley bottoms or swales, and they commonly have a southeastern exposure.

In marked contrast to the rather tidy denning burrows are the excavations made by foraging badgers. Re-excavating burrows of fossorial rodents is a typical foraging tactic. The site of such feeding looks like it might have been produced by a minor explosion. Drawn by the scent of a tender meal of ground squirrel or pocket gopher, the badger digs with a vengeance, sometimes laying waste an area 2 meters or more in diameter. Over the long term, the badger's activities (which mix materials from various horizons) are a boon to the evolution of the soil.

Locally, Wyoming ground squirrels probably contribute the bulk of the diet. Other ground squirrels and chipmunks are taken, as are pocket gophers. Insects are important in summer, especially for young animals not yet fully able to exploit fossorial prey. Eggs, nestling birds, and young rabbits are eaten when the badger happens upon them. Mice are an important resource in winter when hibernating ground squirrels enjoy the partial protection of a layer of frozen ground. As is true of most carnivores, the badger is active throughout the year, although particularly cold and snowy spells—when foraging might be counterproductive in terms of energy expenditure—may be spent in the den. Badgers are active mostly at night, when they catch their largely diurnal prey napping. However, one sometimes sees the animals about by day as well, especially early and late in the day.

Except briefly during the mating season, badgers are solitary. By disposition, they seem thoroughly misanthropic. More antisocial than shy, they usually shuffle off to the burrow when confronted by humans. The usual gait is a waddling walk, accentuated by the sway of the abundant pelage from side to side. When pressed, the badger stretches its legs to their meager limit and runs. Cornered, they become ferocious: snarling, snapping, baring the teeth, and flattening the body against the ground. Badgers have no habitual enemies except numerous parasites, humans, and motor vehicles; thick hide and abundant fur combine with an unsavory disposition to protect the badger from larger carnivores.

Badgers mate in late summer and implantation is delayed until February. One to four (occasionally five) young are born in late March or April and reared in an unlined den. The young develop quickly and by early summer, one-third grown, they are eating rodents caught by the mother. By late summer or autumn, the young are on their own. Reproductive maturity is attained the second autumn.

Selected References.—Long (1973); Lindzey (*in* Chapman and Feldhamer, 1982).

Western Spotted Skunk
Spilogale gracilis

Description.—The spotted skunk (sometimes called "civet cat," albeit erroneously, for it is neither a civet—a kind of mongoose—nor cat) is notably smaller than its more familiar cousin, the striped skunk. Males are 375 to 450 mm in total length, and females range about 50 mm shorter. The tail is about one-third of the total length. Males weigh about 625 grams, females about 450. The color is distinctly patterned black and white. *Field Recognition.* – Small size; pattern of discontinuous white stripes on black background.

Distribution and Habitat. –The western spotted skunk is a species of western North America, ranging from southern British Columbia to southern México and from the Pacific Coast eastward to Colorado and central Texas, where they live in rocky, broken terrain with brushy cover. Rocky Mountain National Park provides little suitable habitat, but the species is known from the western margins of Estes Park and it occurs eastward through the foothills, especially along the major canyons, such as the Big Thompson and the Saint Vrain.

Natural History. –The petite spotted skunk invites comparison with its larger, more widely known relative, the striped skunk. The spotted skunk is better adapted to dry environments, more decidedly nocturnal, more weasel-like in shape and progression, less social and less parasite-ridden, a more graceful and agile climber, and (admittedly a personal judgment) smellier. These are secretive animals. Often they live in quite close proximity to people – even in occupied buildings – but escape all but olfactory surveillance. Away from people they den in rock shelters, in burrows abandoned by ground squirrels, badgers, or coyotes, beneath brushpiles, or in hollow logs. They do not hibernate, but they may den up to avoid extended periods of adverse winter weather.

Spotted skunks are opportunistic feeders on small mammals, insects, birds and their eggs, and fruit of various kinds. Seasonal abundance is a stronger determinant of diet than is preference. Carrion is important in winter. A taste for garbage and small size mean that they are not infrequently trapped in rubbish cans.

Like other skunks, this species is adequately protected from all but the hungriest predators by powerful secretions of anal musk glands. Owls sometimes prey on spotted skunks, and traffic takes a toll where the animals are abundant. Parasite-load may be heavy, and nematode damage frequently is seen in the frontal sinuses of the skull.

Western spotted skunks breed in September. Development is suspended at an early stage, and the blastocyst floats free in the uterus for six to seven months until implantation occurs in April. A litter of about four young is born in May, the total duration of pregnancy being 210 to 230 days. The young are altricial. Covered with fine hair, the characteristic pattern of markings is distinctive. Eyes and ears are closed, but the claws are developed and neonates can crawl about feebly. At about 4 weeks the eyes open, and the teeth erupt a week later. Thereafter, growth is rapid, with full size being attained at three months. Females typically are reproductively active their first autumn, and at least some males are also.

Selected References. — Howard and Marsh (*in* Chapman and Feldhamer, 1982).

Striped Skunk
Mephitis mephitis

Description. —The striped skunk is familiar beyond any real need for description. Adult males are 625 to 750 mm in total length, of which the full tail comprises over one-third (235 to 325 mm). Females range about 40 mm shorter. Weights of males range to 4.5 kilograms (10 pounds) or more, with an average near 3 kilograms; females average about 2.5 kilograms. As in many other mammals, seasonal change in weight may be great. The ground color is jet black (sometimes wearing and bleaching to deep reddish brown) with a pair of continuous white lateral stripes that extend from the back of the head to the base of the bushy black and white tail. *Field Recognition.* —Large size; continuous white stripes on black background.

Distribution and Habitat. —The striped skunk occurs throughout most of the United States, Canada south of Great Slave Lake and Hudson's Bay, and northern México. In Colorado, the species occurs essentially statewide, and it may be expected throughout Rocky Mountain National Park, except at highest elevations. Striped skunks utilize a wide variety of habitats. Locally, they occur about the margins of parks and meadows, in streamside woodlands, and in aspen groves. They are probably most abundant about human settlements, including resort villages and campgrounds.

Natural History. —Striped skunks are nearly omnivorous, eating insects, small mammals, birds and their eggs, amphibians, and fruit, as well as carrion and garbage. Although mostly nocturnal, they sometimes are seen by day. The den may be a "hand-me-down" from another mammal or it may be excavated anew. Dens under rocks, logs, and buildings are common. A nest is built of grasses and leaves. Southeastern slopes typically are selected for dens, to catch the first warming rays of morning sun. (This sense for the value of solar energy is a behavioral trait common to many kinds of mammals.) Striped skunks are not hibernators and they may be active year-round, but they often spend extended periods asleep during cold, snowy weather. If stored fat is depleted, striped skunks will dig out through a cover of snow to feed.

For protection, skunks are highly dependent upon the educability of potential predators. Most vertebrates show skunks a decided deference. Skunks are fitted with paired, anal musk glands which fill muscular reservoirs with fluid. In situations calling for active defense, the skunk raises its tail and relaxes the anal muscles to expose the ducts. Fluid is expelled in a double stream which spreads to a fine mist. The spray is controlled with disconcerting accuracy. The musk is an effective deterrent because of its odor and its painful—if short-term—effect on the eyes. Once initiated, would-be predators seldom have need for a refresher course. Although perhaps less audacious than the diminutive spotted skunk, striped skunks show fear of no other species. They thus are unwary of traffic—a menace against which their defense is obviously inappropriate—and frequently they become casualties on the highway. Indeed, their great susceptibility to traffic fatality leads most of us to imagine them to be much more abundant than they actually are. Occasional skunks fall prey to especially hungry foxes, coyotes, and large raptorial birds, but their malodorous carcass is staple fare for no predator. Internal and external parasites are abundant, and skunks are important carriers of rabies. The foregoing maladies stem in part from the striped skunk's gregarious denning habits.

Striped skunks breed in March or early April. Mating is accompanied by complex "pacification" behavior. Gestation takes about two months and two to 10 (average about five) altricial young are born in May or June. The young develop rapidly and are weaned within two months. Although independent by fall, they may den with the mother through the first winter, breeding first as yearlings.

Selected References.—Godin (*in* Chapman and Feldhamer, 1982); Verts (1967); Wade-Smith and Verts (1982).

River Otter
Lutra canadensis

Description.—This is a large, torpedo-shaped, aquatic mammal, with a long, round tail. Adults range in total length from 1000 to 1300 mm, and the tail is about half the length of the head and body, 350 to 500 mm in length. The webbed hind foot is 110 to 140 mm long and the short ears are obscured by the fur. Adult otters weigh 5 to 10 kilograms.

The dense fur of the upper parts is rich brown in color, and the venter is paler, to grayish or silvery brown.

Observers might confuse the semi-aquatic mink with the otter. The otter is much the larger of the two (about twice the size of a mink and five or more times the weight). The color is dark brown above and silvery white below. The feet are webbed and the tail is notably thickened at the base, tapering to the end. The slippery trails common near beaver ponds sometimes are thought to be the well-known "slides" used by river otters. However, such trails are worn by beavers and used by a number of other species, including muskrats and mink. *Field Recognition.* – Large size, aquatic habitat.

Distribution and Habitat. –The river otter once ranged from Alaska southward through most of Canada and the United States (except for parts of the Desert Southwest) to the northern border of México. The species has been extirpated from much of its former range.

Natural History. –To my knowledge, native river otters never have been observed in Rocky Mountain National Park, although tracks have been reported from Wild Basin. Early records of this large, aquatic mustelid are scattered throughout Colorado, on most major drainage systems. E. R. Warren – the pioneer Colorado mammalogist – speculated that the seasonally variable flow of the state's streams might explain the otter's historical rarity here.

In the 1970s, the Colorado Division of Wildlife began to reintroduce otters to the state, using stocks obtained from Louisiana, Minnesota, Wisconsin, New York, Michigan, and Arkansas. One of the sites for reintroduction was the Kawuneeche Valley, on the west side of Rocky Mountain National Park. Between 1978 and 1984, 43 otters were planted in the area. Several of those animals were fitted with radio transmitters. The otters moved an average of about 13 kilometers (range 1 to 47) to establish home ranges averaging 18 kilometers long in summer, 7 kilometers long in winter. At this time, it is not known if a reproducing population has been established.

The animals are active both day and night. They are largely restricted to aquatic and subaquatic habitats, such as streamside marshes and willow thickets. Fish provide the bulk of the diet in all seasons, occurring in all otter scats found in the Park. Fish to 38 centimeters long were taken; suckers were eaten more often than were trout. Rodents and invertebrates also are eaten.

Otters breed in spring, but the blastocysts do not implant until the following January or February, and one to four young (typically twins) are born in March or April. Females breed again while lactating. Females breed first as yearlings, most males at two or more years of age. The young are altricial, being born blind and toothless, but fully furred. The eyes open at five weeks.

Selected References.—Mack (1985); Toweill and Tabor (*in* Chapman and Feldhamer, 1982).

FAMILY FELIDAE—CATS

From an evolutionary and structural standpoint, the cat family is a very compact group, nearly all species being active carnivores which hunt by stealth. Three species of native cats occur in Colorado. All of them are known from Rocky Mountain National Park. There are some 35 species in the family, which is distributed throughout the world except for Australia and Antarctica. How many genera there are in the family is largely a matter of taxonomic taste; the range from one classification to another is from two to nearly two dozen. The uncertainty even reaches to the local fauna. Some authorities place our cats in two genera, *Felis* and *Lynx*; we follow a growing (but possibly ephemeral) consensus and treat them all in a single genus.

Mountain lion
Felis concolor

Description.—When full-grown, female mountain lions may be 2 meters in total length and weigh 35 to 60 kilograms (80 to 130 pounds), whereas males may be 2.5 meters long and weigh in excess of 90 kilograms. The tail is long, round, and slender, comprising 30 to 40 percent of the total length.

The color is variable both individually and geographically. In our area, the upper parts range from grayish to reddish brown, darkest on the ears and the tip of the tail. The belly is white. Unlike the smaller, short-tailed bobcat and lynx, the upper parts are not spotted (hence the specific name, *concolor*). The young are marked with irregular grayish to blackish spots, but the obviously long tail readily distinguishes mountain lions of any age from other local cats. *Field Recognition.*—Solid-colored back; long, rounded tail.

Distribution and Habitat.—The mountain lion—also called puma or cougar—once enjoyed the largest geographic range of any native American mammal—from northern British Columbia southward to Argentina. From large parts of their former range they have retreated in the face of civilization. Occasional individuals are reported from Rocky Mountain National Park, mostly in summer. Most lions probably follow the deer herds into the lower canyons outside the Park to winter. Mountain lions are not particularly rare in parts of southern and western Colorado, and they appear to be making a gratifying comeback in the foothills of the Eastern Slope, even in the face of an expanding human population. Most recent reports in the Park are from lower elevations, on either side of the Continental Divide. Mountain lions are most abundant in broken rimrock country with good cover of brush or woodland. Extensive stands of heavy timber are avoided, where populations of large herbivores, the preferred diet, are low in such communities. Also, open grasslands provide inadequate cover for a large predator that hunts largely by stealth. Mountain lions move through virtually any kind of habitat in search of suitable hunting grounds, and at one time they must have been present—at least occasionally—throughout the Park, although most common as residents at lower elevations.

Natural History.—In the minds of many, the mountain lion is the ultimate American predator. Smaller than the bears, less fleet than the wolf, less audacious than the coyote, it is the cougar's stealth, its majestic silence, that inspires awe. And for good reason, for the strength and grace of the mountain lion are impressive by any standard. It is little wonder that fact and fancy are so thoroughly mixed wherever the puma is concerned.

The dietary staple of Colorado pumas is venison, provided by the abundant and ubiquitous mule deer. A study in Utah and Nevada indicated that some 75 percent of the diet was provided by deer and that an adult puma required an average of one deer per week for its sustenance. Occasional elk and bighorn sheep are also taken, as are smaller mammals, including beaver and porcupines. Newly weaned kittens and very old individuals may prey on smaller animals, including rabbits, smaller rodents, and birds, and they may eat some carrion. Where domestic livestock is grazed untended in mountain lion range, some loss may be expected. (The subspecific name of our local race is *F. c. hippolestes*, derived from Greek roots meaning "horsethief.")

Mountain lions may travel 40 kilometers in a single night in search of a meal. The animals track the prey by "following their noses," although the sense of smell seems to be developed less well than among some members of the dog family. Most hunting is done at night. The basic tactic is that of a housecat on a grand scale. The lion stalks silently to within a few meters of the prey. The approach may be at ground level or from the vantage point of overhanging rocks. As the puma eyes its prey, the tip of the tail twitches from side to side. A single furious but graceful leap usually immobilizes the prey. The crushing force of the leap or a piercing bite to the nape of the neck dispatches the quarry. Cats are highly adapted to this style of predation. The jaw is hinged tightly in the skull, providing good leverage, but the mandible can be lowered to provide a very wide gape. The canine teeth grasp and puncture the prey. The cheekteeth are very sharp and the movement of the jaw is tightly limited to a single plane; hence the teeth function almost exclusively as shears.

The propulsive force for the prodigious leap comes from the hind limbs, and the shoulders are constructed to cushion the landing. The collarbone of felids is well developed as a shock-absorber. It also allows the front limbs some lateral mobility. These specializations preclude the development of a sustained, rapid gait, but the bounding rush of an adult mountain lion can overcome a fleeing deer at a distance of up to 50 meters.

The lion often moves its prey to a secluded spot before feeding. Larger prey is dragged, and smaller prey is carried in the mouth. The ability of pumas so laden to jump into trees or high onto boulders is legendary. There is a tendency to dine from a carcass and then to cover the leftovers with leaves, snow, or soil. The lion may return to take a meal from the carcass several times until it is consumed or until it begins to spoil. This is especially true of a female confined to a small area with her young. Males, on the other hand, tend to wander more widely and may eat but little from a single carcass. Overall, the economy is one of "feast or famine"—after gorging, an individual may retreat to rest in an inaccessible spot for three or four days. While eating, the animals are nervous and assertive, and there is little sharing of prey, except by a mother with her cubs. The animals lap blood eagerly and are known to subsist without free water for lengthy periods in dry areas.

Rock shelters, shallow caves, heavy thickets, and eroded banks provide suitable dens, which are not "improved" by the occupant. Perhaps because no nest is built and dens are used only a short time, cougars usually harbor a light load of external parasites. Fleas and ticks do inhabit pumas, however, as does a variety of endoparasitic worms. Other than parasites, cougars have no serious enemies other than humans. Some rabies is known. Occasional fights among mountain lions cause death, and males have been known to kill young abandoned by their mothers. Otherwise, natural mortality probably results mostly from starvation due to ineffective hunting (because of broken or age-worn teeth) or from injury inflicted by other pumas or by the antlers or hooves of intended prey.

The breeding structure is promiscuous, and males may fight for dominance and the right to mate with a particular female. The animals breed first at two to three years of age. One to six (mode about three) kittens compose a litter, born after a gestation period of 13 to 14 weeks. Births occur mostly in summer, with a peak in July, but have been reported from every month of the year. The 400-gram young is blind at birth, but the eyes open by about two weeks of age. They nurse for from four to five weeks, and then milk is replaced gradually by fresh meat. Kittens reach a weight of about 4.5 kilograms (10 pounds) in eight weeks; at six months of age, they weigh 12 to 20 kilograms, and yearlings may weigh over 24 kilograms. The pelage of juveniles is variously spotted and the tail is ringed. Kittens play together near the maternal den. Injury is fairly common during these bouts of play, and spinal damage in pumas is rather common. The young may remain with the mother for two years. If a litter of cubs is lost at birth, estrus occurs almost immediately. Otherwise, females probably breed only every other year.

Mountain lions are extremely wary of humans, and settlement would have had an adverse effect on their numbers even if there had not been deliberate attempts to control or eliminate mountain lions over much of their range. When fleeing danger, pumas head for rough, inaccessible country. Pursued, they readily take to the trees. One can hardly say that they climb trees; the first "step" is often a graceful leap of 3 to 5 meters to the lowest branch. Unprovoked attacks on humans are reported very rarely. Indeed, the fear of humans is so strong that a mother may abandon her kittens to flee. Only disturbing a feeding individual is predictably dangerous. Mountain lions do kill domestic pets such as dogs and housecats.

Selected References. – Currier (1983); Hornocker (1970); Dixon (*in* Chapman and Feldhamer, 1982); Young and Goldman (1942).

Lynx
Felis lynx

Description. — Because of the similarity of the two species, this description is made as a comparison between the lynx and the bobcat. The lynx is the decidedly larger animal — 825 to 950 mm or more in total length, to 16 kilograms (35 pounds) in weight, with longer legs, a shorter tail (100 to 125 mm long), and larger feet. In color, the lynx is paler, tending toward grayish white rather than reddish. The markings overall are less pronounced and the forelimbs lack prominent black markings. The tail has a solid black tip rather than an incomplete black ring. Furthermore, the ears have loose, black tassels, nearly as long as the ear itself, rather than a well-defined point. Habitats of the animals also differ, the lynx being a species of heavy forest, the bobcat living in woodland or shrubland on broken terrain. Bobcat and lynx often are treated as members of a distinctive genus, *Lynx. Field Recognition.* —Tail black-tipped; ears with long, open tassel; habitat heavy forest.

Distribution and Habitat. —The lynx is a circumboreal animal, ranging from Scandinavia across northern Asia and Canada and southward in the United States along the Rockies to southern Colorado, at least formerly. The present status of the species in Rocky Mountain National Park is uncertain. The lynx ranks with the wolverine as our least known carnivore. Lynx apparently once occurred here regularly if sparingly, but records are hard to authenticate. The mountain bobcat, large and pale, looks more like a lynx than does any other subspecies of bobcat. Nearly every summer, some observer — familiar with reddish bobcats elsewhere in the country — reports the local bobcat as a lynx. Careful attention to detail is essential if we are to establish the presence of the lynx in the Park.

Natural History. —Differences in habitat between the lynx and the bobcat are profound, and they go far to explain the minor differences in habits. Snowshoe hares are a dietary staple for lynx in the north and presumably would be here as well. Squirrels, mice, and birds are also eaten, as is carrion in poor years. Food caching behavior is known. The lynx is active throughout the year. Individuals have a home range of around 15 to 20 square kilometers, more or less dependent on the productivity of prey populations.

The reliance of the lynx on the snowshoe hare is widely known. Snowshoe hares are subject to wide, periodic fluctuations in numbers. The reproductive success of the lynx seems to be tied to these fluctuations. Kittens are produced each year, but only in years of peak reduction of hares do the young survive to weaning. An average litter of four young is produced in April or May after a gestation period of about two months.

Selected References. – McCord and Cardoza (*in* Chapman and Feldhamer, 1982); Tumlison (1987).

Bobcat
Felis rufus

Description. –The bobcat is the smallest of our native cats. Males range from 825 to 925 mm in total length, the stubby tail being 130 to 160 mm long. Females are smaller on the average, ranging between about 730 and 975 mm, with a tail 120 to 150 mm long. As is true in many other mammals, a full pelage gives the bobcat a deceptively large appearance. This is heightened by the presence of a "ruff" on the face. Weights range from about 5.5 to 8 kilograms (12 to 20 pounds), with exceptionally large males weighing in excess of 10 kilograms.

The color of bobcats is highly variable in our area because this is a region of contact between rather distinctive geographic races, a reddish foothills race and a paler mountain subspecies. In both forms, grayish hairs predominate, the amount of reddish-tipped hairs in the pelage being the principal variable. Strong black markings are present. The ears are pale in front, rimmed with black behind, and come to a sharp point. The end of the tail has incomplete rings of black above and a distinct white "pencil" at the very tip. The bobcat can be confused with no local species other than the lynx; for comparisons, see the account of the latter species. *Field Recognition.* –Tail with incomplete black rings; ears without obvious tassel, coming to definite point; habitat open woodland or shrubland.

Distribution and Habitat. – Bobcats range from coast to coast and from southern Canada to northern México. Permanent settlement has altered the overall range very little, although the animals do avoid human populations. Bobcats range virtually statewide in Colorado and are present in suitable habitat throughout Rocky Mountain National Park. This is an animal of "patchy" country – woodland, shrubland, and forest-edge. Unbroken forest and open parkland are traversed only to reach areas of better game or better cover.

Natural History. — Bobcats are legendary for their ferocity and perhaps rightfully so, but their secrecy is at least as noteworthy. Often the animals are fairly common in an area where they are thought to be nonexistent. Nocturnal habits and a penchant for rough country make them hard to spot. Keen eyes and ears, gracefully silent movements, and a thorough distrust of humans further the conspiracy. Occasional individuals freeze at the roadside in the beam of headlights and sometimes a rockclimber inadvertently flushes one from a daytime retreat. The best evidence of their presence is the occasional footprint, especially obvious in snow. Bobcats are active throughout the year.

Bobcats are highly evolved as predators, pound-for-pound as capable as any. The long, retractable claws are sharpened continually. The canine teeth are long and thin, rapier sharp. The cheekteeth oppose each other in a scissor-like cutting action. Single bobcats occasionally kill deer which may outweigh them by five to ten times. The staple prey under most conditions is rabbits and hares, sometimes comprising three-quarters of the diet. A rabbit is a package of food large enough to make serious hunting worthwhile. The bobcat waits motionless beside a gametrail, or stalks the unsuspecting prey, slinking on the belly, the tail twitching like a furry metronome. Then, with one or two bounds, the prey is surprised and overcome. Though rabbits are a staple, about anything beaver-sized or smaller that moves is taken occasionally — shrews, mice, woodrats, squirrels, marmots, birds (songbirds as well as ground dwellers), and even porcupines. Pocket gophers are eaten but rarely are excavated actively. Most hunting is done on the ground although bobcats climb well and swim readily. Carrion is taken when other food is scarce. A circuitous route 8 to 15 kilometers long is an evening's foraging round. Days are passed in unimproved shelter — rocky clefts, caves, windthrown trees — usually a new retreat each day. Only females with kittens have a permanent den. The usual gait is a stealthy bounding run. When pressed, they can move quickly, but they seldom rely on speed while hunting.

There is a justifiable tendency to compare the bobcat with its domesticated cousin, the housecat. They are similar in structure, function, and "spirit." Both are beautifully adapted predators, both are curious but cautious, and both are mostly aloof (one prudently, the other arrogantly) from humans. Bobcats sharpen their claws and bury their dung; they even purr. Both are furiously defensive, snarling and hissing, rolling on the back and raking the adversary's belly with the claws.

Bobcats harbor parasites, including fleas, nematodes, and tapeworms, although their transient lifestyle and their usual independence of carrion make them less prone to parasitism than are some other carnivores. Bobcats have few serious, habitual enemies other than humans. Larger carnivores can hardly afford the "expense" involved in preying actively on other carnivorous species. They are too few in number to be a dependable resource and the usual (and ecologically more sound) course is to get solar energy via the shortest route possible—from a primary consumer, a vegetarian. The best bet—and the most common situation in the wild—is for carnivores to avoid each other, even other members of the same species. Mutual avoidance eventually spaces the individuals out rather evenly over available habitat. Bobcats are solitary animals, their aloofness breaking down only during the breeding season.

Females are polyestrous and may breed any month, although most breeding occurs from January through September, with a distinct peak in March and April. With a gestation period of about 60 days, most young—altricial, weighing less than a pound—are born in May and June. Litters average three to four kittens, although the range is·one to six. The eyes open at nine days of age. At about two weeks, the kittens begin to play among themselves, an important learning activity which continues until the litter separates. The young are weaned at about two months. The father has no part in the care of the kittens (although rare exceptions have been noted). A mother with kittens is dangerous, to a person or to the kittens' father. If the litter is disturbed, the den is abandoned and the young are moved. Nursery dens may be under rocks, roots, brushpiles, or even old buildings; any hollow, in fact, that is well concealed and needs little or no excavating.

Selected References.—Makar (1980); McCord and Cardoza (*in* Chapman and Feldhamer, 1982); Van Wormer (1963); Young (1958).

Bighorn Sheep.

XI. *Order* ARTIODACTYLA
Even-toed Hoofed Mammals

THE ARTIODACTYLS INCLUDE our largest extant native mammal, the wapiti, or American elk, and are some of the most familiar and conspicuous members of our fauna. Four species are resident in the area, the bison once lived here, and the moose – introduced to Colorado – is becoming common on the west side of Rocky Mountain National Park.

Artiodactyls are members of a large – taxonomically informal – group of mammals, the "ungulates," so-called because they walk on their ungules ("nails" or hooves). Ungulates are adapted to the task of covering long distances with minimal effort. In so doing, they have sacrificed the versatility of the primitive, five-toed mammalian limb.

Our native ungulates are all ruminants, a subgroup of artiodactyls with a complex digestive system. The ruminant "stomach" is composed of four compartments, termed (in order from front to back) rumen, reticulum, omasum, and abomasum. The rumen is the largest compartment. Rumen and reticulum knead the food; bacteria in these compartments begin the breakdown of cellulose by fermentation. From the reticulum, the partially digested food – now called "cud" – is regurgitated, and the animal "chews its cud," a process more properly called rumination. Then the cud is reswallowed and passed (via a short-cut) to the omasum, where muscular walls rework the food mechanically. From there the food passes to the abomasum; there food is processed chemically by secretions of gastric glands. Close examination of the ruminant "stomach" reveals that only the abomasum has a structure comparable to the stomach of other mammals. The anterior three compartments are actually elaborate modifications of the esophagus.

A structure as complex as the ruminant "stomach" must have considerable adaptive significance. What might that be? Obviously, the apparatus serves to maximize the nutrients derived from plant material by allowing separate compartments for specialized bacterial action, but that is not the whole story. The ruminant "stomach" also allows the animal to harvest large amounts of forage rapidly. Then the individual retreats to the safety of cover (or the safety of its herd), regurgitates the meal a little at a time, and processes the material properly at a leisurely pace. The ruminant digestive apparatus is probably a major key to the evolutionary success of the artiodactyls. Overall, the order includes 185 living species, arranged in 79 genera representing nine families. The five families of ruminants include 90 percent of the species.

FAMILY CERVIDAE — DEER

Deer occur throughout the northern continents and in South America, but they are absent from Australia and sub-Saharan Africa. (In Australia, wallabies fill the deer's role and in Africa, antelope and other bovids do the same.) There are about 35 Recent species of deer, four of which occur (or have occurred) in Rocky Mountain National Park.

Wapiti, or American Elk
Cervus elaphus

Description. —The wapiti, or American elk, is second in size only to the moose among members of the deer family. Bulls stand 1.5 meters (5 feet) tall at the shoulder and weigh 340 kilograms (750 pounds) or more; mature cows are smaller, weighing about 225 kilograms (500 pounds). In fresh fall pelage, the rump-patch and tail are yellowish tan and the sides are gray-brown. In striking contrast, the head and neck are blackish brown. Females usually show less contrasting coloration than do bulls. The pelage bleaches and wears through the winter and is replaced in spring by a shorter, more reddish summer coat. *Field Recog-*

nition. —Large size; dark colored head and paler body; tail narrow and without black tip.

Distribution and Habitat. —Once the wapiti ranged across North America from the eastern seaboard to the West Coast, and from northern British Columbia, central Ontario, and New York southward to New Mexico, Texas, Louisiana, and Georgia. This is a holarctic species, known as "red deer" in Eurasia. Except for small, reintroduced populations, the wapiti now is restricted to the western part of the continent where, subject to careful management, the animals are assured a secure future, as long as their habitat is not degraded further.

In Rocky Mountain National Park, the wapiti lives in forest-edge situations with lush herbage, where they feed in openings, staying near enough to the trees to retreat to cover if necessary. Alpine tundra is grazed in summer, but krummholz and subalpine parks are more common habitat. Large open parks at moderate elevations (Horseshoe, Moraine, Hollowell) provide winter range. There are distinct seasonal migrations.

Natural History. —The wapiti is less elusive and more abundant than the bighorn sheep, but certainly is second to none of our fauna in its thoroughly regal mien. "Wapiti" is of Amerindian derivation. Unfortunately, it is mostly a "textbook name," rare in popular usage. The result is some minor international confusion. In Eurasia, the name "elk" is applied to the animal we call "moose" (*Alces alces*), and the "wapiti" of the Old World are called "red deer."

Wapiti have not always been abundant in the Park. According to the memoirs of Milton Estes, when permanent settlers established themselves in Estes Park in 1860, "great bands of elk . . . were everywhere." But in the half century that followed, the wapiti was nearly extirpated by market-hunting (to which this large, gregarious species was especially susceptible) and by competition with domestic livestock for winter range. Strict protection and reintroduction (from the Yellowstone area of northwestern Wyoming) reestablished the herds. Acquisition of Beaver Meadows and Horseshoe and Moraine parks provided some winter range within Rocky Mountain National Park. Now population control is a chronic problem. Recent estimates of the winter resident wapiti population range around 1700 individuals.

Unlike mule and white-tailed deer, the American elk is mostly a grazer, feeding on grasses and forbs rather than shrubs. A study on Specimen Mountain indicated that grasses provided 85 percent of the diet. Diet changes with the season, the principal forage at any given time being the fastest growing, most succulent (and often the most nutritious) species. Some browse is taken, especialy in winter when shrubs may comprise 90 percent of the diet for short periods. Bark and twigs of aspen are eaten commonly. Evidence of this habit is widespread in the Park; look for stunted saplings and for long, deep "claw marks" on the bark of mature aspen, two meters or more above ground. These marks are not made by bears but by the teeth of the wapiti.

The animals feed mostly just after dawn and near dusk, with intervals of grazing and resting occupying the daylight hours. At night, they retire to the cover of forest. The same trails are used continually, becoming quite worn. The bed-ground is used repeatedly, but a given individual seems not to lie in the same spot on successive nights.

The wapiti is a gregarious animal. Herding behavior is strong evidence that the animals' present-day predilection for forested country is something of an innovation. Herding is a defensive strategy typical of mammals of open country—recall the herds of bison on the prairie, muskoxen or caribou on the tundra, or dolphins in the oceans. Forest species tend to live alone or in small bands. Winter herds of elk are large, including 50 to several hundred individuals of both genders. Winter herds disband as bulls move first to summer range, following the retreating snowline and the advance of green herbage. Cows and calves follow bulls to summer range, and the great herds of winter break up into smaller bands. Copious forage allows more leisurely feeding than in winter, but summer heat and insects seem to cause more discomfort than does the cold of winter, impelling the animals to wallow in mudholes or snowbanks.

The wapiti is alert, with keen senses. They are not usually fast-moving, the typical gait being a walk. When startled, however, they will run, covering ground rapidly with long, graceful strides. Obstacles are hurdled deer-like, with an agility and ease surprising for an animal of such size.

The antlers of a mature bull may weigh 12 kilograms (25 pounds) or more, with a total spread of nearly 1.5 meters. Antlers are made of bone. They are shed (or "cast") in late winter, and replacement begins within two weeks. By early August the antlers are nearly full-grown and covered with "velvet"—tender skin overlying abundant blood vessels. When growth is complete, the mineral-rich blood supply is curtailed and the velvet is shed, usually by vigorous rubbing against trees. This rubbing colors the antlers with pigments from the bark.

Cast antlers are found surprisingly seldom. For other members of the fauna—especially the rodents—the concentrated mineral resource of a cast antler is a real windfall. An old antler is recycled quickly, as gnawing mice and other animals funnel the minerals back into the resource web of the mountain ecosystem.

One cannot age all bulls directly by their antlers, but rough estimates are possible. There is no antler development during the calf's first autumn. The second autumn, "spikes" are present. The third year, three-to five-point antlers are typical. The fourth season and thereafter, a six-point rack is typical, the base generally becoming more massive each year. Damage to the base of the antler may cause aberrant growth in subsequent years. Bulls past their prime may show more than six points, but often they are poorly formed or asymmetric. Antlers of bulls on inadequate range are stunted.

In autumn, profound changes occur among the wapiti. The crisp air of late September carries the bugling of the bulls. The rut is beginning. Bugling actually starts well before the actual mating. Although commonly described as a "challenge" or a "threat," bugling is apparently not quite either of those. In part, at least, bugling is a sort of "safety valve" that releases the tension of the bull's seasonal physiological changes. With the rut, shoulders and neck swell. Antlers are sharpened. Bugling peaks in early October and the most aggressive bulls assert authority over bands of five to 15 cows. Another bull may challenge that authority. Sparring with the massive antlers follows. This activity is more akin to "arm-wrestling" than full-blown combat, but the bouts can result in broken antlers and occasionally males are gored, even fatally. Usually, however, ritual sparring does the trick and the vanquished bull retires to temporary bachelorhood.

Gestation takes about 250 days, and a single calf, weighing about 15 kilograms (30 pounds), is born in June. No special calving ground is used; calves are dropped in snow-free, forested areas around the open parks that constitute the winter range, or they arrive while their mothers are migrating, even as high as alpine tundra. The calf is reddish buff, marked with pale buffy spots. With an odor seemingly detectable only by the mother, the calf remains motionless and is left alone as the cow forages. Like those of other ungulates, the young are mobile—if haltingly so – within hours of birth. The calf develops quickly and usually is weaned by late summer. At six months of age, it may weigh 120 kilograms (250 pounds). Cows are reproductively mature their second autumn, and usually calve first at three years of age. Because of the social structure, bulls do not generally manage to acquire a harem and breed until their fourth or fifth year.

As the largest member of our extant fauna, the wapiti is subject to few enemies. At one time the gray wolf preyed on them and mountain lions still take a few. A pack of coyotes can kill a weakened elk or one immobilized on glaze ice, and coyotes – like bobcats and bears – may kill calves when they happen upon them, but they will not tangle with cows over them. Like other ungulates, the elk harbors parasites, including flukes, tapeworms and roundworms, lice, botflies, and mites, the latter being the contagion of scabies. On good range, a cow may live 15 years or more; males have a somewhat shorter life expectancy.

Selected References. – Harrington (1978); Murie (1951); Peek (*in* Chapman and Feldhamer, 1982); Van Wormer (1969).

Mule Deer
Odocoileus hemionus

Description. – The mule deer stands about a meter high at the shoulder. Bucks weigh to 120 kilograms (250 pounds) or more, does usually 45 to 70 kilograms (100 to 150 pounds). Overall, then, the mule deer is hardly half the size of the wapiti. In color, mule deer are reddish tan in summer, tending to grayish brown in winter. The ears are disproportionately large and the tail is narrow, its bushy black tip contrasting with the white rump patch.

The mule deer differs from the white-tailed deer in its narrow, black-tipped (rather than broad, white, and "flag-like") tail, its conspicuously large ears, and its dichotomous antlers, which branch into equal, Y-shaped parts rather than sprouting several tines off a single main stem.

Field Recognition. – Dichotomous antlers; moderate size; disproportionately large ears; head and neck colored much like body.

Distribution and Habitat. – The mule deer is a western species, ranging from the Great Plains to the Pacific Coast, and from the Canadian territories southward to Baja California, Durango, and Veracruz, México. Mule deer are most abundant in brushy situations, about the margins of meadows, in canyons, and in streamside woodlands. Any opening that supports shrubs will be occupied. Successional shrublands on burned-over areas provide good habitat. Some individuals, especially bucks, summer at or above timberline, especially favoring willow thickets. In short, expect to find mule deer throughout the Park except in the heaviest forest or the most open country.

Natural History.—The mule deer is a large mammal that all but the most hurried visitor may expect to see. Today they are abundant throughout the Southern Rockies. In common with our other ungulates, however, this has not always been true. As plentiful as they are today, it is hard to imagine the situation described by Merritt Cary in his *Biological Survey of Colorado:* ". . . a few mule deer [were reported] in the Estes Park region in 1895, but I heard of none in the foothills of Boulder and Larimer Counties in 1906." This is in dramatic contrast to Milton Estes' description of the situation in 1860, when "deer were everywhere." Today, they are "everywhere" again. Over their range, mule deer have proved remarkably resilient when the pressure of unregulated hunting has been curtailed. Unlike many other ungulates, deer thrive in close proximity to humans, and being browsers, they compete very little with domestic livestock.

The diet consists of shrubbery and herbage. A study conducted on Specimen Mountain indicated that shrubs contributed 73 percent of the diet and broadleafed herbs about 26 percent. Therefore, on good range there is little or no competition with elk or bighorn sheep, both of which are grazers, or, outside the National Park, with domestic livestock. Food preference shifts with the season, emphasizing species that are growing most actively and thus are most succulent. Actively growing tissues also are the most nutritious, so selectivity goes beyond mere taste. Conifers are browsed on poor range, especially in winter, when competition with elk may become severe. Mule deer feed mostly at night, seemingly oblivious to weather, and retire to heavy cover to spend the day.

Seasonal migrations occur between summer and winter ranges, but this is somewhat less marked than in the wapiti (perhaps because the animals move in smaller groups). Snow seems to drive the animals down for the winter, and snow's retreat draws them back to summer range. Bucks often summer at or above timberline, whereas does and fawns occupy subalpine, forest-edge situations. In autumn, about October, they move down, many wintering outside the National Park in the foothills of the Front Range or around Middle Park on the Western Slope.

Mule deer have acute senses of smell and hearing; they see moving objects at great distances, but may be oblivious to a motionless observer at close range. When startled, the deer moves with a mechanical, spring-like, bounding gait that is gracefully effortless almost beyond belief. Under more secure circumstances, they move with a stately, high-stepping walk.

Bucks shed the antlers in December or January and renew them annually. Young-of-the-year do not produce antlers; the second fall, a light, two-point set is typical. The third fall—when the buck is just over two years old—weak, three- or four-point antlers are produced. Older bucks usually have four principal points on either side, and the rack becomes progressively heavier each year. In old age (beyond ten years), or when injured, asymmetric antlers form. Most mature racks have a spread of 60 to 90 cm (about 2 to 3 feet). Occasional "antlered does" are reported; these are hormonal "freaks."

Deer are important primary consumers in local ecosystems. A strong deer population can support good populations of the larger carnivores. The browsing strategy taps a rich food resource and the deer converts its dietary intake into a package of animal protein of convenient size for a larger predator. Hunting rabbits or marmots is a poor investment for a mountain lion. In an energetic sense, deer are "purveyors of vegetation to his majesty, the cougar." Coyotes and bobcats also prey on them, especially young, weak, or snow-bound animals, and wolves once took them as well. Bears kill a few fawns each year, probably just stumbling upon them rather than actively hunting them down. Traffic takes a heavy toll of deer. Maximum longevity is about 20 years.

Deer molt in mid-September, and about that same time the antlers of the bucks mature. In November, the rut begins. With neck and shoulders swollen, mature bucks joust furiously for mating rights, a behavior like that of the wapiti, but without the bugling or securing a "harem." Mating is completed by late December. The bucks, their seasonal belligerence exhausted, may band together loosely, or they may spend the winter in seclusion. Does and young form winter herds separate from the bucks.

Gestation takes about 200 days, and the 4.5 kilogram (10 pound) young are born from June to early July. After the first pregnancy—usually as a two-year-old—does typically produce twins, achieving an average litter size of about 1.6. In common with other kinds of deer, fawns are spotted and without obvious odor. Twin siblings usually are hidden separately, the mother approaching them only to nurse. Within a few weeks, fawns are strong enough to follow their mother. They are weaned in autumn at about 22.5 kilograms (50 pounds).

Selected References. – Anderson and Wallmo (1984); Harrington (1978); Loveless (1967); Wallmo (1981).

White-tailed Deer
Odocoileus virginianus

Description. –The white-tailed deer is a handsome animal, reddish to grayish brown in general color, with a white muzzle and eye ring, and a white rump patch. The animals carry the broad, flag-like tail erect while running. Bucks are larger than does; mature males average about 2 meters in total length, with a tail 300 mm long, and they weigh about 200 kilograms. Does are about 1.7 meters long and weigh about 100 kilograms. The only species with which the white-tailed deer might be confused is the mule deer; for comparison, see the account of that species. *Field Recognition.* –White-edged, flag-like tail.

Distribution and Habitat. –The white-tailed deer is a very widespread animal, ranging from central Canada, throughout most of the United States (except the Great Basin, the Colorado Plateau, and much of the Pacific Coast), as far south in South America as Peru and Bolivia. The animals have arrived in Rocky Mountain National Park only recently. Around the turn of the century, Merritt Cary reported the species from the foothills of the Big Thompson drainage, and from the Laramie River drainage, north of the National Park. From then until the 1950s, white-tailed deer were rare or even absent from Colorado. Then increasingly frequent reports of the species began to be received from the bottom-lands of the eastern plains. In the 1970s, white-tailed deer became increasingly abundant along the foothills of the Front Range. The first records of the species from Rocky Mountain National Park were in 1984. They now have been reported from both sides of the Continental Divide, but they are not at all common.

White-tailed deer are animals of forest-edge situations. In eastern Colorado they appear to occur mostly in riparian communities. Habitat relationships with mule deer have not been studied. Seasonal movements are to be expected, but have yet to be investigated in Colorado.

Natural History. –White-tailed deer are mostly crepuscular, being active at dawn and dusk. Like the mule deer, this is a browser, feeding mostly on woody vegetation. One would predict competition with the mule deer for food or cover, but this has yet to be investigated in Colorado. A large deer needs 2 to 3 kilograms (about 10,000 gross kilocalories) of forage per day. Food items are selected on the basis of nutritive value rather than species; hence, diet changes with the season and the growth stage of particular plants.

The rut occurs in October and November, with the promiscuous males following does in estrus. Normally, all mature females are bred. One to three fawns are born in late May or June after a gestation period of about 200 days. The fawns grow quickly, doubling their 2.5-kilogram birth weight by two weeks, and doubling it again by five weeks. The spotted fawns molt to adult pelage at three months. Thereafter there are two molts annually. Does usually breed first as yearlings, after their second summer, and yearling males participate in the rut. Antlers begin to grow in April, are completed by August, the "velvet" is shed by September, and the antlers are cast in February.

The basic social unit is a doe with fawns of two ages. Adult bucks tend to be solitary or to form bachelor herds. In the mating season, females may become more solitary, driving off the young. After the rut, fairly large herds may form, sometimes including both adult does and bucks. Even within these herds, most interaction is between the doe and her offspring.

Predators include coyotes, bobcats, and humans (in terms of harvest and number of hunters, this is the most important big game animal in North America). Where white-tailed deer are abundant, many are killed by vehicles. Natural maximum longevity is about 10 years.

Selected References. — Hesselton and Hesselton (*in* Chapman and Feldhamer, 1982); Jones *et al.* (1983).

Moose
Alces alces

The moose is a circumboreal species. It is not a native resident of Colorado, but occasional individuals have wandered in on their own over the past century, perhaps from northwestern Wyoming. Moose are wide-ranging animals and sometimes they herd with wapiti or even domestic cattle. In the early 1850s, Milton Estes shot a moose in the park that bears his name. Other early Coloradan moose records are from the vicinity of Steamboat Springs and from southwest of Meeker.

In 1978, the Colorado Division of Wildlife introduced moose to North Park, northwest of Rocky Mountain National Park. These animals now inhabit the National Park, especially at lower elevations on the west side of the Park, above the Grand Lake entrance. However, they also have been observed on the eastern side of the Divide at Boulder-Grand Pass, at Jim's Grove on Longs Peak, at Tundra Curves on Trail Ridge Road, and near Milner Pass. The most suitable habitat for the moose locally is the wet willow communities of the Kawuneeche Valley, the headwaters of the Colorado River.

Selected References.—Coady (*in* Chapman and Feldhamer, 1982); Franz-mann (1981).

FAMILY ANTILOCAPRIDAE—PRONGHORN

The pronghorn is the sole survivor of an endemic American family (often ranked as a subfamily of the Bovidae). Antilocaprids had a greater diversity in the geologic past than they do today, with perhaps a dozen genera, all but one of which became extinct before the end of the Pleistocene Epoch.

Pronghorn
Antilocapra americana

The pronghorn no longer occurs in Rocky Mountain National Park, and its early status in the area is poorly known. North Park remains a stronghold of these fleet and beautiful animals, and Middle Park once was prime pronghorn range. Milton Estes, in his memoirs of the early 1860s, mentioned the pronghorn among game species hunted about Estes Park for sale in Denver markets.

Selected References.—Kitchen and O'Gara (*in* Chapman and Feldhamer, 1982); O'Gara (1978).

FAMILY BOVIDAE—CATTLE, SHEEP, GOATS, AND ALLIES

The Bovidae includes the majority of living artiodactyls, the greatest diversity being among the antelope of the Old World. The family is native worldwide except for South America and Australia, and several domestic species are cosmopolitan. Colorado has two native bovids; the bighorn sheep persists in Rocky Mountain National Park and the bison once occurred here.

Mountain Sheep, or Bighorn Sheep
Ovis canadensis

Description. – Mountain sheep vary widely in color over their range. In our area, adults are a rich brown above in fresh spring pelage, and then pale gradually through the season to grayish brown or almost white. The prominent rump patch is white and continues uninterrupted down the hind legs. The backs of the forelegs are also white. Both sexes have horns. Those of the ewes are spike-like. The massive, spiralling horns of the ram taper gradually. Unlike the antlers of the deer family, horns are not shed, but grow continually from the base, laying down "annual rings" which permit the approximate aging of individuals. A ram with a three-quarter curl is about 10 years old.

Mature males stand a meter (about 40 inches) high at the shoulder and weigh about 180 kilograms (400 pounds). Ewes are about 88 cm (35 inches) high and weigh less than half as much as rams, usually less than 70 kilograms (about 150 pounds). *Field Recognition.* – Both sexes with horns; white rump and legs.

Distribution and Habitat. – Within historic times, the bighorn sheep ranged in western North America from central British Columbia southward to Baja California, and from the Sierra Nevada eastward to the badlands and pine-clad escarpments of the Dakotas and Nebraska. Existing populations are scattered within those historical limits, restricted by human encroachment to the more remote parts of the West.

Over its wide range, the bighorn lives in a wide variety of habitats, from desert valleys (such as Death Valley), canyons, and arid mountain ranges to alpine tundra in the Rockies. The animals generally prefer open situations. In Colorado, they now occur at higher elevations – usually avoiding forested country – but once they migrated in winter to lower elevations, even to the edge of the Great Plains. Once present throughout Rocky Mountain National Park, bighorns now occur chiefly in the Never-Summer Range, the Mummy Range, and along the Continental Divide north of Flattop Mountain. In 1977, 20 bighorns were moved to the Cow Creek drainage from the Tarryall Range near Pikes Peak. This population now undergoes a seasonal migration, wintering on MacGregor Mountain, in Black Canyon, and along Cow Creek, and moving to summer range on Mummy Mountain above Lawn Lake. Visitors frequently see these sheep along the Fall River Road east of the Park entrance.

Natural History. – Bighorn sheep have come rightfully to be the animal symbol of the Rocky Mountain National Park, and they have been selected as the official state mammal of Colorado. Bighorns are impressive mammals indeed. In their rugged native haunts they portray a wild grandeur sufficient to match their majestic home. But despite their majesty as silhouettes against the alpine skyland, the bighorns' erratic behavior permits occasional moments of amusingly informal abandon. The scrambling play of lambs among the rocks and the headlong running of their startled elders down the most precipitous slopes hardly suggest a thorough composure.

Except during the breeding season – which extends from November to January with a peak in December – the daily round of activity consists of alternate periods of feeding and rest (and rumination). At midday the entire band usually stops grazing for siesta. As is true of other mammals of open country, bighorns have keen eyesight and detect the slightest movement at great distances. No one individual serves as sentinel; all are alert for danger, real or imagined.

Bighorn bands are variable in size and composition, ranging from a few individuals to several dozen. Rams band together in summer and forage at higher elevations than do ewes and lambs. Bighorns are mostly grazers, the bulk of the diet, under good range conditions, being grasses and sedges. In a study of food habits of bighorn sheep, elk, and mule deer on Specimen Mountain, grasses provided 88 percent of the diet of bighorns and forbs 12 percent. Browsing was minimal. As a result there was little dietary overlap with mule deer, which emphasized browse. The bighorns' predilection for ridgeline tundra meadows takes them out of potential competition with elk, which tend to graze in krummholz stands and subalpine parks and meadows. Sheep may ingest mud for its salt content, as at Sheep Lakes in Horseshoe Park or on Specimen Mountain. At dusk the animals retire for the night to a bedding ground in a rocky area. Often the same ground is used continually for long periods, and especially favored sites may be used year after year.

During the breeding season, the usually disorderly and nervous behavior of bighorns gives way to utter chaos. Usually a single ewe comes into estrus at a time. She is singled out by mature rams for attention. As the ram approaches, the ewe runs off for a few meters and then stops. The ram follows, but if another ram joins the chase, the budding romance gives way to duelling. Fighting consists mostly of head-on butting, the massive horns absorbing most of the shock. No holds are barred, however, and kicking the flanks and butting about the shoulders are not uncommon. The victor earns the right to mate. But at times a third ram will mate with the ewe while she watches the principals in their pugilistic ritual. Under these promiscuous conditions, virtually all ewes are bred. Females breed first their third year; males mature their fourth, but typically do not actually manage to breed until seven or eight years old.

The gestation period is about 174 days, and lambing peaks at the beginning of June. Lambing grounds typically are in remote places with precipitous slopes, providing the precocial young with maximal protection. Single births are the general rule, although twinning has been recorded. Lambs play near the ewes. Milk is supplemented by occasional herbage as early as two weeks after birth and the young are weaned in mid- to late autumn.

Before settlement, bighorns made rather lengthy seasonal migrations, wintering in the foothills and along the western margin of the plains. In some parts of Colorado they still winter mostly on south-facing slopes at moderate elevations and follow the retreating snowline to summer range in the alpine tundra, rams preceding ewes and young. In the vicinity of Rocky Mountain National Park, however, civilization interrupted the migrations of the typically wary sheep. Until the 1977 reintroduction, most sheep remained above timberline throughout the year, grazing in winter on tundra blown free of snow.

Prior to permanent settlement, bighorn sheep were abundant in what is now Rocky Mountain National Park. By 1900, however, they had been virtually eliminated by market and trophy hunters, by habitat disturbance (especially by competition with domestic livestock for winter range), and by introduced sheep diseases, such as scabies. With the establishment of the National Park the population began to recover, partly because of an actual recovery of the local population and partly because sheep from surrounding areas concentrated in the newly established wildlife sanctuary. In the 1920s, a new decline began, owing to concentration of the animals year around on what had been summer range. Apparently crowding led to mineral and protein deficiencies and an increase in lungworm and other endoparasitic diseases. The addition of Horseshoe Park to the National Park provided mineral-rich winter range, although sheep sporadically return to the alpine. Horseshoe Park is a place where many visitors observe bighorns.

Coyote predation on lambs and wolves certainly took a toll formerly. The mountain lion preys on bighorns, but probably is not sufficiently abundant to cause appreciable mortality on a long-term basis. Despite their broad hooves and remarkable agility, accidents—including avalanches—claim sheep from time to time. Most mortality today is from disease, especially lungworm and associated pneumonia. Poor nutrition on inadequate range weakens the bands and increases their susceptibility to infection. Other parasites weaken the animals further. Persistent crowding of bands by visitors can cause stress in bighorns, which may predispose them to death from otherwise sublethal disease. Maximum longevity in the wild is 15 to 20 years.

Selected References.—Geist (1971); Lawson and Johnson (*in* Chapman and Feldhamer, 1982); Goodson (1978); Harrington (1978); Moser (1962); Packard (1946); Shakleton (1985); Stevens and Hanson (1986).

Bison
Bison bison

The last native bison in Colorado were killed in the Lost Park area (in Park County, southeast of Jefferson) in 1897. The last known native bison in eastern Colorado was killed near Springfield in 1889, and the last remnant in northwestern Colorado was killed at Cedar Springs (west of Craig) in 1884. Today, bison occur in the state only in semi-domestication.

The history of the bison in Rocky Mountain National Park is rather poorly known. Certainly these magnificent animals were not abundant in the area by the time literate settlers arrived to report on the native fauna. Milton Estes made no mention of the bison or its remains in his memoirs. Abner Sprague came to the area in 1868, eight years after Estes arrived. He noted bison remains near the north end of Estes Park, while enroute to the North Fork of the Big Thompson River near the present site of Glen Haven. In about 1878, Sprague found a bison skull on Hague's Peak, above 3550 meters (12,000 feet). About the same time, he found the nearly fresh carcass of a bison at the south end of North Peak.

Other early localities of bison remains include: Horseshoe Park, east of Mary's Lake, McCreery Gulch (south of Gem Lake), Moraine Park, Dunraven Meadows, Lost Lake (near the headwaters of the North Fork of the Big Thompson), Tuxedo Park, and Grand Lake. Thatchtop

188

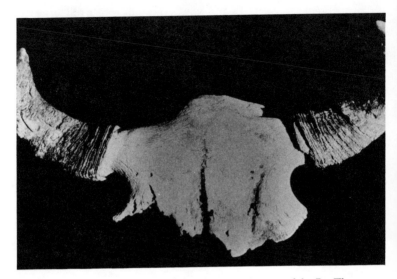

Remains of a bison skull discovered near the headwaters of the Big Thompson River in 1981. *National Park Service*

Mountain was known to the Arapahoes as "the Buffalo Climb," and Buffalo Pass—to the north of the National Park—was so-named by Indians. Long Gulch (near Mount Olympus) was used by the Arapahoe as a buffalo trap. In 1981 two skulls and other remains of bison melted out of the snowfield below Icefield Pass, on the headwaters of the Big Thompson River at an elevation of 11,600 feet.

Obviously, the bison was once important in the mountain ecosystems of our region. Apparently the animals were migratory. The Arapahoe found them to be a rather undependable resource in the area. Occasional individuals or bands ranged above timberline and greater concentrations lived at intervals on open parklands. The bison is a rightful member of the native fauna. However, the present-day National Park has too little range to support the animals as anything but captives and is far too small to accommodate the animals' migratory tendencies.

Selected References. —Fryxell (1928); Reynolds, Glaholt, and Hawley (*in* Chapman and Feldhamer, 1982).

Ringtail.

XII. SPECIES OF POSSIBLE OCCURRENCE

THE FAUNA OF any area is a dynamic assemblage of species. Some species undergo seasonal migrations. Others disappear from the fauna from time to time to enter hibernation or dormancy. Geographical ranges change on time scales of years or millenia, as climatic change leads to change in the resource base. Superimposed on these natural patterns are changes in response to human involvement – deliberate or not – in native ecosystems.

Because of this dynamism, and because some species are just difficult to observe, it is nearly impossible to list and describe accurately an entire fauna for a particular area. Of the 65 species described in this book, about 50 have been documented in Rocky Mountain National Park or Arapaho National Recreation Area by museum specimens and/or confirmed observations of animals or their certain sign. Of that number, at least five species (gray wolf, grizzly bear, river otter, pronghorn, bison, and perhaps the wolverine) have been extirpated within historic time. (The river otter now is being restored on the west side of the Park.) The moose was of occasional natural occurrence over the last century in northern Colorado; resident populations of the animals have been introduced in North Park in recent years by the Colorado Division of

Wildlife, and moose may now be considered residents of Rocky Mountain National Park. Mountain goats (*Oreamnos americana*) have been introduced to Colorado by the Division of Wildlife, beginning in the 1940s. It is conceivable that they will one day wander into the Park from the south. The introductions nearest to Rocky Mountain National Park have been in the Gore Range and on Mount Evans. According to David R. Stevens, Park Biologist, mountain goats will not be allowed to become established in the Park.

In addition to the species of documented occurrence in Rocky Mountain National Park, the presence of the following ten species is so highly probable that I have included accounts of them in text with little explanatory comment: dwarf shrew, small-footed myotis, big brown bat, silver-haired bat, hoary bat, Townsend's big-eared bat, Colorado chipmunk, rock squirrel, Mexican woodrat, and gray fox. Each of these species is known from Larimer, Boulder, and/or Grand counties from habitats that are abundant in Rocky Mountain National Park or Arapaho National Recreation Area.

Furthermore, five additional species are of possible occurrence, either at present, in the near future, or in the recent past. These species are included in the keys (Appendix I) and brief accounts of them appear below. The difference between species of probable occurrence and those of possible occurrence obviously is a matter of degree, and in the last analysis the treatment here of a particular species was a subjective judgment.

Merriam's Shrew (*Sorex merriami*). — Merriam's shrew is of moderate size, larger than the dwarf shrew and considerably smaller than the water shrew. They are paler in color than other shrews in our area, grayish drab above grading to paler grayish on the flanks and becoming white below. The animals occur in western United States, from western Nebraska and the Dakotas to California, and from Washington and Montana southward to Arizona and New Mexico. In Colorado, records are scattered at moderate elevations both east and west of the Continental Divide. The animals have not yet been documented in Rocky Mountain National Park, but judging from what is known of the ecological distribution of the species, one would strongly suspect that it will eventually be found, either at lower elevations in the vicinity of Estes Park or in Arapaho National Recreation Area. Nearest records of occurrence are in the foothills near Fort Collins and Boulder. Preferred habitat includes sagebrush, coniferous woodland, and grasslands. The altitudinal range of the species in Colorado is about 1500 to 2850 meters (5000 to 9500 feet). For further information on this species, see Armstrong and Jones (1972).

Fringed Myotis (*Myotis thysanodes*).—The fringed myotis is so-called because of a conspicuous fringe of stiff hairs along the trailing edge of the interfemoral membrane. It is a species of western North America, from British Columbia to Chiapas, México. The local distribution of the animals along the eastern margin of their range in Colorado, Wyoming, and western South Dakota is poorly documented. Because the fringed myotis often has been found in open ponderosa pine woodland, it may be expected along the eastern boundary of the National Park. The closest record of occurrence is from near Fort Collins. O'Farrell and Studier (1980) provided a summary of information on this species.

Sagebrush Vole (*Lagurus curtatus*).—This small, short-tailed vole occurs under cover of sagebrush stands, especially when there is a grassy understory. It is a runway builder. It frequently has been found in association with Merriam's shrew. Sagebrush voles occur north of Fort Collins, in the Laramie River Valley, and in North and Middle parks, and thence northwestward to Washington State. The locality of record nearest the National Park is at Hot Sulphur Springs, in Grand County. The animals may possibly be present in drier situations in Arapaho National Recreation Area. Carroll and Genoways (1980) summarized our knowledge of the biology of this species.

Ringtail (*Bassariscus astutus*).—The ringtail—sometimes inappropriately called "ringtailed cat" or "civet cat"—is a distinctive animal. About the size of a housecat, it almost looks like an artist's composite, with the head of a fox, the lithe body of a squirrel, and a long, showy tail a step beyond the raccoon's. The ringtail occurs from Colorado, extreme southwestern Wyoming, and Oregon southward to Oaxaca, México. In Colorado, the animals are present on both sides of the Continental Divide, but are more common on the Western Slope. In 1954, a ringtail was reported from Grand County, south of Hot Sulphur Springs, signalling its possible occurrence in Arapaho Recreation Area, and more recently there have been intriguing reports of the animals from the foothills of Boulder County, southeast of the National Park. Ringtails inhabit rough, broken country with shrubby vegetation. The animals eat rodents, insects, berries, and some carrion. They are strictly nocturnal and are so secretive that they often are fairly abundant in areas where they remain unnoticed. Armstrong (1982) reviewed some literature on this species.

Black-footed Ferret (*Mustela nigripes*).—This is doubtless the rarest mammal in North America. It surely does not occur at present in Rocky Mountain National Park or immediately adjacent areas. However, it may once have occurred in what is now Arapaho National Recreation Area. This speculation is based on the fact that there is in the Denver Museum of Natural History a specimen of the black-footed ferret taken in Middle Park in 1888. Sagebrush habitat suitable for ferrets is present now (and was then) around Granby and Grand Lake. However, white-tailed prairie dogs, the principal food of black-footed ferrets in the general vicinity, were not reported from Middle Park by the early naturalists (e.g., Cary, 1911). Hence, the ferret population that once apparently lived there may not have been particularly prosperous. Hillman and Clark (1980) reviewed the literature on the black-footed ferret.

APPENDIX I: KEY TO MAMMALS OF ROCKY MOUNTAIN NATIONAL PARK AND VICINITY

This is a "dichotomous key," so-called because it is based on pairs of choices. Pairs of alternatives are called "couplets." From each couplet, select the alternative description best applicable to the mammal in question. The alternative will lead either to another couplet or to the name of a species or group of species. An attempt has been made to use both external and cranial characters. This allows the user to identify whole animals observed in the field as well as odd skulls that might be picked up.

Here is a prudent rule of thumb: *never trust a key.* Any key may use some characters that are difficult to observe or involve some subjective judgment. Follow the key through to reach a preliminary best guess at the identity of an organism. Then refer to accounts of species to make certain that the description fits the mammal in question. Illustrations and characteristics of habitat may also be important at this point.

KEY TO ORDERS OF MAMMALS

1. Forelimbs modified for flight ....BATS, KEY B.
   Forelimbs not modified for flight.........................2.
2. Stance bipedal; body mostly hairless; tail absent; snout reduced; eyes directed forward; thumb apposable; digits with nails; cerebral cortex greatly enlarged; metabolic energy augmented with fossil fuels; communication between non-overlapping generations cultural as well as genetic .....PRIMATES–Humans–*Homo sapiens*, p. 73. Stance quadrupedal; body well-haired; tail present; snout prominent; eyes directed more or less laterally; thumb (if present) not apposable; digits with claws or hooves; cerebral cortex not markedly developed; metabolic energy not augmented with fossil fuels; communication between non-overlapping generations only genetic ....3.

3. Upper incisors absent; males, at least, with horns or antlers
.... ARTIODACTYLS, KEY F.
   Upper incisors present; without horns or antlers ....4.
4. Canine teeth present; no pronounced gap (diastema) present between incisors and cheekteeth ....5.
   Canine teeth absent; pronounced gap (diastema) present between
   incisors and cheekteeth ....6.
5. Canine teeth not markedly longer than adjacent teeth ....
   ................................INSECTIVORES, KEY A.
   Canine teeth markedly longer than adjacent teeth ....
                                      CARNIVORES, KEY E.
6. Incisors 2/1; tail shorter than hind foot .....LAGOMORPHS,
                                                        KEY C.
   Incisors 1/1; tail longer than hind foot ...RODENTS, KEY D.

KEY A – INSECTIVORES

1. Total length greater than 150 mm; greatest length of skull, 20 mm
   or more; hindfoot with conspicuous fringe of stiff hairs; color grayish
   black ....Water Shrew (*Sorex palustris*), p. 52.
   Total length less than 120 mm; greatest length of skull, 18 mm or
   less; hindfoot without conspicuous fringe of stiff hairs; dorsal color
   variously brownish, never black ....2.
2. Only three unicuspid teeth conspicuous in lateral view; dorsal color
   dark brown ....Pygmy Shrew (*Sorex hoyi*), p. 47.
   Four or five unicuspid teeth conspicuous in lateral view; dorsal color
   medium brown to pale brown ....3.
3. Third unicuspid tooth obviously smaller than fourth ....4.
   Third and fourth unicuspid teeth of approximately equal size
   ....5.
4. Total length usually 100 mm or greater; habitat primarily moist,
   boggy situations ......Montane Shrew (*Sorex monticolus*), p. 48.
   Total length less than 100 mm; habitat sometimes as above, but also
   in drier, rocky or shrubby areas ....Dwarf Shrew
                                        (*Sorex nanus*), p. 51.
5. Unicuspid teeth markedly robust; color pale grayish above, whitish
   below, tail usually markedly bicolored; habitat relatively dry woodland or brushland ....Merriam's Shrew (*Sorex merriami*), p. 192.
   Unicuspid teeth not markedly robust; color medium brown above,

brownish to buffy below; tail indictinctly bicolored to unicolored; habitat moist, boggy situations ....Masked Shrew
(*Sorex cinereus*), p. 46.

KEY B–BATS

1. Ear relatively long (30 mm or greater), pale, nearly translucent, with prominent, transverse ridges; folded back in resting animal
.... Townsend's Big-eared Bat (*Plecotus townsendii*), p. 69.
Ear short to moderate in length (25 mm or less), dark, not translucent; in resting animal, may be folded forward, but not back ....2.
2. Hairs of back with whitish or silvery tips, at least in part ....3.
Hairs of back without whitish tips ....4.
3. Upper surface of uropatagium densely furred to posterior border; ears short, rounded, well-furred, rimmed with black; size large, forearm greater than 50 mm; total teeth, 32; flight late, swift
.... Hoary Bat (*Lasiurus cinereus*), p. 68.
Upper surface of uropatagium not densely furred to posterior border; ears relatively long, pointed, dark and naked; size moderate, forearm less than 45 mm; total teeth, 36; flight early, very slow
.... Silver-haired Bat (*Lasionycteris noctivagans*), p. 64.
4. Size large, forearm greater than 45 mm; total teeth, 32 ....
Big Brown Bat (*Eptesicus fuscus*), p. 66.
Size small to moderate, forearm about 40 mm or less; total teeth, 38 ....5.
5. Ear relatively long, extending past end of nose when laid forward................Long-eared Myotis (*Myotis evotis*), p. 57.
Ear relatively short, not extending past end of nose when laid forward ....6.
6. Body fur extending on underside of wing to level of elbow; calcar keeled ....Long-legged Myotis (*Myotis volans*), p. 63.
Body fur extending little or not at all onto underside of wing, calcar not keeled ....7.
7. Size smaller, forearm about 33 mm, hindfoot about 8 mm
.... Small-footed Myotis (*Myotis leibii*), p. 60.
Size larger, forearm about 40 mm, hindfoot about 10 mm....8.
8. Posterior border of interfemoral membrane with conspicuous fringe

of stiff hairs ....Fringed Myotis (*Myotis thysanodes*), p. 193.
Posterior border of interfemoral membrane without conspicuous
fringe of stiff hairs ....Little Brown Bat (*Myotis lucifugus*), p. 61.

KEY C–LAGOMORPHS

1. Ear as broad as long; no visible tail; five upper cheekteeth on each
   side of jaw ....Pika (*Ochotona princeps*), p. 77.
   Ear much longer than broad; tail short but obvious; six upper cheekteeth on each side of jaw ....2.
2. Hindfoot less than 105 mm; ear relatively short, usually less than
   65 mm; interparietal bone distinct; pelage dark throughout year
   ....Nuttall's Cottontail (*Sylvilagus nuttallii*), p. 80.
   Hindfoot more than 135 mm; ear relatively long, usually more than
   65 mm; interparietal bone indistinct; pelage dark in summer, white
   in winter ....3.
3. Size moderate; ear less than half the length of hindfoot; hindfoot
   remarkably long; greatest length of skull less than 80 mm; habitat
   willow thickets and brushy openings in dense forest ....
   Snowshoe Hare (*Lepus americanus*), p. 82.
   Size large; ear about two-thirds as long as hindfoot; greatest length
   of skull greater than 90 mm; habitat in open country (mountain
   parks, tundra).....................White-tailed Jackrabbit
   (*Lepus townsendii*), p. 84.

KEY D–RODENTS

1. Pelage of back in part modified to form stout quills; infraorbital foramen larger than foramen magnum ....Porcupine
   (*Erethizon dorsatum*), p. 130.
   Pelage of back not modified to form quills; infraorbital foramen
   various, but smaller than foramen magnum ....2.
2. Tail broad, flattened, nearly hairless; nostrils and ears valvular;
   length of skull greater than 120 mm ....Beaver
   (*Castor canadensis*), p. 109.
   Tail not broadly flattened; nostrils and ears not valvular; length of
   skull less than 100 mm ....3.
3. External, fur-lined cheekpouches present; lips closing behind incisors;
   forefeet strongly clawed, ears and eyes reduced ....

Northern Pocket Gopher (*Thomomys talpoides*), p. 107. External, fur-lined cheekpouches absent; lips closing over incisors; forefeet not obviously strongly clawed; eyes and ears generally prominent .... 4.

4. Tail long (half again as long as body); hindfoot elongate; hind limb modified for jumping; upper incisor grooved ....
Western Jumping Mouse (*Zapus princeps*), p. 128.
Tail short (no longer than head and body); hind limb not modified for jumping; upper incisors not grooved .... 5.

5. Total teeth 20 or 22, four or five upper cheekteeth on each side of jaw; animals diurnal, mostly conspicuous .... 6.
Total teeth 16, three upper cheekteeth on each side of jaw; animals nocturnal (or if diurnal, inconspicuous and secretive) .... 14.

6. Tail short, less than one-fourth total length; length of skull greater than 90 mm .... Yellow-bellied Marmot
(*Marmota flaviventris*), p. 93.
Tail relatively long, more than one-fourth total length; length of skull less than 80 mm .... 7.

7. Habitat mostly in forested areas; habit arboreal; crown of second upper molar as long as wide........................... 8.
Habitat mostly open, rocky, or brushy areas; habit mostly terrestrial or fossorial; crown of second upper molar notably wider than long... 9.

8. Size large (total length greaer than 450 mm); ear tufts large; color black, brown, or gray; three upper premolars ....
Abert's Squirrel (*Sciurus aberti*), p. 102.
Size small (total length less than 350 mm); ear tufts small to moderate; color grayish to reddish brown above, grayish white below; third upper premolar reduced or lacking ....
Chickaree (*Tamiasciurus hudsonicus*), p. 104.

9. Upper parts striped, the stripes continuing onto the head; posterior border of cheekbone opposite first molar................. 10.
Upper parts dappled, or if striped, the stripes not continuing onto the head; posterior border of cheekbone opposite third premolar .... 12.

10. Size small, total length usually less than 210 mm; hindfoot 32 mm or less .... Least Chipmunk (*Tamias minimus*), p. 88.
Size larger, total length usually greater than 210 mm; hindfoot greater than 32 mm .... 11.

11. Dorsal color dusky, paler stripes rather obscure; habitat most above 2400 m (8000 ft) ....Uinta Chipmunk (*Tamias umbrinus*), p. 91.
Dorsal color bright, stripes well defined; habitat usually below 2250 m (7500 ft) ....Colorado Chipmunk (*Tamias quadrivittatus*), p. 90.

12. Upper parts striped..........Golden-mantled Ground Squirrel (*Spermophilus lateralis*), p. 98.
Upper parts not striped................................13.

13. Size larger, total length 450 mm or greater, tail long, rather bushy; habitat in rocky canyons ....Rock Squirrel (*Spermophilus variegatus*), p. 101.
Size moderate, total length less than 350 mm; tail relatively short, narrow; habitat meadows, parklands, forest edge ....
Wyoming Ground Squirrel (*Spermophilus elegans*), p. 96.

14. Size large (total length greater than 450 mm); tail scaly, nearly naked, laterally flattened; hindfeet partially webbed; length of skull greater than 65 mm .... Muskrat (*Ondatra zibethicus*), p. 125.
Size moderate to small (total length less than 450 mm); tail haired, not scaly, not laterally flattened; hindfoot not webbed; length of skull less than 55 mm ....15.

15. Underparts and feet white, ears prominent, not obscured by dense fur; skull not abruptly constricted just anterior to braincase
.... 16.
Underparts and feet dark gray to silvery gray, not truly white; ears not prominent, obscured by dense fur; skull abruptly constricted just anterior to braincase ....19.

16. Size relatively large, total length greater than 300 mm; cheekteeth without true cusps ....17.
Size relatively small, total length 200 mm or less; cheekteeth cusped..18.

17. Size smaller, total length 360 mm or less; tail narrow, not bushy, with black medial stripe; length of skull less than 45 mm; habitat mostly in horizontal rock outcrops in foothills ....
Mexican Woodrat (*Neotoma mexicana*), p. 118.
Size larger, total length 375 mm or greater; tail bushy, grayish above; habitat mostly among granitic rocks of mountains ....
Bushy-tailed Woodrat (*Neotoma cinerea*), p. 117.

18. Tail relatively short, obviously less than 20 mm; dorsal color buffy to reddish brown; greatest length of skull less than 27 mm ....

Deer Mouse (*Peromyscus maniculatus*), p. 114.
Tail relatively long, nearly or quite as long as head and body; ears relatively large, 20 mm or longer; dorsal color grayish brown; greatest length of skull greater than 28 mm . . . .
Rock Mouse (*Peromyscus difficilis*), p. 113.
19. Hairs of back deep reddish brown, sides buffy or yellowish brown, underparts silvery gray to buffy . . . .
Southern Red-backed Vole (*Clethrionomys gapperi*), p. 120.
Hairs of back, sides, and dorsum gray to grayish brown or black . . . . .20.
20. Tail usually greater than one-third total length . . . .
Long-tailed Vole (*Microtus longicaudus*), p. 122.
Tail usually less than one-third total length . . . . .21.
21. Tail markedly short, but little longer than hindfoot; color pale gray . . . . Sagebrush Vole (*Lemmiscus curtatus*), p. 193.
Tail longer, markedly longer than hindfoot; color grayish brown to brown . . . . .22.
22. Size smaller, usually less than 150 mm, tail 35 mm or less; tail speckled with white above; when viewed from above, inner angles of lower molars deeper than outer angles . . . .
Heather Vole (*Phenacomys intermedius*), p. 121.
Size larger, usually greater than 150 mm, tail usually 40 mm or longer; tail not speckled white above; when viewed from above, inner and outer angles of lower molars of equal depth . . . .
Montane Vole (*Microtus montanus*), p. 123.

KEY E – CARNIVORES

1. Hind foot with five toes . . . . .2.
Hind foot with four toes . . . . .14.
2. Tail shorter than hindfoot; size large; total teeth, 42 . . . .
Black Bear (*Ursus americanus*), p. 143.
Tail longer than hindfoot; size small to medium; total teeth 40 or fewer . . . . .3.
3. Tail with banded pattern; musk glands absent; molars 2/2, total teeth, 40 . . . . .4.
Tail without banded pattern; musk glands present; molars 1/2, total teeth, 39 or fewer . . . . .5.
4. Dark bands on upper surface of tail only; tail approximately equal

202

to head and body; length of skull 100 mm or less . . . .
    Ringtail (*Bassariscus astutus*), p. 193.
Dark bands on tail complete; tail obviously shorter than head and
body; length of skull 110 mm or more . . . .
    Raccoon (*Procyon lotor*), p. 146.
5. Body relatively stout, tail less than one-third length of head and
body . . . . .6.
Body relatively slender, or if heavier-bodied, tail longer than one-
third length of head and body . . . . .7.
6. General color dark, blackish brown above and below, with pale
stripe on sides; no stripe on forehead; premolars 4/4 . . . .
    Wolverine (*Gulo gulo*), p. 156.
General color pale, upper parts grayish buff to reddish brown, muzzle
and feet black; prominent white stripe on head, continuing for variable distance onto back; premolars 3/3 . . . .
    Badger (*Taxidea taxus*), p. 157.
7. Toes webbed; size large, condylobasal length of skull greater than
90 mm, total length greater than 100 mm . . . .
    River Otter (*Lutra canadensis*), p. 162.
Toes not webbed; size small to moderate, condylobasal length of
skull less than 85 mm, total length less than 800 mm . . . . . . .8.
8. Color of back a pattern of white on black throughout the year; audi-
tory bullae small, flat . . . . .9.
Color of back not patterned, usually a shade of white or brown;
auditory bullae inflated . . . . .10.
9. Back marked with two continuous white stripes; size large, total
length 600 mm; length of skull greater than 70 mm . . . .
    Striped Skunk (*Mephitis mephitis*), p. 161
Back marked with four or more lines of irregular white spots; size
smaller, total length less than 500 mm; length of skull less than
70 mm . . . . . . .Western Spotted Skunk (*Spilogale gracilis*), p. 159.
10. Tail brown to tip; condylobasal length of skull usually greater than
65 mm . . . . .11.
Tail with prominent black tip; condylobasal length of skull usually
less than 55 mm . . . . .12.
11. Color golden brown above, pale brown to orangish below; habitat
forest, habit arboreal; premolars 4/4 . . . .
    Marten (*Martes americana*), p. 149.
Color brownish above, brown below; habitat riparian, habit semi-

aquatic; premolars 3/3 . . . . Mink (*Mustela vison*), p. 154.

12. Size smaller, total length less than 250 mm, tail less than 70 mm; condylobasal length of skull less than 40 mm . . . .
Ermine (*Mustela erminea*), p. 153.

Size larger, total length greater than 300 mm, tail greater than 100 mm; condylobasal length of skull greater than 40 mm . . . . . . 13.

13. Body and tail yellowish white; face marked with prominent black mask; feet black . . . Black-footed Ferret (*Mustela nigripes*), p. 194.
Body and tail brownish in summer, orangish to brownish below, pure white in winter; face without prominent black mask, feet not black . . . . Long-tailed Weasel (*Mustela frenata*), p. 150.

14. Claws not retractable; muzzle elongate . . . . 15.
Claws retractable; muzzle foreshortened . . . . 17.

15. Tail with mane or crest of stiff, black-tipped hairs; temporal ridges pronounced, lyre-shaped . . . .
Gray Fox (*Urocyon cinereoargenteus*), p. 141.
Tail without mane of stiff, black-tipped hairs; temporal ridges indistinct or V-shaped . . . . 16.

16. Color usually reddish-yellow above, buffy to white below; tip of tail white; postorbital process thin, concave; length of skull less than 150 mm . . . . Red Fox (*Vulpes vulpes*), p. 139.
Color grayish above, white below; feet pale; tip of tail black; postorbital process thick, convex; length of skull greater than 170 mm . . . . Coyote (*Canis latrans*), p. 136.

17. Tail long, more than one-third total length; length of skull greater than 150 mm . . . . Mountain Lion (*Felis concolor*), p. 164.
Tail short, less than one-fifth total length; length of skull less than 130 mm . . . . 18.

18. Tip of tail black above and below; ears with prominent black tufts; feet notably large . . . . Lynx (*Lynx lynx*), p. 168.
Tip of tail black above, white below; ears at most slightly tufted; feet not notably large . . . . Bobcat (*Lynx rufus*), p. 169.

KEY F—ARTIODACTYLS

1. Frontal appendages horns (keratinous sheath over a bony core) . . . . 2.
Frontal appendages antlers (branching structure of bone) . . . . . 5.

2. Horns branched . . . . . Pronghorn (*Antilocapra americana*), p. 183.

Horns not branched ....3.

3. Horns smooth, without annular ridges ....

Bison (*Bison bison*), p. 187.

Horns rough, with annular ridges ....4.

4. Horns of males robust (increasingly so with age), strongly curved into posteriorly-directed helix; lacrimal pits present; coat not shaggy, color brown with white rump patch ....

Bighorn Sheep (*Ovis canadensis*), p. 184.

Horns of both sexes of moderate size; slightly curved posterolaterally; lacrimal pits absent; coat shaggy, white, without contrastingly colored rump patch ....

Mountain Goat (*Oreamnos americanus*), p. 192.

5. Antlers palmate (the branches flattened), rounded at the tips; nasal bones noticeably short; profile humped at shoulders; throat with prominent dew lap ....Moose (*Alces alces*), p. 182.

Antlers not palmate, pointed at tips; nasal bones relatively long; profile not humped at shoulders; throat without prominent dew lap ....6.

6. Antlers with prominent brow tine; upper canines present.......

Wapiti, or American Elk (*Cervus elaphus*), p. 174.

Antlers without prominent brow tine; upper canine absent...7.

7. Tail narrow, white with black terminal tuft; antlers branching dichotomously, anterior and posterior beams nearly equal ......

Mule Deer (*Odocoileus hemionus*), p. 178.

Tail broad, brown above, white beneath; antlers with single main beam, not branching dichotomously ....

White-tailed Deer (*Odocoileus virginianus*), p. 181.

APPENDIX II: GLOSSARY

agonism: contesting behavior among individuals of same species.

altricial: born at a relatively undeveloped and helpless stage of development (compare *precocial*).

alveolus: socket in jaw in which mammalian tooth is set.

ambulatory: walking locomotion.

antler: bony derivative of frontal bone of skull typical of males of deer family (compare *horn*).

arboreal: tree-dwelling.

auditory bulla: bony case enclosing sensory apparatus of ear.

baculum: stiffening rod of bone in penis of many mammalian groups; also called *os penis*.

bicolored: of two distinct colors.

biocides: chemicals developed to kill living things; a near synonym of "pesticide," but preferable because term "pesticide" presumes objective definition of "pest," which is probably impossible.

boreal: northern.

bristle: short, stiff hair.

calcar: spur of cartilage or bone that projects inward from ankle of some species of bats forming partial support for uropatagium.

canine: anteriormost tooth in maxillary bone; tooth specialized for piercing and/or grasping; primitive mammals have one canine tooth on either side of jaw, above and below.

carrion: remains of dead animals.

cecotrophy: consumption of specialized, nutritive "fecal" pellets (=reingestion).

cheekpouch: distensible storage space in cheeks of some rodents.

cheekteeth: collective term for molars and premolars; i.e., all teeth posterior to canine.

circumboreal: occurring around the Northern Hemisphere.

cloaca: common chamber for products of urogenital and digestive tracts; from the Latin for "sewer."

convergence: evolutionary phenomenon in which organisms of separate ancestry come to resemble each other in some way.

cranial: pertaining to skull.

crepuscular: active at dawn and/or dusk (compare *diurnal, nocturnal*).

cursorial: running locomotion.

deciduous: capable of being shed (said of teeth, antlers, placentae, leaves of woody plants).

delayed implantation: suspension of embryonic development after first few cell divisions and prior to embedding (implantation) in wall of uterus.

diastema: gap between teeth in jaw due to evolutionary loss of teeth and/or elongation of jaw bone.

dichotomous: branching into two equal parts; Y-shaped branch.

digitigrade: standing on the digits (toes, fingers).

dispersal: movement of individuals from place of birth to place of reproduction (compare *migration*).

distichous: arrangement of hairs of tail in lateral rows, producing flattened appearance.

diurnal: active by day (compare *nocturnal, crepuscular*).

dormancy: extended, deep sleep, often during periods of resource scarcity or severe weather.

dorsal: pertaining to back (compare *ventral*).

ecotone: area of overlap between adjacent, distinctive biotic communities.

ectoparasite: external parasite (usually insect, mite, tick).

endemic: restricted in occurrence to a particular place.

endoparasite: internal parasite (usually roundworm, flatworm, protist, bacterium).

endothermy: "warm bloodedness"; maintenance of constant body temperature despite variation in environmental temperature.

estrous: of, relating to, or characteristic of estrus.

estrus: "heat"; period of maximal sexual reproductivity of female.

extirpation: local extinction.

family: taxonomic category above genus and below order; familial names of animals end in suffix "-idae."

feces: solid wastes of digestive processes.

fellfield: stone-strewn ground.

feral: pertaining to domestic animal reverted to wild state, or at least escaped from domestication into native ecosystems.

foramen: "hole"; opening in skull or other bone, usually for passage of nerves, muscles.

foramen magnum: large opening connecting cranial cavity and spinal column, through which spinal cord enters brain.

forbs: "forest herbs"; broadleafed herbaceous plants.

form: shallow depression, usually beneath shrub or other cover, occupied by rabbits and hares.

genus: taxonomic category comprised of one or more closely related species.

gestation: period between fertilization and parturition, or birth.

guard hairs: stiffer, longer, outer hairs of pelage; overlie underfur.

hectare: metric unit of land area, a square 100 meters on a side, 10,000 square meters; there are 100 hectares to the square kilometer; a hectare equals about 2.47 acres.

heterodont: teeth within toothrow of several kinds (incisors, canines, premolars, molars in primitive mammal) specialized for various functions (compare *homodont).*

hibernaculum: place in which hibernation is passed.

hibernation: regulation of physiology to minimum, especially in winter.

holarctic: occurring in the Northern Hemisphere, both New and Old Worlds.

holotype: type specimen; specimen upon which name of a species or subspecies is based.

home range: area covered by an individual in its daily round of activities (compare *territory).*

homodont: teeth all roughly the same; no specialization within toothrow (compare *heterodont).*

horn: covering of keratin (the structural protein of hair and nails) over bony growth of skull; typical of family Bovidae (compare *antler).*

implantation: burial of early embryo in wall of uterus prior to development of placenta.

incisor: nipping or gnawing teeth; in primitive mammals, three on either side of jaw, above and below.

infraorbital foramen: opening in skull below orbit, or eye socket.

interfemoral membrane: flap of skin between hindlimbs of many bats, including tail (=uropatagium).

interparietal: bone forming posterior part of skull cap, bounded laterally by parietals, posteriorly by occipital.

Krummholz: woodland of stunted, crooked trees at upper treeline; from the German.

lateral: pertaining to the sides of the body (compare *medial*).

mammary gland: milk-producing gland of female mammals (and source of name of class).

mean: arithmetic average.

medial: pertaining to the midline of the body (compare *lateral*).

metabolism: sum of chemical processes in an organism.

migration: movement of individuals, mostly access to new feeding grounds or hibernacula, usually seasonal, cyclic (compare *dispersal*).

mode: in a series of values for a particular variable, the most common value.

molar: most posterior cheekteeth, usually adapted to grinding; not present in deciduous ("milk") dentition; in primitive mammals, three in each toothrow, above and below.

molt: normal loss and replacement of hair; typically seasonal.

monoestrous: having one estrous cycle (and hence, one breeding period) annually (compare *polyestrous*).

monogamous: mating system in which individual (of either sex) has single mate.

natatorial: locomotion by swimming.

occlusion: functional contact between upper and lower teeth.

order: taxonomic category above level of family and below level of class.

ovulation: release of egg cell from follicle of ovary.

parasite: consumer organism which derives its nourishment from another organism (the "host"), but normally does not actually kill the host.

parturition: act of giving birth.

pelage: coat of hair and derivative structures (quills, bristles, vibrissae, etc.).

placenta: composite structure produced by female mammal and developing embryo, across which nutrients, gases, and wastes move between maternal and fetal bloodstreams.

plantigrade: standing on sole of foot, with toes, foot bones, and distal parts of ankle in contact with ground.

polyandrous: mating system in which female has more than one mate (compare *polygynous*, *polygamous*).

polyestrous: having more than one estrous cycle (hence, the possibility of more than one breeding period) annually (compare *monoestrous*).

polygamous: mating system in which individuals have more than one mate; a general term in which gender is not specified (compare *monogamous, polyandrous, polygynous*).

polygynous: mating system in which one male mates with several females (compare *polyandrous, polygamous*).

postorbital process: projection of temporal bone behind eye socket (orbit).

post-partum estrus: estrus immediately following parturition.

precocial: born in relatively well developed and independent state (compare *altricial*).

premolar: cheekteeth of variable structure and function located ahead of molars; present in deciduous ("milk") dentition; in primitive mammals, four in each toothrow, above and below.

rabies: infectious viral disease of nervous system.

raptor: bird-of-prey; general term for eagles, hawks, falcons, and owls.

reingestion: consumption of specialized, nutritive "fecal" pellets (=cecotrophy).

riparian: river or streamside habitat.

saltatorial: locomotion by jumping.

scabies: contagious disease caused by burrowing of certain mites beneath skin.

scansorial: locomotion by scampering or climbing.

scat: droppings, feces.

scrotum: sac in which testes of most mammals are carried during active spermatogenesis.

species: group of actually or potentially interbreeding individuals reproductively isolated from other such groups.

spermatogenesis: sperm production.

supraorbital shield: bony projection of frontal bone above eye socket.

taiga: coniferous forest; derived from the Russian.

talus: slope of fragmented rock.

taxonomy: scientific study of classifications.

temporal ridges: prominences on temporal bones serving as points of attachment for temporal muscles that close the jaw.

territory: portion of home range defended (actively or passively) by individual against other individuals of same species (see *home range*).

thecodont: teeth set in sockets (*alveoli*).

torpor: partial suspension of physiologic activity; deep sleep.

tularemia: contagious bacterial disease typified by intermittent fever.

type locality: place at which holotype (type specimen) was collected.

type specimen: holotype; specimen upon which name of a species or subspecies is based.

underfur: short, often dense, insulating coat beneath guard hairs of many mammals.

unguligrade: standing on the hooves.

unicuspid: tooth having single cusp or point.

urogenital tract: the common ducts and openings of the urinary and reproductive systems.

uropatagium: interfemoral membrane; flap of skin between hind limbs of many bats, including tail.

uterus: "womb"; muscular organ of female mammal in which young are carried before birth; wall of uterus participates in formation of *placenta*.

valvular: capable of being closed.

ventral: pertaining to belly or underside (compare *dorsal*).

vestigial: non-functional remnant of former structure or function.

vibrissae: "whiskers"; stiff, touch-sensitive hairs.

APPENDIX III: DERIVATION OF
SCIENTIFIC NAMES

THE FORMAL NAMES of science are invaluable in classifying and retrieving information. Noting that two species have the same generic name (*Peromyscus maniculatus* and *Peromyscus difficilis*, for example) makes an evolutionary statement, suggesting that these are closely related species. At least part of what we know about the biology of the abundant, widespread, and well-studied deer mouse is probably true as well for the more scarce, less widespread, and relatively poorly studied rock mouse.

However, for most people, actually learning scientific names of organisms is a waste of time and energy; it is quite enough to know where to "look up" the names. A few persons need to know zoological names for professional purposes, because they use them all the time. A few others actually enjoy knowing their biological acquaintances on a formal basis. It is for the last-named few that this section is included.

One of the easiest ways to remember scientific names is to know their derivation. Scientific names are Latin or have a latinized form (or at the very least are treated grammatically as if they were Latin). Many are classical names for the animals to which they apply (*alces, felis, lupus*). Other names are commemorative, honoring naturalists of note (*hoyi, merriami, townsendii*). Others are descriptive of the animals (*nanus, cinereus*), their habitat (*palustris*), or their geographical range (*canadensis*). Some are even humorous (the specific epithet for the blue whale, the largest animal that has ever lived on Earth, is *musculus*, "little mouse").

Because scientific names of genera and species are written in a foreign language, they are underlined in manuscript and italicized in print. (By convention, proper names of higher taxonomic categories—families, orders, classes, phyla—are not underlined, however.) A very useful reference for tracking down the etymology of scientific names is Borror (1971).

The following list of derivations is included because knowing the source of a name often helps one to remember it. Please do not mistake this mnemonic device, however, for anything else. Despite their Latin name, individuals of the species *Homo sapiens* are not necessarily wise, either individually or collectively, and *Lasionycteris noctivagans* does not *mean* "night-flying shaggy bat" any more than everyone named Smith is a metalworker or everyone named Fletcher makes arrows. Rather, the scientific name *means* the biological entity to which it is applied. (Abbreviations, L=Latin, G=Greek.)

aberti: for J. W. Abert (1820–1897), military explorer-naturalist of the Southwest.

Alces: "elk" (L).

Antilocapra: compound of two other generic names, *Antilope* (the Old World blackbuck) and *Capra* (goats).

arctos: "bear" (G).

astutus: "skilled" (L).

Bassariscus: diminutive form of *bassaris*, "fox" (G).

Bison: "bison," from Germanic *wisent*, "bison."

canadensis: pertaining to Canada.

Canis: "dog" (L).

Castor: "beaver" (G).

Cervus: "deer" (L).

cinereoargenteus: cinereo-, "ashen" (L), + -argenteus, "silvery" (L).

cinereus: "ashen," "gray" (L).

Clethrionomys: clethriono-, pertaining to the alder (G), + -mys, "mouse" (G).

concolor: con-, "together" (L), + -color, "color" (L).

curtatus: "short" (L).

difficilis: "difficult" (L).

dorsatum: pertaining to the dorsum (L), or back.

elegans: "elegant" (L).

Erethizon: erethi-, "irritate" (G), + -zon, "animal" (G).

erminea: latinized form of French *hermine*, "ermine."

evotis: ev-, "good" (G), + -otis, "ear" (G).

Felis: "cat" (L).

flaviventris: flavi-, "yellow" (L), + -ventris, "belly" (L).

frenata: "brindle" (L).

fuscus: "brown" (L).

Gulo: "glutton" (L).

hemionus: hemi-, "one-half" (G), + *-onus,* "ass," "mule" (L).

Homo: "self" (G).

hoyi: for P. R. Hoy (1816–1892), pioneer naturalist in Wisconsin.

hudsonicus: pertaining to Hudson's Bay.

intermedius: "between" (L).

Lagurus: lag-, "rabbit" (G), + *-urus,* "tail" (G).

Lasionycteris: lasio-, "shaggy" (G), + *-nycteris,* "bat" (G).

Lasiurus: lasio-, "shabby" (G), + *-urus,* "tail" (G).

lateralis: pertaining to "side" (L).

latrans: "barking" (L).

leibii: for one Dr. Leib of Philadelphia, who collected the holotype.

Lepus: "hare" (L).

longicaudus: longi-, "long" (L), + *-caudus,* "tail" (L).

lotor: "washing" (L).

lucifugus: luci-, "light" (L), + *-fugus,* "flee" (L).

lupus: "wolf" (L).

Lutra: "otter" (L).

lynx: "cat" (G).

maniculatus: pertaining to *manicula,* "little hands" (L).

Marmota: latinized form of French *marmotte,* from Late Latin *musmontanus,* "mountain mouse."

Martes: "marten" (L).

Mephitis: "foul odor" (L).

merriami: for C. Hart Merriam (1855–1942), first Chief, Bureau of Biological Survey, U.S. Department of Agriculture, and first President, American Society of Mammalogists.

mexicana: pertaining to México.

Microtus: micr-, "small" (G), + *-otus,* "ear" (G).

montanus: "mountain" (L).

Mustela: "weasel" (L).

Myotis: my-, "mouse" (G), + *-otis,* "ear" (G).

nanus: "small" (G).

Neotoma: neo-, "new" (G), + *-toma,* "cut" (G).

nigripes: nigri-, "black" (L), + *-pes,* "foot" (L).

noctivagans: nocti-, "night" (G), + *-vagans,* "wandering" (L).

nuttallii: for Thomas Nuttall (1786–1859), pioneer American naturalist.

Ochotona: latinized form of *ochodona,* the Mongol name for pika.

Odocoileus: odo-, "tooth" (G), + *-coileus,* "hollow" (G).

Ondatra: latinized form of Huron name for muskrat.
Oreamnos: oreo-, "mountain" (G), + -amnos, "lamb" (G).
Ovis: "sheep" (L).
palustris: pertaining to swamp or marsh (L).
Peromyscus: pero-, "defective" (G), + -myscus, "mouse" (G).
Plecotus: plec-, "folded" (G), + -otus, "ear" (G).
princeps: "first," "chief" (L).
Procyon: pro-, "before" (G), + -cyon, "dog" (G).
quadrivittatus: quadri-, "four" (L), + -vittatus, "stripe" (L).
rufus: "red" (L).
sapiens: "wise" (L).
Sciurus: sci-, "shade" (G), + -urus, "tail" (G).
Sorex: "shrew" (L).
Spermophilus: spermo-, "seed" (G), + -philus, "lower" (G).
Spilogale: spilo-, "spotted" (G), + -gale, "weasel" (G).
Sylvilagus: sylvi-, "forest" (L), + -lagus, "rabbit" (G).
talpoides: talpo-, "mole" (L), + -id, "like" (G).
Tamias: "distributor" (L).
Tamiasciurus: compound of two other generic names, *Tamias* and *Sciurus*.
Taxidea: derivative of *taxus*?
taxus: "badger" (L).
Thomomys: thomo-, "heap" (G), + -mys, "mouse" (G).
thysanodes: thysan-, "fringed" (G), + -odes, "like" (G).
townsendii: for J. K. Townsend (1809–1851), explorer and naturalist of the American Northwest.
umbrinus: "shady" (L).
Urocyon: uro-, "tail" (G), + -cyon, "dog" (G).
Ursus: "bear" (L).
variegatus: "variegated," "variously colored" (L).
virginianus: pertaining to Virginia.
vison: French for mink.
volans: "flying" (L).
Vulpes: "fox" (L).
Zapus: za-, "excessive" (G), + -pus, "foot" (G).
zibethicus: from *zibeth*, an Indian civet.

LITERATURE CITED

Allen, G. M. 1939. Bats. Harvard University Press, Cambridge. 368 pp.

Anderson, A. E., and O. C. Wallmo. 1984. Odocoileus hemionus. Mammalian Species, 219: 1–9.

Anderson, S., and J. K. Jones, Jr., eds. 1984. Orders and families of recent mammals of the world. John Wiley and Sons, New York, xii + 686 pp.

Armstrong, D. M. 1972. Distribution of mammals in Colorado. Monogr., Univ. Kansas Mus. Nat. Hist., 3: i–x + 1–415.

―――――. 1975. Rocky Mountain mammals. Rocky Mountain Nature Assoc., Estes Park, viii + 174 pp.

―――――. 1977. Ecological distribution of small mammals in the Upper Williams Fork Basin, Grand County, Colorado. Southwestern Nat., 22: 289–304.

―――――. 1982. Mammals of the Canyon Country. Canyonlands Natural History Assoc., Moab, Utah, 273 pp.

Armstrong, D. M., B. H. Banta, and E. J. Pokropus. 1973. Altitudinal distribution of small mammals along a cross-sectional transect through the Arkansas River watershed, Colorado. Southwestern Nat., 17: 315–317.

Armstrong, D. M., and J. K. Jones, Jr. 1971. Sorex merriami. Mammalian Species, 2: 1–2.

Barbour, R. W., and W. B. Davis. 1969. Bats of America. Univ. of Kentucky Press, Lexington, 286 pp.

Bear, G. H., and R. M. Hansen. 1966. Food habits, growth and reproduction of the white-tailed jackrabbit in southern Colorado. Tech. Bull., Agric. Exper. Sta., Colorado State Univ., 90: i–viii + 1–59.

Bekoff, M. 1977. Canis latrans. Mammalian Species, 79: 1–9.

Bekoff, M., and M. C. Wells. 1980. The social ecology of coyotes. Sci. Amer., 242: 130–148.

——. 1986. Social ecology and behavior of coyotes. Adv. Study Behav., 16: 251–338.

Black, H. L. 1974. A northern temperate bat community: structure and prey population. J. Mamm., 55: 138–157.

Borror, D. J. 1971. Dictionary of word roots and combining forms, 11th printing. Mayfield Publishing Co., Palo Alto, iii + 134 pp.

Brown, L. N. 1967a. Ecological distribution of six species of shrews, and comparison of sampling methods in the central Rocky Mountains. J. Mamm., 48: 617–623.

——. 1967b. Seasonal activity patterns and breeding of western jumping mice (Zapus princeps) in Wyoming. Amer. Midland Nat., 78: 460–470.

——. 1969. Reproductive characteristics of the Mexican woodrat at the northern limit of its range in Colorado. J. Mamm., 50: 536–541.

——. 1970. Population dynamics of the western jumping mouse (*Zapus princeps*) during a four-year study. J. Mamm., 51: 651–658.

Buchholtz, C. W. 1983. Rocky Mountain National Park, a history. Colorado Assoc. Univ. Press, Boulder, xii + 255 pp.

Burt, W. H., and R. P. Grossenheider. 1952. A field guide to the mammals. Houghton Mifflin Co., Boston, xxi + 200 pp.

Carleton, W. M. 1966. Food habits of two sympatric Colorado sciurids. J. Mamm., 47: 91–103.

Carroll, L. E., and H. H. Genoways. 1980. Lagurus curtatus. Mammalian Species, 124: 1–6.

Cary, M. 1911. A biological survey of Colorado. N. Amer. Fauna, 33: 1–256.

Chapman, J. A. 1975. Sylvilagus nuttallii. Mammalian Species, 56: 1–3.

Chapman, J. A., and G. A. Feldhamer. 1982. Wild mammals of North America. Johns Hopkins, Baltimore, xiii + 1147 pp.

Cinq-Mars, R. J., and L. N. Brown. 1969. Reproduction and ecological distribution of the rock mouse, Peromyscus difficilis, in northern Colorado. Amer. Midland Nat., 81: 205–217.

Conaway, C. H. 1952. Life history of the water shrew (Sorex palustris navigator). Amer. Midland Nat., 48: 219–248.

Costello, D. F. 1966. The world of the porcupine. J. B. Lippincott, Philadelphia. 157 pp.

Currier, M. J. P. 1983. Felis concolor. Mammalian Species, 200: 1–7.

Douglas, C. L. 1969. Comparative ecology of pinyon mice and deer mice in Mesa Verde National Park, Colorado. Univ. Kansas Publ., Mus. Nat. Hist., 18: 421–504.

Eisenberg, J. F. 1981. The mammalian radiations. Univ. Chicago Press, xx + 610 pp.

Errington, P. L. 1963. Muskrat populations. Iowa State Univ. Press, Ames, x + 665 pp.

Estes, M. 1939. The memoirs of Estes Park. Bull., Colorado State College Library, 6: 1–14.

Farentinos, R. C. 1972. Social dominance and mating activity in the tassel-eared squirrel (Sciurus aberti ferreus). Anim. Behav., 20: 316–326.

Fenton, M. B., and R. M. R. Barclay. 1980. Myotis lucifugus. Mammalian Species, 142: 1–8.

Finley, R. B., Jr. 1958. The wood rats of Colorado. Univ. Kansas Publ., Mus. Nat. Hist., 10: 213–552.

———. 1969. Cone caches and middens of Tamiasciurus in the Rocky Mountain Region. Misc. Publ., Univ. of Kansas Mus. Nat. Hist., 51: 233–273.

Forsyth, D. J. 1976. A field study of growth and development of nestling masked shrews (Sorex cinereus). J. Mamm., 57: 708–721.

Franzmann, A. W. 1981. Alces alces. Mammalian Species, 154: 1–7.

Frase, B. A., and R. S. Hoffmann. 1980. Marmota flaviventris. Mammalian Species, 135: 1–8.

Friedrichsen, T. T. 1977. Responses of rodent populations to visitors in a national park. Unpubl. MS thesis, Colorado State University, Fort Collins, xi +98 pp.

Fritzell, E. K., and K. J. Haroldson. 1982. Urocyon cinereoargenteus. Mammalian Species, 189: 1–8.

Fryxell, F. M. 1928. The former range of the bison in the Rocky Mountains. J. Mamm., 9: 129–139.

Geist, V. 1971. Mountain sheep, a study in behavior and evolution. Univ. Chicago Press, Chicago, xv + 383 pp.

Goodson, N. J. 1978. Status of bighorn sheep in Rocky Mountain National Park. Unpubl. MS thesis, Colorado State Univ., Fort Collins, xv +190 pp.

Halfpenny, J. C. 1986. A field guide to mammal tracking in western America. Johnson Publishing Co., Boulder, xi + 161 pp.

Hall, E. R. 1951. American weasels. Univ. Kansas Publ., Mus. Nat. Hist., 4: 1–466.

———. 1981. The mammals of North America. John Wiley and Sons, New York, 2 vols.

Hansen, R. M. 1960. Pocket gophers in Colorado. Bull., Exper. Sta., Colorado State Univ., 508-S: 1–26.

Hansen, R. M., and J. T. Flinders. 1969. Food habits of North American hares. Sci. Ser., Range Sci. Dept., Colorado State Univ., 1: i–ii + 1–18.

Hansen, R. M., and A. L. Ward. Some relations of pocket gophers to rangelands on Grand Mesa, Colorado. Tech. Bull., Agric. Exper. Sta., Colorado State Univ., 88: 1–20.

Harrington, F. A., Jr. 1978. Ecological segregation of ungulates in alpine and subalpine communities. Unpubl. PhD thesis, Colorado State Univ., Fort Collins, xii + 152 pp.

Hatt, R. T. 1927. Notes on the ground squirrel, Callospermophilus. Occas. Papers, Univ. of Michigan Mus. Zool., 185: 1–22.

———. 1943. The pine squirrel in Colorado. J. Mamm., 24: 311–345.

Hennings, D., and R. S. Hoffmann. 1977. A review of the taxonomy of the Sorex vagrans complex from western North America. Occas. Papers, Mus. Nat. Hist., Univ. Kansas, 68: 1–35.

Hill, J. E., and J. D. Smith. 1984. Bats, a natural history. Univ. Texas Press, Austin, 243 pp.

Hillman, C. W., and T. W. Clark. 1980. Mustela nigripes. Mammalian Species, 126: 1–3.

Hoffmann, R. S. 1958. The role of reproduction and mortality in population fluctuations of voles (Microtus). Ecol. Monogr., 28: 79–109.

Hoffmann, R. S., and J. G. Owen. 1980. Sorex tenellus and Sorex nanus. Mammalian Species, 131: 1–4.

Hoffmeister, D. F., and V. E. Diersing. 1978. Review of the tassel-eared squirrels of the subgenus Otosciurus. J. Mamm., 59: 402–413.

Hornocker, M. G. 1970. An analysis of mountain lion predation upon mule deer and elk in the Idaho Primitive Area. Wildl. Monogr., 21: 1–39.

Humphrey, S. R., and T. H. Kunz. 1976. Ecology of a Pleistocene relict, the western big-eared bat (Plecotus townsendii) in the southern Great Plains. J. Mamm., 57: 470–494.

Husar, S. L. 1976. Behavioral character displacement: evidence of food partitioning in insectivorous bats. J. Mamm., 57: 331–338.

Jenkins, S. H., and P. E. Busher. 1979. Castor canadensis. Mammalian Species, 120: 1–8.

Johnson, D. R. 1967. Diet and reproduction of Colorado pikas. J. Mamm., 48: 311–315.

Johnson, K. 1981. Social organization of a colony of rock squirrels (*Spermophilus variegatus*, Sciuridae). Southwestern Nat., 26: 237–242.

Jones, J. K., Jr., D. M. Armstrong, and J. R. Choate. 1985. Guide to mammals of the Plains States. Univ. Nebraska Press, xvii + 371 pp.

Jones, J. K., Jr., D. M. Armstrong, R. S. Hoffmann, and C. Jones. 1983. Mammals of the Northern Great Plains. Univ. Nebraska Press, xii + 329 pp.

Jones, J. K., Jr., D. C. Carter, H. H. Genoways, R. S. Hoffmann, and D. W. Rice. 1982. Revised checklist of North American mammals north of Mexico, 1982. Occas. Papers Mus., Texas Tech. Univ., 80: 1–22.

Keith, J. O. 1965. The Abert squirrel and its dependence on ponderosa pine. Ecology, 46: 150–163.

King, C. M. 1983. Mustela erminea. Mammalian Species, 195: 1–8.

King, J. A., ed. 1968. The biology of *Peromyscus* (Rodentia). Spec. Publ., Amer. Soc. Mammal., 2: i–viii + 1–593.

Kunz, T. H. 1982a. Lasionycteris noctivagans. Mammalian Species, 172: 1–5.

———, ed. 1982b. Ecology of bats. Plenum, New York, xviii + 425 pp.

Kunz, T. H., and R. A. Martin. 1982. Plecotus townsendii. Mammalian Species, 175: 1–6.

Lechleitner, R. R. 1969. Wild mammals of Colorado. Pruett Publishing Co., Boulder, xvi + 254 pp.

Long, C. A. 1973. Taxidea taxus. Mammalian Species, 26: 1–4.

———. 1974. Microsorex hoyi and Microsorex thompsoni. Mammalian Species, 33: 1–4.

Lotze, J. H., and S. Anderson. 1979. Procyon lotor. Mammalian Species, 119: 1–8.

Loveless, C. M. 1967. Ecological characteristics of a mule deer winter range. Tech. Publ., Colorado Game, Fish and Parks Dept., 20: 1–124.

MacClintock, D. 1970. Squirrels of North America. Van Nostrand Reinhold Co., New York, vi + 184 pp.

Mack, C. M. 1985. River otter restoration in Grand County, Colorado. Unpubl. MS thesis, Colorado State University, Fort Collins, xiii + 133 pp.

McKeever, S. 1964. The biology of the golden-mantled ground squirrel. Ecol. Monogr., 34: 383–401.

Makar, P. W. 1980. Bobcat and coyote food habits and habitat use in Rocky Mountain National Park. Unpubl. MS thesis, Colorado State University, Fort Collins, vii + 32 pp.

Meaney, C. A. 1983. Olfactory communication in pikas (*Ochotona princeps*). Unpubl. PhD thesis, Univ. of Colorado, 125 pp.

Mech, L. D. 1974. Canis lupus. Mammalian Species, 37: 1–6.

Merritt, J. F. 1981. Clethrionomys gapperi. Mammalian Species, 146: 1–9.

Merritt, J. F., and J. M. Merritt. 1980. Population ecology of the deer mouse (*Peromyscus maniculatus*) in the Front Range of Colorado. Ann. Carnegie Mus., 49: 113–130.

Mills, E. A. 1914. The story of Estes Park, third edition. Privately published, Estes Park, 99 pp.

———. 1919. The grizzly, our greatest wild animal. Riverside Press, Cambridge, 284 pp.

Moser, C. A. 1962. The bighorn sheep of Colorado. Tech. Publ., Colorado Game and Fish Dept., 10: 1–49.

Murie, O. J. 1951. The elk of North America. The Stackpole Co., Harrisburg, PA, 376 pp.

———. 1954. A field guide to animal tracks. Houghton Mifflin Co., Boston, xii + 374 pp.

Mutel, C. F., and J. C. Emerick. 1984. From grassland to glacier, a natural history of Colorado. Johnson, Boulder, x + 238 pp.

Nash, D. J., and R. N. Seaman. 1977. Sciurus aberti. Mammalian Species, 80: 1–5.

Neff, D. J. 1959. A seventy-year history of a Colorado beaver colony. J. Mamm., 40: 381–387.

Nelson, R. A. 1979. Handbook of Rocky Mountain plants. Skyland Publishers, Estes Park, 331 pp.

Nowak, R. M., and J. L. Paradiso. 1983. Walker's mammals of the world, 4th ed. Johns Hopkins Univ. Press, Baltimore, 2 vols. (Vol. III of First Edition, by E. P. Walker, 1964, was a comprehensive bibliography.)

O'Gara, B. W. 1978. Antilicapra americana. Mammalian Species, 90: 1–7.

Oaks, E. C., P. S. Young, G. L. Kirkland, Jr., and D. F. Schmidt. 1987. Spermophilus variegatus. Mammalian Species, 272: 1–8.

Packard, F. M. 1946. An ecological study of the bighorn sheep in Rocky Mountain National Park, Colorado. J. Mamm., 27: 3–28.

Ross, A. 1967. Ecological aspects of food habits of insectivorous bats. Proc. Western Found. Vert. Zool., 2: 205–263.

Rue, L. L., III. 1964a. The world of the raccoon. J. B. Lippincott, Philadelphia, 145 pp.

———. 1964b. The world of the beaver. J. B. Lippincott, Philadelphia, 155 pp.

———. 1969. The world of the red fox. J. B. Lippincott, Philadelphia, 204 pp.

Schoonmaker, W. J. 1968. The world of the grizzly bear. J. B. Lippincott, Philadelphia, 150 pp.

Scott, J., D. M. Armstrong, S. J. Bissell, and J. Freeman. 1984. The bats of Colorado: shadows in the night. Colorado Div. Wildl., Denver, 22 pp.

Shakleton, D. M. 1985. Ovis canadensis. Mammalian Species, 230: 1–9.

Shump, K. A., Jr., and A. U. Shump. 1982. Lasiurus cinereus. Mammalian Species, 185: 1–5.

Skryja, D. D. 1974. Reproductive biology of the least chipmunk (Eutamias minimus operarius) in southeastern Wyoming. J. Mamm., 55: 764–795.

Smith, A. T. 1975. The distribution and dispersal of pikas: influences of behavior and climate. Ecology, 55: 1368–1376.

———. 1978. Comparative demography of pikas (Ochotona): effect of spatial and temporal age-specific mortality. Ecology, 59: 133–139.

Smith, C. C. 1968. The adaptive nature of social organization in the genus of three (sic) squirrels Tamiasciurus. Ecol. Monogr., 34: 383–401.

Smolen, M. J., and B. L. Keller. 1987. Microtus longicaudus. Mammalian Species, 271: 1–7.

Sorensen, M. W. 1962. Some aspects of water shrew behavior. Amer. Midland Nat., 68: 445–462.

Southwick, C. H., S. C. Golian, M. R. Whitworth, J. C. Halfpenny, and R. Brown. 1986. Population density and fluctuations of pikas (Ochotona princeps) in Colorado. J. Mamm., 67: 149–153.

Spencer, A. W., and D. Pettus. 1966. Habitat preferences of five sympatric species of long-tailed shrews. Ecology, 47: 677–683.

Stevens, D. R., and D. D. Hanson. 1986. The range use and movements of an introduced bighorn sheep population 5 years after establishment. J. Colorado-Wyoming Acad. Sci., 18(1): 51.

Stinson, N., Jr. 1978. Habitat structure and species diversity on north and south-facing slopes in the Colorado Lower Montane Zone. Southwestern Nat., 23: 77–84.

222

Svendsen, G. F. 1979. Territoriality and behavior in a population of pikas (*Ochotona princeps*). J. Mamm., 60: 324–330.

Telleen, S. L. 1978. Structural niches of *Eutamias minimus* and *E. umbrinus* in Rocky Mountain National Park. Unpubl. PhD thesis, Univ. of Colorado, ix + 141 pp.

Trimble, S. 1984. Longs Peak, a Rocky Mountain chronicle. Rocky Mountain Nature Association, Estes Park, 109 pp.

Tumlinson, R. 1987. Felis lynx. Mammalian Species, 269: 1–8.

Turner, R. W. 1974. Mammals of the Black Hills of South Dakota and Wyoming. Misc. Publ., Univ. Kansas Mus. Nat. Hist., 60: 1–178.

Tuttle, M. D., and L. R. Heaney. 1974. Maternity habits of *Myotis leibii* in South Dakota. Bull. So. California Acad. Sci., 73: 80–83.

Van Wormer, J. 1963. The world of the bobcat. J. B. Lippincott, Philadelphia, 128 pp.

———. 1966. The world of the black bear. J. B. Lippincott, Philadelphia, 163 pp.

———. 1969. The world of the American elk. J. B. Lippincott, Philadelphia, 159 pp.

Vaughan, T. A. 1969. Reproduction and population densities in a montane small mammal fauna. Misc. Publ., Univ. Kansas Mus. Nat. Hist., 51: 51–74.

———. 1974. Resource allocation in some sympatric subalpine rodents. J. Mamm., 55: 764–795.

———. 1986. Mammalogy, third edition. Saunders College Publ., Philadelphia, vii +576 pp.

Verts, B. J. 1967. The biology of the striped skunk. Univ. Illinois Press, Urbana, xii + 218 pp.

Wade-Smith, J., and B. J. Verts. 1982. Mephitis mephitis. Mammalian Species, 173: 1–7.

Wallmo, O. C. 1978. Mule and black-tailed deer. Pp. 31–41 *in* Big game of North America (J. L. Schmidt and D. L. Gilbert, eds.). Stackpole Books, Harrisburg, xv + 494 pp.

Wadsworth, C. E. 1969. Reproduction and growth in *Eutamias quadrivittatus* in southeastern Utah. J. Mamm., 50: 256–261.

Warner, R. M., and N. J. Czaplewski. 1984. Myotis volans. Mammalian Species, 224: 1–4.

White, J. A. 1953. Taxonomy of the chipmunks *Eutamias quadrivittatus* and *Eutamias umbrinus*. Univ. Kansas Publ., Mus. Nat. Hist., 5: 563–582.

Williams, O. 1952. New phenacomys records from Colorado. J. Mamm., 33: 399.

Woods, C. A. 1973. Erethizon dorsatum. Mammalian Species, 29: 1–6.

Young, S. P. 1958. The bobcat of North America. The Stackpole Co., Harrisburg, PA, xi + 193 pp.

Young, S. P., and E. A. Goldman. 1944. The wolves of North America. Amer. Wildl. Inst., Washington, xvi + 636 pp.

———. 1946. The puma, mysterious American cat. Amer. Wildl. Inst., Washington, xiv + 358 pp.

Young, S. P., and H. H. T. Jackson. 1951. The clever coyote. The Stackpole Co., Harrisburg, PA, xv + 411 pp.

Zegers, D. A. 1984. Spermophilus elegans. Mammalian Species, 214: 1–7.

APPROXIMATE CONVERSION FACTORS, METRIC-ENGLISH MEASUREMENTS

Linear Measurements

To convert *inches* to *millimeters*, multiply by 25.

To convert *millimeters* to *inches*, multiply by 0.04 (that is, divide by 25).

To convert *inches* to *centimeters*, multiply by 2.5.

To convert *centimeters* to *inches*, multiply by 0.4 (that is, divide by 2.5).

To convert *feet* to *meters*, multiply by 0.3.

To convert *meters* to *feet*, multiply by 3.3.

Measurements of Weight

To convert *ounces* to *grams*, multiply by 28.

To convert *grams* to *ounces*, multiply by 0.35 (that is, divide by 28).

To convert *pounds* to *grams*, multiply by 450.

To convert *pounds* to *kilograms*, multiply by 0.45.

To convert *kilograms* to *pounds*, multiply by 2.2.

Better Still, Don't Convert— Just Think Metric!

A dime weighs 2.5 grams, a penny 3, a nickel 5, a quarter 6, and a quart of milk weighs almost a kilogram. The "Bic" pen in my pocket is 15 centimeters long and 8 mm thick, and a U.S. dollar bill is 65 mm wide and 155 mm long. For comments on the use of the metric system, see p. 3.

DATE DUE

FEB 12 1999			
	261-2500		Printed in USA